W9-DEG-376

GO TO THE
NET

AL STRACHAN

GO TO THE

TRIUMPH
B O O K S
CHICAGO

●NET

EIGHT GOALS

THAT CHANGED

THE GAME

This is dedicated to the National Hockey
League players who, while not perfect,
possess more admirable qualities than any
other group of people with whom I've ever
been associated.

This book is available in quantity at special discounts for your group or organization. For
further information, contact:

Triumph Books
542 South Dearborn Street
Suite 750
Chicago, Illinois 60605
(312) 939-3330
Fax (312) 663-3557

Jacket image: Bettman/Corbis
Printed and bound in the USA

Published in Canada by
Doubleday Canada, a division of
Random House of Canada Limited

ISBN-13: 978-1-57243-898-9
ISBN-10: 1-57243-898-3

BVG   10 9 8 7 6 5 4 3 2 1

CONTENTS

INTRODUCTION

IT HAS OFTEN BEEN SAID THAT BASEBALL MUST BE A WONDERFUL game to withstand the people who run it.

That's true not only of baseball.

Hockey, too, is a great game—a lot greater than baseball, in my opinion. And it has travelled a much tougher road than baseball when it comes to withstanding the impact of those who have directed its course.

Like most Canadians, I grew up with an inherent love of hockey. One of my fondest early memories is scoring on a breakaway for King Edward VII Public School in a game we won 1–0.

I try not to remember with the same degree of clarity that the only reason I got the breakaway was that I was so far behind the play that there was no one within thirty feet of me. And that the only reason I scored was that I fell as I approached the crease, took a wild swipe at the puck while sliding on my stomach, and somehow batted it past a goaltender who was too confused (or possibly amused) by this unorthodox approach to make the save.

In Windsor, Ontario, in those days, you were either a fan of the Toronto Maple Leafs or the Montreal Canadiens. Even though Detroit was right across the river, the Red Wings were generally viewed as the Evil Empire because they had the right to prevent the Windsor CBC-TV outlet from showing games the rest of the country was watching—and they exercised that right with disgusting regularity.

We were Detroit Tigers fans. We were Detroit Lions fans. But never the Detroit Red Wings.

I switched allegiances on a regular basis, rooting for whichever of the two Canadian-based teams was having a better season at the time. If the Leafs played the Canadiens in the playoffs, my choice that year would be determined by some long-forgotten whim.

As a hockey writer, I followed basically the same principle, but with a slight alteration: now I admired not just the best Canadian team, but the best *NHL* team.

Over the years, I've been accused of being a flack for almost every team in hockey—well, not every team. Only the good ones—a fact that puts the lie to the beliefs of thousands of readers who, upon seeing some criticism in print of their own favourite team, fire off nasty letters accusing me of taking this stance because I live in Toronto and am therefore in the pocket of the Leafs.

Suffice it to say, that isn't a view that would receive a lot of support from the Maple Leafs themselves. As I said, my soft spot is for NHL teams that do well.

At the time I undertook to write this book, no NHL team was doing well. The owners had locked out the players at midnight, September 15, 2004, and there was to be no major-league hockey for the foreseeable future.

Nothing could have had a more profound effect upon the society in which I exist.

The hockey world is like a village, a small community of two thousand or so people in which, to varying degrees, everyone knows everyone else.

A tragedy that affects one member affects everyone. Consider how many hockey people from all over the continent turn out for a funeral for one of their number.

The common thread, the defining characteristic, in this "village" is not the location in which one lives—quite the contrary—but the avocation one holds.

At the core are the players. They are the elite tradesmen. Without them the lifeblood of the village would dry up. The NHL governors would be the landed gentry, the ones who own the means of livelihood. Their managers would be those same people who do that job in hockey—the general managers, coaches and assistant coaches.

The media? Well, they're the village gossips, the ones who spread the news about who is doing what to whom, and how often.

But if you're going to make the analogy work, you have to accept the premise that there are two types of hockey media people/gossips.

There are those who cover a number of sports, whose knowledge of hockey ranges from abysmal to acceptable and who are basically visitors. They are comparable to migrant labourers who merely visit the village when their job demands it.

The other type of media person is the specialist whose life revolves around hockey and who rarely gets involved with any other sport. These are the hometown experts. Some would say they're *idiots savant*, capable of rambling on about the minutiae of the game for hours—even days, weeks, months and years—on end, but incapable of intelligent discourse on any other subject. That may or may not be true. Certainly some of them come perilously close to fitting that description. But for better or worse, this is the group to which I belong.

When you're in this group, you're a genuine resident of the village. You may not be accepted as an insider by everyone, but you are certainly "one of us."

You are recognized and called by name. Like any village

resident, you have your detractors and your confidants. You are part of alliances that evolve and devolve over the years. You share with the other residents the inherent details of life on this planet as they relate to each other—births and deaths, illnesses and recoveries, marriages and divorces, joy and sorrow.

The hockey village isn't just a place to live. It is your life. You can never get away from it.

Other people go home in the evening and watch television. If you do get home at all in the evening—if you're not in an arena covering a game—you watch hockey from cities across the continent.

Other people go out amongst society and discuss a variety of subjects. You go out and face the hockey questions of the day. In the autumn, people want to know about their favourite team's chances. In the winter, it's the issue of the moment—a suspension, a firing, a slump or a hot streak. In the spring, the impending playoffs are the subject *du jour*, as well as the cornucopia of potential trades before the deadline. In the summer, it's the playoffs themselves, followed closely by the draft and the free agents.

Rarely do those you meet in the larger world want to talk to you about the things normal people use as a basis for discourse—recent movies, current events, the weather or the latest political scandal. They want to talk hockey.

Underlying it all is the implicit assumption that if you write about sports for a living, you're mentally incapable of discussing anything else. Either that, or they're simply not interested.

As a result, the inclination of those within the hockey community to rely on each other becomes even more pronounced. You tend to restrict your circle of associates to people of like interests—the other residents of the village. You have friends in every major city in North America, as long as that city has a hockey team.

Your closest friends are people to whom the phrase "Thank God It's Friday" has not the slightest relevance. Saturday and Sunday are working days like all the rest. There will be days off, but not generally on a weekend.

All of which is to say that when hockey is your life, not your pastime, and the owners decide to shut down your sport—as they did in 2004—you know how the people of Morrisburg, Ontario, felt when they learned that the government had decided to flood their town in order to create the St. Lawrence Seaway.

This is hockey's darkest hour, and unfortunately, there's no reason to put any faith in the adage that the darkest hour is just before dawn.

Hockey has had its ebbs and flows, its peaks and valleys. Like the other sports, it has evolved over the years, and a cursory study of natural history would indicate that the course of evolution is not a steady one. There are periods of rapid progress and periods of slow, gradual development. And periods of stagnation.

We don't know what the game will be like when it comes back after this latest trauma, but we do know where it has been. At the moment, by virtue of stirring victories in both the 2004 World Cup and the 2002 Salt Lake City Olympics, not to mention other recent triumphs in junior hockey, women's hockey and the world championships, Canada is the reigning hockey power in the world.

The Tampa Bay Lightning (one of those teams that annoyingly uses a singular form for its nickname) is/are the holders of the Stanley Cup and the first team in history to hang on to it for more than a year without having to face a challenge.

There was another occasion—in 1919—when the Cup was not awarded, but at least regular-season hockey was played, and the Stanley Cup final, between the Seattle Metropolitans and the Montreal Canadiens, did get underway. Unfortunately, it was halted after two games by the Spanish influenza epidemic.

When the NHL returns, assuming it does, a new era will be inaugurated, one that will continue until it faces some immutable force that sends the game in another direction.

There have been a number of such forces over the years. Sometimes that force appears in the form of a person: Maurice Richard, Bobby Orr or Wayne Gretzky, for example. These are just some of the people who have changed the game forever merely by playing it. Sometimes, it's a political development, such as the decision of the Soviet Union to put its national team on the same stage as many of the NHL's finest in 1972 and to steadily increase its exposure thereafter. Sometimes it's an infusion of new ideas, like those the Europeans brought to North America when they came over in force in the 1980s.

But whatever the catalyst, each era tended to have a turning point, a defining moment, marked by a goal that represented, if not the very pinnacle of the era, then at least the point at which it could be said that the hockey seen before that goal was not the same as the hockey seen after it.

This book is not just an examination of those goals, but an insight into the factors that brought those goals into being and the ramifications of their being scored.

Not all of those ramifications could be seen as positive. Before the owners shut down the NHL, it was not in particularly good shape. The entertainment value was not all it should have been, and certainly not all it used to be.

Scoring decreased steadily throughout the 1990s, and the league frantically tinkered with the rules, usually with little success. One of the attempted improvements, the video review, led to the fiasco during the 1999 Stanley Cup finals, when Brett Hull of the Dallas Stars scored a hotly disputed goal against the Buffalo Sabres. The subsequent controversy put an abrupt end to the video phase of hockey's evolution.

But scoring remained low, even though more cities were being awarded franchises. By 2001, NHL commissioner Gary

Bettman's dream of a thirty-team league had finally become a reality. The NHL now boasted teams in such unlikely locales as Georgia, Ohio, Tennessee and North Carolina.

So pleased was Bettman by this development that it seemed almost churlish to point out that the league had been in two of those states fairly recently and had failed rather miserably.

The earlier Georgia incarnation had been the Atlanta Flames, which drew moderately well. But in those days, hockey teams were in great demand and Calgary entrepreneurs who wanted a team for their city simply made a bid that was too enticing to turn down.

When the Atlanta franchise was originally awarded, management ran a name-the-team contest and, despite a number of other attractive options (Ice-holes being one of the more entertaining) they settled for Flames, a reference to the fact that General Sherman had burned down the city of Atlanta in 1864 during the American Civil War.

In 1980, the Atlanta Flames packed their bags and went to Calgary, and with no better ideas coming to the fore, the nickname went unchanged, even though there was no evidence that Calgary had ever been put to the torch.

The earlier Ohio team was the infamous Cleveland Barons, the least successful franchise of the modern era. The Barons started life as the California Seals in 1967 and operated under such aliases as the Oakland Seals and the California Golden Seals while exhibiting a stunning degree of ineptitude, before finally moving to Cleveland in 1976.

After two years of ignominy, the Barons merged with the Minnesota North Stars, thereby ending their short NHL life with barely a whimper.

The merger of the Barons and North Stars had resulted in a seventeen-team NHL, but the hockey climate was somewhat different when the Columbus Blue Jackets re-established an Ohio presence in the twenty-first century. Now, there were thirty teams, and as a result, it became fashionable among fans to announce that the league was "watered down" and "diluted" and that there was not sufficient talent available to support such a bloated body.

It was a widely accepted theory, and one that fans seemed to find logical. They saw low-scoring hockey, which was a relatively recent development. They saw thirty teams, which was definitely a recent development. They decided that there must be a correlation.

Using that criteria, ants are so painfully shy that whenever you look at them through a magnifying glass on a bright day, they burst into flames from embarrassment.

The flaw in the watered-down-league theory was this: if you ever watched an NHL team scrimmage, you saw some wonderful hockey. The simple facts were there to observe—but not for everyone, because NHL practices aren't open to the public. However, they *are* open to the media, and a lot of people who sit behind microphones and pontificate about the lack of NHL skills could have done themselves—and their listeners—a great service by extricating themselves from their comfortable ruts and going to watch a morning skate.

Once there, they could hardly help but notice the obvious. The players who were in the league when it reached the thirty-team plateau were much faster, stronger and more skilled than their predecessors.

A player on a third or fourth line ten years earlier would have had no chance of cracking one of these modern-day lineups. The enforcers of 1990 could hardly skate. Slow defencemen were the norm.

To put it bluntly, the contention that the newly created thirty-team league was—or is now—watered down is simply wrong.

The problem, it seems, is that many observers confused talent level with parity. If there's not much difference between the good and bad teams, they said, the talent must be diluted. Therefore, they continued, if the lockout were to result in the elimination of six teams, the overall product would be the better for it.

In fact, the opposite is true. The gap between the league's elite teams and its bottom-feeders had indeed narrowed, but that was due to a *proliferation* of talent, not a lack of it.

The NHL had evolved into a low-scoring league not because the offensive players were poor, but because the defensive players were good. And in this era, everybody is a defensive player.

A few years ago, a good forward with a head of steam could get around most defencemen. A wicked shot from the wing would often become a goal. A backup goalie was rarely able to win a game. Only a small percentage of forwards were considered to be good two-way players.

None of those assertions can be made anymore. Forwards skate backwards or forwards equally well and with astonishing alacrity. They forecheck at breakneck speed. They backcheck at whatever speed it takes—and do so with determination. A defenceman carrying the puck out of his own end looks up and sees six defenders facing him. A decade ago, a checking forward would skate alongside his mark, thereby leaving himself open to a nifty shift. Today, that checking forward skates backwards like a defenceman, much better able to react to any move.

If a defenceman skates so poorly that a forward can go around him, he's in the minor leagues, not the NHL. Like the forwards, the NHL defencemen are much better. Even the giants (and increasing numbers of them are giants) are so nimble, and so quick in their lateral movements, that they can keep even the most explosive skaters to the outside.

Keeping all this in mind, what would happen if you compressed the league by six teams? You would eliminate 20 per cent of the league and therefore 20 per cent of the jobs. Then, even though the talent gap between the best and worst players is already narrower than it has ever been, it would become smaller still. There would be even less hope of making a productive offensive play, even less hope of getting away from a checker, and even less hope of finding a weak spot in the opposition's defence. Getting rid of six teams wouldn't energize the spectacle. It would make it more moribund than ever.

Consider another point. On every other occasion that the NHL has expanded, offensive production has increased. The same phenomenon has taken place in other leagues.

But ever since the NHL's most recent expansion, offensive production has fallen steadily. Why? Because there's so much available talent. There are no patsies. If the talent weren't there, the evidence would manifest itself in high-scoring games.

Getting rid of six teams is not the answer.

In a peripheral matter, Bettman likes to make the point that the games are intense and hard-fought. Indeed they are. There's room to criticize hockey's end, but not its means. The games are low-scoring and have few brilliant plays, but that's because the intensity level is so high.

And that's a direct result of the presence of thirty competitive teams. In the eighties, when the NHL was a twenty-one-team league, sixteen of those teams made the playoffs. The quality teams rarely needed to break a sweat before April.

Today, when sixteen teams are in the playoffs and fourteen are out, every regular-season point is important. There are no cruise-control nights.

In his days playing goal for Montreal in the seventies, Ken Dryden used to categorize his shutouts as "working" or "non-working." Some nights, he did little more than lean on his stick. Games like that are almost nonexistent these days.

Also worthy of consideration is the fact that hockey needs geographical diversity if it is to grow. In today's world, the sports industry is ruled by the television industry. And the television industry is ruled by ratings. The NHL couldn't continue to allow the existence of all those black holes all over the American TV map.

Those who think thirty teams are too many will pounce on that point. "You can't sell hockey in those markets," they say. "Look at all the empty seats!"

You can look at the empty seats if you want. But where do you see them? You see them in cities where the team is doing poorly. The location of the market has much less to do with it.

When the Florida Panthers were heading for the Stanley Cup finals in 1996, the arena was packed every night. Once the Panthers became awful, they played to mostly empty seats. Hockey is hugely popular in Dallas—and has been ever since the Stars started to win.

The Colorado Avalanche has sold every seat since moving to Denver from Quebec in 1995. In their first season, the Avs won the Stanley Cup, and they've been competitive ever since. When the Anaheim Mighty Ducks were winning in the nineties, the Pond was full. When the Ducks went into a tailspin, so did the attendance. When the Ducks advanced to the Stanley Cup finals in 2003, the Pond was sold out again.

Were there any empty seats in Carolina in 2002 when the Hurricanes made their run to the finals? Not a one.

Conversely, Calgary had lots of empty seats that season, so many that it closed off entire sections of the Saddledome. It's not just the southern markets that find themselves with almost-empty arenas. But in the early nineties, there had been a waiting list in Calgary for season tickets. And when the Flames returned to the Stanley Cup finals in 2004, all those mothballed seats were put back into service and Flames tickets were the hottest commodity in town.

Today, Detroit is called "Hockeytown" and is seen as one of the league's core cities, home of one of the franchises that epitomize success. Few remember that when Mike Ilitch bought the team, it was one of the league's weak sisters and attendance was so poor that, for one full season, he gave away a new Ford every night in an attempt to get fans to buy tickets.

Fans buy tickets in the hope of watching a winner. So the problem with a thirty-team league is not that some teams will settle in unfamiliar markets or wear exotic uniforms. It is that, simply by sheer weight of the numbers, there will be far too many losers. Each year, there's one winner and twenty-nine losers. The average fan's favourite team will win the Cup once every thirty years.

Fans want to see a winner, yet it's obvious that with all those teams—and the occasional emergence of a dynasty—most won't get their wish.

That's one of the reasons for the allure of international hockey. Canadian fans in Vancouver, who have to be able to remember the 1915 Millionaires to have seen a Stanley Cup winner; or in Toronto, where the drought stands at thirty-eight years; or in Ottawa, where the Cup hasn't resided since 1923, can finally support a team that they can call their own and that has a good chance of winning: Team Canada.

Some of the goals examined in this book involve Team Canada—not necessarily because they brought glory to the nation, but because they changed the face of the entire game, including the product offered by the National Hockey League.

When Team Canada plays, everyone in the hockey world watches, and the best players are in the spotlight. The way the various incarnations of Team Canada have played over the years, and the lessons they have learned during international competition, have affected the sport at all its levels.

Sometimes, as in the case of the Challenge Cup of 1979, the guardians of the sport in North America were forced to finally come to grips with the fact that the young players of the Soviet Union were getting better coaching and better direction than their counterparts on this side of the Atlantic Ocean.

Five years later, in the 1984 Canada Cup, there was evidence that important steps had been taken. For the first time since the emergence of the USSR as a hockey power, Canada allowed the Soviets to dictate the style of play, but beat them at their own game—without resorting to the kind of violence that had done considerable damage to the nation's image as a hockey power during earlier confrontations.

While all this was going on, hockey was changing at the league level as well. The famous game between the Montreal Canadiens and the Boston Bruins in the 1979 playoffs, when Bruins coach Don Cherry got caught with too many men on the ice, made a splash that sent ripples across the entire hockey pond.

Hockey went through a number of eras prior to the ones examined in this book, and in each case, you can pinpoint one goal that defined that era.

A full examination over the lifetime of the NHL would have required the inclusion of a lot more goals, but I opted to settle, for the time being at least, on those that I personally witnessed, in games that I covered either for the Montreal *Gazette*, *The Globe and Mail* or the *Toronto Sun*. The earliest goal examined here takes place in 1979, the latest in 2002.

My hope is that these games are so memorable that hockey fans, upon seeing the bare statistical report that begins each chapter, will say, "Oh yes, I remember that goal."

My further, and more fervent, hope is that those same fans will say, after reading the chapter, "I didn't know all those things had been going on behind the scenes."

Either way, perhaps this reflection on some of the more glorious moments in the history of hockey will go some distance, however small, towards reminding those who love this sport that no matter what the NHL governors do, hockey is far too good and far too much a part of our heritage to remain forever in its current dire straits.

THE GOAL: FEBRUARY 11, 1979.

Game three of the Challenge Cup best-of-three final.
Scored by Boris Mikhailov (assisted by Alexander Golikov)
at 5:47 of the second period. Team USSR 6, Team NHL 0.

THERE WAS NO NATIONAL HOCKEY LEAGUE ALL-STAR GAME IN 1979. Instead, there would be further proof that Canadian hockey was the best in the world. At least, that was the theory.

Instead of the meaningless time-waster pitting the Campbell Conference all-stars against those from the Prince of Wales Conference, Team NHL would face the Soviet Union in a best-of-three series called the Challenge Cup.

The site was to be the famed Madison Square Garden in New York, and the underlying premise was that the spectacle would be so attractive to the sports fans of the United States that a lucrative network television contract for the NHL would surely become little more than a formality.

For all intents and purposes, Team NHL was Team Canada. Granted, three Swedes—Borje Salming, Ulf Nilsson and Anders Hedberg—were added to an otherwise all-Canadian roster, but Salming was the only one who would play regularly. Halfway through the first game, Nilsson and Hedberg decided to do some freelancing during a power play and coach Scotty Bowman immediately yanked them off the ice and never sent them out again.

"I was really mad," explained Guy Lafleur, the other NHL forward on the power play at the time. "I was all alone waiting for the pass and those two kept passing the puck back and forth with Salming in our own zone. Three times they had a chance to pass to me and they didn't. I finally got so mad I went to the bench."

Shortly afterwards, so did Hedberg and Nilsson. But unlike Lafleur, the Swedes stayed there.

In fact, Bowman was so miffed at the Swedish duo that he scratched them for the whole of the second game as well, and gave them only minimal ice time in the third.

Bowman had instituted a precise game plan, and in those days he was a true taskmaster—not as severe as his Soviet counterpart Viktor Tikhonov, perhaps, but as demanding a coach as any in the NHL. If Hedberg and Nilsson wanted to do things their own way, they could do it when they were playing for the New York Rangers, not for him.

At the time of the tournament, Canada was considered to be the world's top hockey nation. Therefore, it had by far the most to lose in this matchup. If the Soviets lost the series, they could repeat what they had said a few times before it began: "We consider the International Ice Hockey Federation's world championship to be the true barometer of hockey supremacy. This is just an exhibition series." But if the Soviets won, the shock to the Canadian psyche would be a further devastating blow to a country that was in something of a funk. The seventies were not the happiest of times for Canada.

The Parti Québécois had come to power in Quebec, and the very fabric of the nation was threatened. On the economic front, the inflationary spiral soared unabated, the dollar was in a precipitous slide and the labour unions were flexing their muscles with increasing regularity.

One of the few sources of Canadian national pride—perhaps the only one of any consequence to most blue-collar Canadians—was the fervent belief that when it came to the game Canada had invented, Canadians were the best in the world. To the average Canadian fan, this would be no mere three-game exhibition series. It was democracy versus Communism, the maple leaf versus the hammer and sickle, the game's traditional masters versus the steadily improving challengers.

The Canadian roster was loaded with the stars of the day. People like Lafleur, Bobby Clarke and Lanny McDonald were among the league's top scorers. Don Marcotte and Bob Gainey were considered to be the elite checkers. Ken Dryden and Gerry Cheevers were the top goalies.

The defence? Well, that might be something of a problem. Larry Robinson, Denis Potvin, Serge Savard and Salming were there, but this was not a golden era for NHL defencemen. The few at the top were great, but depth was a luxury the Canadians did not possess. Rounding out the blueline corps were Barry Beck and Robert Picard.

The Challenge Cup was the first series of this nature since the famous 1972 Summit Series, but in the interim, the two countries had been involved in a number of skirmishes at varying levels.

In the 1976 Canada Cup, the USSR had lost 3–1 to Canada in the round-robin segment of the tournament and hadn't advanced to the final, which Canada won by defeating Czechoslovakia.

There had also been assorted club matches—in which the Soviets had built a somewhat ominous 10–5–2 edge, even though all seventeen games were played in North America.

Canada had resumed participation in the annual world championship in 1977, but sent only players whose NHL teams had been eliminated from the playoffs. As a result, the Canadians were soundly trounced, but no one back home considered that to be of any import, since most of the country's best players were unavailable.

The Challenge Cup was the first head-to-head, best-against-best series in seven years, and even though the

Soviets were masters of the self-serving lie, they could not deny that they were bringing a powerhouse team.

"We are taking to New York twenty-four players, our best lineup," said Tikhonov.

Well, sort of. They weren't taking Viacheslav Fetisov, the brilliant young defenceman who, ten years later, made his way to the NHL and starred for nine years with the New Jersey Devils and Detroit Red Wings. Boris Alexandrov, who had the Montreal Canadiens gaping when they watched him in practice prior to the December 31, 1975, game between the Canadiens and Central Red Army, wasn't there either. Even though he had proved himself to be a brilliant player, perhaps the most talented in the entire Soviet system, he had become too aware of that talent for their liking. He wasn't sufficiently subservient. He enjoyed his vodka. He didn't exhibit the proper deference to Comrade Coach, whoever that might have been at the time. So he was banished from the national team.

There was no room for individualism in the Soviet system. Even though the national team was composed of "players," what those people did with the game could hardly be described as play. They *worked* at hockey. There was no fun in their game, and certainly no joking at practice. Their lives were rigidly structured, both on and off the ice. If they were travelling out of the country, they were accompanied by KGB guards; and, with extremely rare exceptions, they were not allowed to talk to the media.

Prisoners in Canadian penitentiaries had an easier life than those "players." The Soviets worked hard for eleven months of the year, and if they won the world championship—but only if—they were rewarded with a month at a resort on the Black Sea.

"I think the biggest edge they had back then was in conditioning," recalled Bowman in a 2005 interview. "They don't have that edge today, but they did then because they played for eleven months a year.

"I know that in the seventies, their complete team in VO2 testing was in the mid- to high seventies. [VO2 testing measures the oxygen an athlete can process; the more oxygen you use, the fitter you are.] There was no team like that in the NHL. For example, in Montreal we used to test the players and the highest we ever had was Bob Gainey. He was 73. Lafleur was somewhere around 70." And the lowest? "Pete Mahovlich. He was 35." But he wasn't that far behind the others, Bowman said. "We had a lot of our defencemen in the 40s. Jacques Laperriere was 42 or something like that. If you got to 59 in the NHL, you were considered to be in good shape."

Of the twenty-four players on the 1979 Soviet squad, eleven were in the army, four were in the navy and two were in the air force. Long stretches away from home were the norm for them, so when Tikhonov left Moscow with his team, he didn't see any need to rush to New York. Instead of travelling directly from the Soviet Union to North America, the entourage went first to the Netherlands for a three-week training camp.

Why the Netherlands, of all places? Because it was there that Tikhonov's operatives had been able to find a rink that had exactly the same dimensions as Madison Square Garden.

Once in the Netherlands, they operated on Eastern Standard Time—not European time, but New York time.

They went back to Moscow for two days, then flew from there to New York, with a refuelling stop in Newfoundland. Throughout, they continued to operate on Eastern Standard Time. The idea was that when they finally arrived in the United States, on the Sunday night prior to Thursday's opening game of the tournament, the effects of jet lag would be minimal.

While they were in Holland, they followed their usual regimen—at least two practices a day, combined with a fair amount of dry-land training and soccer in the off-hours "to keep in shape."

The NHL, meanwhile, was playing its full schedule. The Challenge Cup had been squeezed into a slightly extended all-star break, but there certainly would be no three-week training camp for the NHLers. They were to have no more than two practices in which to prepare for the strongest Soviet team in history.

Propaganda was a very important tool for those who ran the Kremlin in those days, and because sporting events were so widely watched, the Soviets put a lot of effort—not all of it within the bounds of legality outside the USSR—into building teams that would be the world's best.

Failure was not tolerated, and when the team coached by Boris "Chuckles" Kulagin lost twice to Sweden at the 1977 world championship in Vienna and failed to win the gold medal, Kulagin was replaced by Tikhonov and his Challenge Cup assistant, Vladimir Yurzin.

After examining the areas in which the Canadians had found success, those two incorporated some tactical changes into their game prior to the Challenge Cup. The Soviets began shooting a bit more than they once did, no longer necessarily waiting for the perfect opportunity to score. Once in a while, although not very often, they even voluntarily gave up possession of the puck and opted for the Canadian dump-and-chase style.

In 1972, all the bodychecking had been one way: Canadians gave, Soviets took. But now the Soviets, especially defencemen like Sergei Babinov, were capable of administering the occasional crunching body check.

"He is about as close to our style as any of their defencemen," said Bowman. "He's chunky, a Leo Boivin style. He likes to hit people and he gives the puck to his partner a lot rather than control the play."

There had also been some sartorial and tonsorial changes to the Soviet squad. When their predecessors had arrived in Canada for the 1972 Summit Series, there was no doubt that these guys were fresh from the backwaters of Europe. They dressed in clothes that had long since gone out of style in North America, and their personal hygiene left a lot to be desired. If you were in an elevator with them, you'd never forget the experience.

But when the Soviet squad arrived in New York in 1979, the players looked just like American businessmen. Their hair was stylishly long, but neatly coiffed. When they were lounging around the hotel, they tended to wear identical sweatsuits, but if the occasion demanded a little more formality, they had a blazer-and-slacks ensemble. If the occasion were more formal still, they all wore elegant black suits with grey pinstripes. And if it were more formal than that, they still wore their suits. They did, after all, represent a Communist regime. The NHL staged a black-tie testimonial dinner for former league president Clarence Campbell during the run-up to the tournament and offered to rent tuxedos for all the Soviets. They declined. There were limits to their transition into North Americans.

They sampled the New York nightlife as any visiting businessmen might—although their tours were more structured than most. They were not allowed to travel in small groups, only in larger groups accompanied by KGB men.

The veteran forward Vladimir Petrov was their designated tour organizer, and their liaison with the NHL was Aggie Kukulowicz, a Russian speaker who worked for Air Canada and was a regular part of the Canadian entourage whenever the Russians were involved.

On the day after the Soviets arrived in New York, Petrov approached Kukulowicz. "Aggie, my friend," he said, "we want to go to a movie. We want a movie with a lot of sex, a lot of music, a lot of action and a sense of history."

His group went to see *Superman*.

Since the Manhattan showing of *Superman* didn't feature Russian subtitles, they took along their own interpreter, who recited the dialogue in Russian despite frequent shouts from other patrons of "Keep it down back there!" or the more succinct "Shut up!"

The others on the team who wanted to see the same type of movie—save the requirements of music, action and history—went to Times Square. The movies in that seedy district didn't require any translation of dialogue.

Despite signs that the Russians were becoming more attuned to modern ways, Bowman wasn't anticipating any major surprises. He had been Canada's head coach in the 1976 Canada Cup, and his Canadiens had twice faced Soviet club teams. He said that he intended to have Team NHL use basically the same style as his Canadiens—a high-tempo, defensively aware approach.

The most obvious difference would come in the forechecking, he said. The Canadiens, because they were better skaters than most teams in the league, tended to apply maximum forechecking pressure. Not only were they not afraid to go after the puck behind the opposition's net, but there were occasions when an entire forward line might be back there. Given the Soviets' speed and passing skills, Team NHL would have to be more cautious.

"One long pass beating two or three people would be disastrous," said Bowman on the eve of the tournament. "You can't let them trap too many guys. Patience is a big factor. You can't go charging after them."

But on the other hand, it would be equally disastrous to sit back and let the Soviets come to Team NHL.

"You've got to be in motion," Bowman said. "You've got to be constantly circling and moving."

Furthermore, that circling and moving had to be done in the centre of the rink, where the Soviets liked to operate.

Former NHL player Andre Boudrias, later a member of the Canadiens' front-office staff, had done some scouting of the Soviets on Bowman's behalf.

"They're still playing basically the same kind of game," he said. "They're coming out up the middle. And if they're stopped at the blue line, they won't shoot it in. They'll go back and regroup and come up the middle again."

But no matter how skilled the Soviet forwards might be,

any wizardry they intended to perform required possession of the puck. And that's where Bowman hoped to thwart them. His Canadiens invariably ran up a decided advantage in puck-possession time, and he wanted Team NHL to do the same.

"How good do you think Guy Lafleur is defensively?" he asked. "Average? Below average? The point is that it doesn't really matter because he has the puck so much. With the Canadiens, our offence is our best defence. If the offence is working, that provides the defence. We have to play the Soviets the same way."

In a perfect example of how these international games raised the calibre of hockey on both sides of the Atlantic Ocean, Bowman wanted his team to borrow something from the Soviet style. He wanted them to increase their already high possession time. He wanted them to be judicious in their shot selection because a bad shot was a low-percentage play that would probably result in lost possession—or even worse, an odd-man rush. And he wanted them to eschew the dump-and-chase style. Again, it was a matter of maintaining puck possession.

In the press conferences, Tikhonov would downplay his team's abilities and the importance of the series. But at the same time, he would talk about "surprises" that were to be forthcoming. Bill Torrey, the general manager of Team NHL, refused to take Tikhonov's musings seriously. "I'm pretty sure we know what they've got in mind when they say they might surprise us," he said, "and we're ready for it."

Oh really? How ready?

"I'd rather not say what we have in mind."

Team captain Bobby Clarke (he was Bobby back then, but after his retirement he became Bob) admitted that the players had some nagging doubts about what they might encounter, but were determined not to let themselves be psyched out.

"There's no sense letting them get us worried with their talk about surprises," he said. "We'll just go out there and see what they're doing and worry about it then."

But despite the bravado, even before the series had started, the Canadians had concluded after two practices that their defence corps was probably no match for the Soviet forwards. A hasty call was made to Montreal's Guy Lapointe, who had been excused from the team because of a mild attack of pneumonia. "Forget your chest pains," he was told. "Get yourself to New York as fast as possible."

It had become apparent to Bowman and his staff that he needed seasoned, fleet defencemen to handle the likes of the Soviets' rising star, Helmut Balderis.

"He's a real sniper," said Bowman. "He has a hard shot and he plays on the wrong wing. He's a left-handed shot on the right wing. He has tremendous acceleration. He's an Yvan Cournoyer type, but he's a big one. He likes to play up and he also likes to put pressure on the defence on the outside. He's the guy they try to hit on the fly."

Hence the call to Lapointe.

Every such development was scrutinized in minute detail in Canada. In the United States, and even in New York itself, the reaction was little more than a yawn. On the eve of the series, the *New York Times* made no mention of it whatsoever. The *Daily News* made an oblique reference in a story about Bobby Orr being awarded the Lester Patrick Trophy for outstanding contributions to hockey in the United States. Only the *New York Post*, which was more of a sports paper than the others, ran a pair of small, general-interest pieces.

The American TV networks, whose patronage had been openly courted and for whose convenience the series had been situated in New York, managed, for the most part, to express a profound disinterest.

Vladislav Tretiak, the Soviet goalie who would later be inducted into the Hall of Fame, would have preferred a change of venue.

"I'm treated very well here and I don't want to say anything that would be detrimental to the people in New York," he said, "but I am sorry these games are not being played in Canada. When you're playing in arenas where people understand hockey, you can play very well.

"Let's face it. When we are talking among ourselves, we don't call them Team NHL, we refer to them as Canadians. We can't very well call them Americans, can we?"

He was right, of course, and it's a suggestion that has been taken to heart here. It makes sense to refer to this team as Canadians, even though Salming was taking a regular shift.

Tretiak was probably the most famous of all the Soviet hockey players at that time. He had been brilliant in the 1972 series and downright spectacular in the December 31, 1975, game between the Canadiens and Red Army which ended in a 3–3 tie.

Tretiak had just published a book, *The Hockey I Love*, essentially a diary of his hockey-playing exploits, and some signings had been scheduled in the New York area. Because of this, he was granted a rare exemption from the regimented schedule that was imposed on all the other players.

I was the sports editor of the Montreal *Gazette* at the time, and the late Don Ramsay of *The Globe and Mail* was a close friend. We saw Tretiak wandering around the hotel by himself and asked Kukulowicz if he could arrange an interview. Interviews with Soviet players were all but nonexistent in that era—even in the Soviet Union—but because of his affinity for hockey fans in Toronto and Montreal, Tretiak agreed.

He was wary at first, but soon opened up. He spoke just a little English and sometimes, when Kukulowicz was translating his remarks, he would hear an English word he understood and blurt out some more Russian to embellish the answer. He looked at the notes Ramsay and I were scribbling and pointed at them. "It looks like the Japanese translation of my book," he laughed.

Speaking of the book, where were the royalties going? Was he getting un-Communistically rich off it?

"I wish I knew," he said with a rueful grin. "I don't have any figures."

Perhaps it would make him a rich man.

He laughed at that, then grew serious. "I think you know me well enough from the way I play hockey," he said, "that you know I don't really care about royalties. It is much more important to me that my book is a success and that people read it, than to get the royalties."

He admitted, however, that he did enjoy the notoriety.

"Because of my book and my hockey playing," he said beaming, "people recognize me. Everybody in the Soviet Union knows who I am. When our plane landed in Gander on the way here, everybody recognized me.

"The only place they don't know me is in New York."

Like most goalies, Tretiak was a student of the game and he was willing to discuss its evolution, especially with regard to the Canadian and Soviet styles.

"The number one change that has taken place since 1972 is that the Canadians take us seriously now," he said. "Previously, they considered us to be children. Their attitude is different now. They treat us as equals.

"In fact, maybe the Canadian style has adopted a bit of the European game. When you look at the total package, what you see is a more balanced game.

"At first, it was a case of one team trying to carry the puck and the other trying to knock them off it. Now, both sides are capable of solid play."

When Tretiak ran out of time and had to leave for his book signing, we wished him well, shook his hand and thanked him. We were just leaving when Kukulowicz called us back. Tretiak had more to say.

"Please convey my regards to all Canadian hockey fans," he said. "You are in the two biggest Canadian cities and I would like the people to know that I especially like to come to Canada because people there truly like hockey.

"I would say that the three countries which really love the game are the USSR, Czechoslovakia and Canada.

"Personally, I very much regret that these games aren't being played in Canada. Series like this should be held in Canada."

Even though the big American networks were paying no attention to the series, the press contingent was both large and cosmopolitan. With three Swedish stars on the team, a large number of Swedish writers had arrived, including one notorious drunk who, on the press bus to the opening game, stood up and delivered a tirade to the North American media about Swedish athletes.

His point was that, even though Sweden was well represented in sports like tennis, hockey and soccer, all the best Swedes stayed at home. "Sounds like two World Wars," muttered someone in the crowd. Thinking that the line had been delivered by *Toronto Sun* writer Jim Hunt (it hadn't), the tipsy Swede attacked Hunt.

Hunt was probably the oldest guy on the bus, but fortunately, the Swede was too inebriated to do any damage before he was pulled off, and the media horde on the bus, gossips to the core, dashed into the rink more concerned with relating the tale of the encounter than setting up for the game.

According to later reports, the Swede was moved out of sports and in a subsequent posting he distinguished himself at an ambassador's reception by getting roaring drunk, falling down the stairs, throwing up and swearing loudly at a perplexed dignitary, a series of actions that got him reassigned once more. The line concerning Swedish neutrality became a part of hockey lore and was used for years afterwards. It even appears again in this book.

As for New York hockey fans themselves, they turned out in full force, despite the lack of network attention. For the series opener on Thursday night, Madison Square Garden was sold out.

In keeping with the overall Soviet approach, the players' sweaters were a bit more modern than they had been in 1972, but the numbers on their backs still looked as if they had been designed in the 1940s.

The game started with no one sure what to expect from this new-look Soviet team, and only sixteen seconds in,

Lafleur made Tretiak look more like an author than a goal-tender. He took a precision pass from Clarke, moved in on goal, faked Tretiak to the ice, then stepped around him and slid the puck into the net.

After that, the Canadians played a virtually perfect game. They followed Bowman's instructions to the letter and dominated in time of possession. Because the NHLers were playing opponents who, at that stage, weren't as devoted to a checking game as those they faced during the regular season, they were able to be more creative than usual, and they made the most of that rare opportunity. "The Soviets don't have a patent on pretty passing plays, you know," laughed NHL forward Steve Shutt.

The Canadians blocked the middle all night long; they provided tenacious forechecking and delivered some bone-crunching body checks. But through it all, they were very conscious of the potential of the Soviet team and were careful to become neither reckless nor overconfident.

"We wanted to make sure they didn't start wheeling," said Shutt. "They play the puck from one defenceman to the other defenceman to the centre. The centre is the key guy in their play. We blocked off that play and it caused them a bit of difficulty."

In short, they bottled the Soviets up. "They like to play for the home run," said NHL defenceman Serge Savard. "They're always going for the long pass. We have to make sure they don't get away with it."

"We didn't let them get started," said Savard's colleague Larry Robinson. "We were taking the man after he made the pass. Their patterns often call for a man to go to a spot for a return pass. If he's not there because he has been taken out, the pass goes wild."

Only six minutes after Lafleur scored, Gilbert Perreault made a dazzling rush up the middle, then set up Mike Bossy to make it 2–0. The wily Soviet veteran Boris Mikhailov tried to get his team going when he scored five minutes later, a development that did not come as a surprise to Bowman.

"He's very crafty," he said. "He's as crafty a player as they have. He's not a big guy, but he's quite an agitator. He's always in the mix-ups and he uses his stick. He's excellent at finishing plays."

But before the first period ended, Canada made it 3–1. Bob Gainey swept around Soviet defencemen Sergei Starikov, waited until Tretiak went down to one knee, then snapped a forehand shot over his shoulder.

When Bossy stole the puck from Gennady Tsygankov and set up Clark Gillies for a backhanded goal in the second period, the game was as good as over, even though the Soviets did narrow the gap to 4–2 in the third period.

This domination on the part of Team NHL had been greeted with roars of approval from the enthusiastic New York crowd, but when the NHLers went into a defensive shell in the third period, they grew a bit testy—especially since there was no sign of their local heroes, Hedberg and Nilsson.

"We want the Swedes," they chanted. "We want the Swedes."

They weren't getting them. Bowman left them on the bench. He knew the importance of defence in this series, and his charges were producing a superb game. He wasn't about to reward those who weren't contributing. He also knew he would need a lot more than two strong offensive periods to win this series, and already, dark clouds loomed on the horizon.

In the third period, Tikhonov started to use a line of three youngsters who played together for Gorky Torpedo in the USSR: Mikhail Varnakov, Alexander Skvortsov and Vladimir Kovin. If you were a Team NHL fan, it seemed reasonable to assume that this line's success was attributable to the Canadians' devotion to defence by that stage of the game. But then again, maybe it was the Soviets' speed and tenacity that allowed the trio to bottle up every

Canadian line they faced. They were quietly doing to the NHLers what the NHLers had just been doing to them.

Canadian fans were euphoric with the final result, but those closer to the game realized that it probably wouldn't continue to be this easy. En route to its 4–2 series-opening victory, Team NHL had produced a virtually perfect game, while the Soviets, as anyone who looked at the proceedings impartially could see, had played well below their capabilities.

Soviet forward Vladimir Golikov was asked, in view of this latest defeat at the hands of the Canadians, when he thought Soviet hockey might reach the level of the NHL. "Tomorrow," he said.

"The Russians played lousy," said Harry Sinden, who had coached Team Canada in the 1972 series. "It's true you only play as well as the other team lets you, but they were making bad plays and bad passes even when they weren't being bothered."

"You wait and see," offered Torrey. "The Russians can adjust. They're in this to be the best."

"Don't start celebrating yet," warned Alan Eagleson, the head of the NHL Players' Association, "We've got [referee] Viktor Dombrowski on Saturday so we'll be playing the whole game shorthanded."

The referee in the series opener had been the late John McCauley, a wonderful man who went on to become the National Hockey League's head of officiating. After the game, he was minding his own business, having a sandwich in a nearby restaurant with the game's linesmen, when a man walked up to him and punched him in the eye. It wasn't an irate hockey fan, just someone who, judging by a remark he made, had been offended by the conversation he had overheard.

McCauley's sight in his left eye was so badly damaged that he had to be hospitalized. After a long stretch of recuperation, his sight finally was finally restored to the point that he thought he might be able to get back to officiating.

But when he gave it a try, he realized he couldn't do it and he retired to work for the league in an administrative capacity.

McCauley was an excellent referee, probably the most respected in the NHL at the time. His judgment was impeccable, and he had a wry sense of humour that he often used to defuse potentially volatile situations.

Occupying the other end of the refereeing spectrum was Dombrowski, who had attained an unparalleled level of infamy during the 1972 Summit Series—in Canada, that is. In the USSR, he was so highly regarded that he had been all but incorporated into the team.

The Soviets had insisted that one of their referees be included in the officiating rotation for the Challenge Cup, and Dombrowski was the man. Actually, he was more than the man. He was one of the boys. He skated with the Soviet squad when they practised, making passes and taking shots on the goalies. He travelled with the team and was a full-fledged member of the entourage, eating with them and going on their excursions.

"I've lost count of how many games he has ruined when I've been coaching," said the late Billy Harris, the coach of Team Canada '74 and a veteran of international hockey. "He can't skate. He can't keep up with the play."

But then again, by the time the end of game two rolled around, neither could the Canadians.

They started well enough, building a 4–2 lead when Robinson scored with a little more than five minutes gone in the second period. But Tretiak hadn't been particularly sharp and had allowed those four goals on only seven shots. He was about to step up the level of his performance dramatically. Robinson's goal turned out to be the last that Team NHL would get, not only in that game, but in the entire series.

Tikhonov took Bowman's tactics from the opening game and threw them right back in his face. This time, it was the Soviets who were doing the heavy forechecking, not the Canadians. The Gorky Torpedo line continued its domination.

"They forechecked the hell out of us in our own end," said Clarke in a somewhat redundant but nevertheless graphic appraisal. "In fact, it seemed we played the entire game in our own end. They were intense. They knocked us off the puck every chance they got. They were simply better than we were."

And they did it under atrocious conditions. Madison Square Garden officials, true to their usual disdain for hockey, had rented the building to a track meet on Friday. With the Saturday game scheduled as an afternoon affair, in hopes of attracting a TV audience, the ice conditions were appalling.

Not that the NHLers could use that as an excuse. It was clear that the Soviets were better in the skill aspects of the game, and the bad ice probably saved the NHL from a more lopsided loss.

Despite pockmarked, rutted ice, the Soviets built a strong edge in time of possession. Although the puck was bouncing like an India-rubber ball, they still managed to complete passes and stickhandle well enough to keep the puck away from the Canadians. Statistics on such matters weren't very precise in those days, but there were suggestions afterwards that the time of possession broke down roughly to a 70–30 split.

As it was, the two-goal lead started to evaporate when Dombrowski lived up to his billing and sent off Barry Beck for rattling Alexander Skvortsov into the boards with such force that his helmet flew off. The check was clean by NHL standards, but not by Dombrowski's.

It was the kind of call referees tend to assess upon a team that is enjoying a two-goal lead, and the Soviets took advantage of it. Again, it was Mikhailov who came to the fore. The thirty-four-year-old veteran was the captain of the Soviet team, and he was making it clear why he had been accorded that honour. He was starting to take charge of the series and turn the momentum around.

He was playing with the kind of fervour not usually seen in the Soviet system. It had often been said that the Soviets took a robotic approach to the game, and on most occasions, that observation was valid. They rarely showed emotion, and in the early meetings between the two countries, they shocked Canadians by not even raising their sticks in jubilation after scoring a goal—they just went back and awaited the face-off.

Certainly there was dedication to the task at hand. They always worked hard. If they didn't, the coach would let them know about it in no uncertain terms as soon as they returned to the bench.

But there could be no denying the fact that in many games, they did indeed play like machines—finely tuned machines, perhaps, but machines nevertheless.

Suddenly, midway through the series, it was clear that Mikhailov was no machine. He was playing like a human being—an excited and highly committed human being. There was an extra jump in his step, an extra pop in his checks. And remarkably enough, the Soviets were indeed laying on the checks. If they weren't outhitting the NHLers, they were definitely matching them hard check for hard check.

With the Soviets on the power play as a result of Beck's penalty, the Canadians were under intense pressure. As the seconds ticked away, it appeared that they might escape unscathed, but with five seconds left, Mikhailov, set up in the slot, snapped a shot past goaltender Ken Dryden to narrow the gap to 4–3.

Bowman always found goals of that nature to be demoralizing. "It always hurts more when you've killed most of the penalty and then they get one," was his contention.

Shortly afterwards, with another face-off deep in the Canadian end, he sent out the always reliable Clarke to take the draw. If there was one area in which the Canadians excelled against the Soviets, it was face-offs, and Bowman, who revelled in studying statistics long before the practice became fashionable, knew it. By the time the series ended, the Soviets had gained possession on only 36 per cent of the draws. The NHLers were so dominant in the first game that afterwards, Clarke was quoted as saying he wasn't even sure the Soviets were trying on the face-offs.

But they won this one. Viktor Zhluktov beat Clarke cleanly, getting the puck to Sergei Kapustin, who promptly beat Dryden. The Soviets had scored twice in forty-five seconds.

The MSG crowd was quiet, but leading the cheers for the Soviets was Mikhailov—on the bench, leaning over and banging the boards with his stick, not the kind of activity normally associated with the reserved, dispassionate Soviets.

By now, the Canadians were on their heels, and the Soviets poured it on. Only 1:31 into the third period, Moscow Dynamo forward Vladimir Golikov popped in his second of the series, and that was all the Soviets would need.

Even though the Canadians tried resolutely to mount a counterattack, the Soviets, especially the Gorky Torpedo line, shut them down, so much so that Canada was able to muster only six shots in that third period, an astonishingly low total for a team packed with offensive stars desperately seeking a tying goal and playing in an era of free-wheeling hockey.

Yet such was the Soviet domination that those six shots represent the highest Canadian total of any period in that game. The NHL stars had been outshot 31–16.

Now the Canadians were up against the wall. They had to play a rubber match on Sunday night, their third game in four days. Given the sticky New York ice and the Soviets' overwhelming superiority in conditioning, the prospects were far from rosy.

But if there was one area in which Canadian hockey far excelled, it was physical intimidation. Clarke and his

Philadelphia Flyers, aptly nicknamed the Broad Street Bullies, had won the Stanley Cup twice in the seventies. The Montreal Canadiens had won the next four Cups by adding enough enforcers to their core talent to keep the Flyers and Boston Bruins—and knuckle-draggers all over the league—at bay.

Bench-clearing brawls were common in the NHL, and the oft-repeated dictum of former Toronto Maple Leafs president Conn Smythe that if you couldn't beat them in the alley, you couldn't beat them on the ice, was questioned by no one. Every Canadian fan knew that the winning goal in the 1972 Summit Series had been provided by Paul Henderson, but they also knew that the turning point in that series was Clarke's vicious slash on Valery Kharlamov, which broke the Soviet superstar's ankle and got rid of the biggest thorn in Team Canada's side.

So, faced with adversity in the 1979 Challenge Cup, the Canadians knew what to do. Get physical. Or, to put it a touch more succinctly, play dirty.

They knew they couldn't be too openly aggressive because Bowman had warned them about the danger of taking penalties. But there was nothing to stop the marginal infractions, such as Bryan Trottier giving Skvortsov a face-wash with his glove after the whistle, or Lanny McDonald faking a butt-end to the stomach of Balderis with the clear implication that the next one might not stop at a fake. Don Marcotte, always a solid checker, took advantage of the situation to be more solid than ever—and not always with his elbows down. Beck flattened anyone who came close. The Canadians used their whole arsenal of cross-checks, elbows, slashes and any other nefarious method that might come to mind. Yet they somehow came out of it unpenalized—Dombrowski had worked his one game and was through for the series.

But if the Canadians were expecting the Soviets to roll over, they would be disappointed. Mikhailov, as the clear leader of the Soviet squad, was a prime target, but he bounced up from every check, even the wicked slash across the legs delivered by the surprise netminder of the day, Gerry Cheevers.

"Nobody else on that team ever said a word," recalled Clarke in 2005, "but he was always screaming at them on the ice. He was their leader, no doubt about it."

As for hockey, the Canadians weren't terribly impressive. The first period had almost reached the halfway mark when they got their first serious scoring chance, and it was clear that their conditioning—or the lack thereof—was starting to take its toll.

They were giving all they had if it appeared that they might create a good offensive opportunity, but when the Soviets turned the play around, the Canadians were invariably trailing behind in the slipstream.

They managed to hang in throughout the first period, but the feeling in the press box during the intermission was that if the Soviets were to get a lead and force the Canadians to try to mount a comeback, the result might not be pretty. By this stage of the series, the Soviets were clearly superior to the Canadians in the finesse areas of the game, and if the NHL players were to get trapped while trying to tie the score, the Soviets would make them pay the price. After all, by the time that first period ended, the Canadians had played almost fifty-five minutes without scoring.

Canadian fans recalled Bowman's explanation of his strategy in this series: "If the offence is working, that provides the defence." But the offence wasn't working.

And the Canadians weren't even facing Tretiak any longer. Tikhonov, in a masterful psychological ploy, had started his "backup" goalie Vladimir Myshkin, a short, blond, pudgy twenty-four-year-old of whom they had virtually no knowledge. As it turned out, Myshkin was the designated goalie of the future, but such was the Soviet penchant for secrecy that none of the Canadians knew that at the time.

The breaking point came not far into the second period. Mikhailov, sporting the number 13 that was worn by no NHL player at the time, was proving to be unmanageable.

At times, he exhibited the grace of Jean Beliveau as he floated around the Canadian defence. At other times, he turned on the jets and went flying down the wing. In the battles in front of the net, he stood his ground, resolutely refusing to concede the area he had claimed as his own.

Off the ice, with his crumpled nose and battle-scarred face, he looked more like an aging middleweight fighter than a hockey player. But on the ice, he possessed all the qualities that would have made him an all-star in the NHL.

The Canadians were still managing to preserve the scoreless tie when the Soviets mounted an attack. Golikov moved through the neutral zone, then fed Mikhailov as he crossed the blue line.

Beck was waiting for him, but the crafty Mikhailov made a deke as if he were going to leave a drop pass, one of the Soviets' favourite ploys. Naturally enough, Beck reacted to the move, and for an instant was frozen as he started to move towards the phantom pass before realizing that it wasn't there.

That gave Mikhailov the split second he needed to unleash his wicked wrist shot undeterred. In those days, the butterfly style of goaltending had not been popularized. Goalies were encouraged to remain standing as long as possible. As a result, the most dangerous shots were the ones directed towards the corner and about six inches off the ice. They were too low for the goalie to get a glove on, and a pad save required the goalie's leg to travel the maximum distance.

That is exactly where Mikhailov put his shot, and Cheevers never had a chance.

The dam had been breached.

There was no doubt as to which had been the better team to this point. The Canadians had been hanging on, but they were gasping. They clearly lacked the conditioning of the Soviets. The press corps had been of the opinion that if the Canadians could perhaps get a goal of some sort, even a lucky one, they might be able to make it stand up. But if the Soviets were the ones who scored first, the outlook was grim.

In typical fashion, the disheartened, frustrated Canadians tried to redouble their intimidation, but it backfired. Only forty seconds after Mikhailov's goal, Marcotte was sent to the box, and the Soviets scored again on the ensuing power play.

This much must be said about the players who play international hockey for Canada. They may get beaten and they may make mistakes. Sometimes, rarely, they even give their country cause to be ashamed. But they never lack heart.

Down by two goals to a team that was fitter and more skilled, they knew they were in deep trouble. Only a miracle could save them now. Still, they kept trying.

But when Cheevers allowed a soft goal to make the score 3–0 in the third period, the fire went out. The Soviets were eager to stoke the propaganda machine and prove that they were the best in the world, and by the time the game finished, the score was a humiliating 6–0.

Philadelphia Flyers owner Ed Snider, of all people, decreed that it was "the worst disgrace in hockey history." There were plenty of hockey fans in that era who would have said that when it came to hockey disgraces, Team NHL '79 would have to go a long way to surpass the teams that Snider's organization had put on the ice. Still, there was no shortage of shame in Canada. The plight of the national game, as exhibited by the Challenge Cup debacle, was even discussed in the House of Commons.

Canadians had consoled themselves for years with the assertion that their hockey players were the best in the world, and it had just become painfully evident that they weren't. Every player on the Soviet team was a superb skater. The same claim could not be made about the NHL team.

"There were two big factors in their favour in that series," recalled Bowman. "One, they had a balanced team. They didn't worry much about matching lines or power-play units. Whoever's turn it is, that's who goes on.

"That's why they always wanted to play these series with twenty-two players, whereas we used twenty in the NHL. They had two goalies and twenty skaters because they wanted to play four units of five.

"I tried it for a while when I was in Detroit, and it makes sense. If five guys play together all the time, they get to be a lot better than guys who just come together and play with different guys all the time.

"The other thing they had going for them was the conditioning. They'd had those five-man units go on and off, but in those days, some of our guys would stay on two minutes because they paced themselves and the game wasn't as fast. Some guys, like Phil Esposito, would stay on for two and a half minutes You didn't push all the time. You went when you had to go.

"The Russians had those two big edges—the conditioning and the five-man format."

The skill level exhibited by the Soviets was higher as well. And their conditioning level wasn't merely superior to that of the NHL—it was in another stratum. The truth could no longer be avoided: an era had ended. Canadians were no longer the best hockey players in the world.

The Canadians had given it their best shot. They had sent their best available team. But they had lost. Badly. They could drag out none of the usual excuses. The games were played in midseason, so game-readiness couldn't be an issue. The top coach in the game was behind the bench. The games were all played in an NHL rink in front of a partisan crowd. For two of the three games, they had NHL refereeing.

As Gainey, one of the few Canadian players to come out and meet the media right after the final game, said, "I think we prepared as well as we could. And you can't look at anybody and say he didn't play as hard as he could."

No. But even so, it wasn't good enough.

For years, there had been those in and around the sport who had maintained that while rough, tough hockey was certainly acceptable, too much emphasis had been placed upon intimidation. An oft-repeated joke suggested that the reason Canadian streets were so safe was that all the criminals were playing hockey.

You simply had no hope of coming close to winning in those days if you didn't have a string of enforcers in your lineup. One was never enough. Two gave you a chance. Three would be better. Four meant that you could genuinely count on your stars getting a chance to play.

The violence wasn't confined to the professional ranks. Youngsters growing up with NHL aspirations in that era emulated the performances they saw on television. The goon shows were just as bad in junior hockey—probably worse. And the malaise infected every level of the minor-hockey system.

It was a message that Savard had been delivering privately for some time. But right after the Challenge Cup, when he came out and joined Gainey in an almost-deserted dressing room, he laid his feelings bare.

"We can't say that hockey is ours anymore," he said. "Now we'll have to make some great adjustments to our game."

Such as?

"Maybe now we'll stop trying to develop goons," he said. "There's not too many 5'8" players being drafted in the NHL lately, but there were a lot of them on the ice tonight.

"For the last five years, I haven't let my son play organized hockey because it is so violent. We tried to sell the game with violence back in 1971, '72 and '73," he continued.

"We just got the answer tonight."

There were some extenuating circumstances behind the NHL's inept showing against the Soviets, but not many. However, in fairness, the impact of a rival league, the World Hockey Association, had to be taken into consideration.

Because players in the NHL always knew that they could find a job in the WHA if need be, there was nowhere near as much commitment as there had been when the NHL was a monopoly.

Furthermore, the NHL had expanded from six teams to twelve in 1967, then added two more teams in 1970. And two more in 1972. And another two in 1974. Toss in the twelve WHA teams that came into existence in 1972, and it stands to reason that the calibre of major-league hockey in the seventies was not what it should have been—or used to be. Furthermore, it must be kept in mind that no new sources of talent were available to be tapped, as was the case a few years later when the Soviet Union crumbled.

Peer pressure is a major factor in the development of professional athletes. By nature, they are competitive people and they tend to develop their skills much more comprehensively if those around them—be they opponents or teammates—are pushing the limits. But with the top leagues being so watered down, there was very little incentive to improve.

There were other factors. In many venues, the two leagues were fighting for fans. And the best way to get them, they thought, was to fight on the ice. Many a team—in both the NHL and WHA—promoted its product by marketing its mayhem rather than promoting its skilled players.

Little wonder, then, that no Soviet team would want to go into the alley with an NHL team. But on the ice, the Soviets justifiably felt quite confident.

There were those who spoke out against the widespread promotion of violence, but they were in the minority. Less than two months before the Challenge Cup, Dryden put forward his opinions, saying, "Hockey made a terrible error by deciding that they were essentially going to sell themselves on this basis. The first association that uninitiated people had with the game was: hockey means no teeth and fights.

"If the game is to hope to function as a television sport, rather than as a gate-receipts sport, then it needs a mass of acceptance. And surely this is not the way to attain that mass of acceptance. Hockey is still paying for that mistake."

It paid another installment during the Challenge Cup, but there were more negative aspects to the existence of the WHA than the mere promotion of violence.

A major-league sport must have the full-time attention of its overseers, and during the NHL–WHA war, the product was all but ignored. The two sides first tried to put each other out of business, then tried to find a way to merge to their mutual benefit. But there was no united front. Too many within the NHL opposed any attempt at conciliation. Philadelphia's Snider, for instance, was one of those who favoured a merger, while Harold Ballard, owner of the Toronto Maple Leafs, was vehemently opposed. The animosity within the NHL was so great that, one morning during a round of league meetings at the Queen Elizabeth Hotel in Montreal, Ballard was informed that a small fire had broken out on Snider's floor the night before.

"I wish I'd known," he growled. "I'd have gone up there and poured gasoline on it."

Each side in this internecine war fired lawsuits at the other, and millions of dollars that could have been allocated to promoting the game or developing its positive aspects were instead squandered on legal fees.

Furthermore, the NHL was never particularly strong after its 1967 expansion, and after 1972 the weak teams suffered even greater difficulties because of the impact of WHA encroachment. Money that could have been better used elsewhere had to be diverted to propping up these weak franchises.

Even when the two leagues decided that it would be better for both if they could effect some form of merger, the focus was still not on hockey. They held approximately twenty meetings in locales all over the two countries— three, if you count the meeting they held in the Bahamas.

In 1972, Team Canada barely scraped past the best team the Soviets could put on the ice. For the next seven years, the Soviets developed their skills and worked towards the day when they would get another chance to face the Canadians head to head.

During the course of those seven years, the NHL had wasted its energy fighting a rival league, fighting on the ice and fighting lawsuits. The game and its development received no attention whatsoever. No wonder the Soviets won so handily.

Nor was the on-ice showing the only disaster to befall the NHL.

The league had made a number of concessions to the TV moguls it hoped to attract, including staging the series in New York and scheduling one of the games on Saturday afternoon. But in a display of what was either incompetence or greed, the NHL insisted on selling board advertising. The big New York affiliates, the flagships of the networks, consequently refused to show highlights because of potential conflicts with their own sponsors, ensuring that the series was played in virtual secrecy as far as TV viewers were concerned.

When the TV ratings for the Challenge Cup finally arrived, they showed that the games had been played before a worldwide audience of approximately 250 million people. But in New York, the response had been a collective shrug. And by the time those numbers came in, the NHL was wishing that the rest of the world had shown the same cavalier attitude as the American networks.

The Challenge Cup fiasco was an embarrassment that the league was never really able to overcome. It continued to try to flog its product to the networks, to little avail.

For the next decade, NHL president John Ziegler tried to rationalize the situation, repeatedly insisting that the NHL was the Cadillac of sports leagues, whereas other sports were the Chevrolets.

But the fact remained that no major U.S. network wanted his game, leaving the league little choice but to sell rights for piddling sums to cable networks—which were then only in their formative stages.

The league's TV people did manage to sell an occasional all-star game here and there, and eventually, a limited number of late-season games in selected markets. But one of the NHL's major problems, which has persisted to this day, has been that inability to rely on significant TV revenues. Without them, the league is chronically short of money, unable to match the salaries that are paid in other major-league sports, and therefore incapable of being profitable enough to avoid labour strife.

Instead of proving its superiority, the NHL had shown the world its weakness, its dearth of skill and its lack of properly conditioned athletes. A country that had been taking the game seriously for no more than a quarter of a century mauled the country that had the richest hockey heritage in the world.

Over the final ninety-five minutes of the series, the NHL players had been outscored 9–0.

"Mikhailov was their captain and I was the captain, so he came up to me after the game to shake hands," recalled Clarke. "He grabbed my hand, leaned towards me so our faces were inches apart, and said, 'Ha, ha, ha.' I wanted to kill him."

When the Challenge Cup was first announced, there had been broad hints from the organizers that this head-to-head matchup might evolve into regular competitions of this nature between the NHL and the Soviet Union.

But after the embarrassing result, those suggestions were quickly forgotten. There was never another Challenge Cup. And it would be a further five long years before Canadians were able to demonstrate, in the 1984 Canada Cup, that their hockey superiority was not a thing of the past.

For those who watched the Challenge Cup, there were

many memorable moments. But for me, the most lasting involved Boris Mikhailov.

Under the stands, after the game, he emerged from the dressing room wearing an ugly purple-and-orange windbreaker of dubious provenance. A crest on the left breast read, "Montreal Hockey Club."

Spotting Alan Eagleson, he broke into a smile, walked over and held up one finger.

"Soviets," he said.

Then he held up two fingers.

"Canada."

Even Eagleson had no response to that.

THE GOAL: MAY 10, 1979.

Game seven of the Stanley Cup semifinal.
Scored by Guy Lafleur (assisted by Jacques Lemaire)
at 18:46 of the third period. Montreal Canadiens 5,
Boston Bruins 4 (overtime).

IN HIS PRIME, GUY LAFLEUR WAS THE MOST TALENTED PLAYER IN the game. With his hair streaming behind him, he would blaze down the right wing, move in on goal and rip a blistering shot that was uncannily accurate.

Goalies didn't venture very far out of their nets in those days, and as a result, there was invariably a space, albeit a narrow one, between their pads and the post. That opening was Lafleur's primary target, and even though the goalies sometimes managed to react in time to block his shots, there were 327 occasions over a six-year span when they didn't.

In his first three seasons with the Montreal Canadiens, Lafleur didn't live up to his billing, scoring just 29, 28 and 21 goals. During his junior hockey career, many had touted him as the best player to emerge in decades, perhaps ever, and when he didn't immediately become the dominant player in the National Hockey League, many of his devotees felt cheated. Considering the torrent of hyperbole that had preceded him, this was hardly surprising.

The less mercurial in the hockey world were willing to wait a little longer, realizing that Lafleur was still a boy playing against men.

Canadiens general manager Sam Pollock had been so impressed by Lafleur's brilliance at the junior level that he had used all the Machiavellian tricks in his extensive repertoire to acquire his services.

First, he fleeced the California Golden Seals by sending them Ernie Hicke and the Canadiens' 1970 first-round draft pick in exchange for the Seals' 1971 first-round pick and Francois Lacombe. Hicke averaged about 16 goals a season over the course of his NHL career, and the Seals used the 1970 pick to take Chris Oddleifson, whom they traded away before he ever played a game for them. They didn't miss a lot—Oddleifson was a gritty player, but he scored only 95 goals in his 524 NHL games.

However, to Pollock's horror, he noticed in early 1971 that the Los Angeles Kings were going through a rough stretch and could conceivably end up being even worse than the abysmal Seals. Should they manage to slide into last place, they would select first in the upcoming June draft.

To thwart this, Pollock acted swiftly. He sent a first-rate player, Ralph Backstrom, to Los Angeles for Gord Labossiere and Ray Fortin. Neither ever played for the Canadiens, nor did Pollock expect them to. The trade was basically a donation to strengthen the Kings.

"Sammy Pollock denies that, but I say it's true," recalled Backstrom with a chuckle. "It was a mutual thing. I told him I wanted to be traded, but he waited and waited, probably to see where to send me.

"The funny thing was that I went up to see him after practice that day, he said, 'You're going to Los Angeles. I've got [Kings owner] Jack Kent Cooke on the phone.'

"It was about noon. I talked to Mr. Cooke and I said, 'I'll be there tomorrow.'

"He said, 'You'll be here tonight! You've got a reservation on the four o'clock flight.'

"I had four hours to go home, tell my wife and family, make all the arrangements, pack for two months and get to the airport."

Sure enough, Backstrom's contributions lifted the Kings clear of the Seals, and Pollock was able to use that coveted first-overall pick to select Lafleur.

For three years it appeared that Pollock's machinations might never pay off, but finally, in his fourth year, Lafleur discarded his helmet and suddenly became the best player in the game.

Many hockey parents of the era insisted that there was no correlation between those two events. Lafleur simply blossomed, they told their sons, and even though he's your favourite player, you don't have to do what he did. Wear your helmet for safety.

The facts were quite different. Lafleur loved the feeling of playing without a helmet. He could feel his hair flowing in the breeze; it gave him a sensation of speed and superiority—almost invulnerability.

Many of today's players experience similar feelings of ambivalence about visors. While they understand the inherent benefits of the protection they provide, they insist that the sensation of their surroundings is inhibited when they wear a visor.

As a garage-league player, as Mario Lemieux would phrase it, the distinction was never quite clear to me. But in 2004 I attended a Canadian Football League game in what was then still known as the Skydome. The game began with the roof closed and nothing seemed to be amiss. Then, late in the first quarter, the roof opened—and all of a sudden, the game seemed different. It was a totally changed atmosphere—a much better and more open atmosphere. The game seemed more alive.

The feelings that Lafleur experienced when he shed his helmet may have been similar. They lifted his spirits in the way that many of us find our moods altered by a bright, sunny day after a week of rain. Rationally, the weather shouldn't make any difference to our lives. It doesn't affect our jobs, our financial status or our everyday concerns. Nevertheless, our surroundings can make us feel better. Similarly, removing his helmet made Lafleur feel better, and in a league where confidence plays a major role in an individual's performance, it made him play better.

When he was flying down the ice with the puck on his stick and his hair trailing in his slipstream, he was a brilliant goal waiting to happen. He was Guy Lafleur, the best hockey player in the universe. He won three Art Ross Trophies, three Lester B. Pearson Awards, two Hart Trophies and five Stanley Cup rings.

In the mid-seventies, Lafleur was on top of the hockey world, but unfortunately for him, there were times when he had to leave the arena. And no matter how he tried, he was never comfortable away from the game.

He was a bundle of contradictions, a man who had no difficulty handling the pressures of being the best player on hockey's most storied team and playing in front of the most demanding fans in the National Hockey League, but who always had great difficulty handling the pressures of everyday life.

"He was a private guy," explained one of his teammates of the era, Doug Risebrough. "I think one of the basic and misunderstood elements of Guy was that he was a shy person in a lot of ways. Here was a guy who was compelled through his hockey abilities to have to be more than just a hockey player.

"I always think of the moments with Guy when you'd go to the practice and he'd be on the ice before you got there. And I always got there early.

"Here was guy who just really liked to be out there shooting the pucks around. And that wasn't just one incident. That was regular.

"I think he was just basically a shy person. My memories of Guy are all positive. I think one of the things about a star player is that if he's a true star, he has to make all the players on the team feel good, and for a guy who's really a shy person, it's a different situation than for a guy who's really outgoing.

"I always had a very basic feeling with Guy that he liked me and he respected me and he appreciated what I did on the ice. It came across with that little smile, that quick smile that would kind of fall away. Whatever you wanted to do on the ice, he'd join in."

Lafleur's longtime linemate Steve Shutt summed it up perfectly one day when asked to comment on suggestions that Lafleur should run for political office at the end of his hockey career. Shutt had no doubt about Lafleur's popularity, but his ability to handle any role away from the rink was another matter. "He'd get elected," said Shutt, "but he'd get lost on his way to his seat."

Even though 1979 is within the memory of many of today's hockey fans, there are many who would hardly recognize the game of that era. There were no ads on the boards back then, and the crease was a simple rectangle that extended out four feet from the goalposts. Markings on the ice were standard throughout the league—and throughout the season, except for the occasional "Season's Greetings" that might be laid down in late December.

A debate over the efficacy of helmets still raged, and most players didn't wear them. Tube skates were on their way out, but were not yet completely gone. Sticks were universally made of wood and the tape was always black. Players' equipment was often battle-scarred and was not an exercise in product placement. The goalies' equipment had not yet ballooned to today's proportions; it was there to stop injury, not take up space, and the flopping, butterfly style of netminding was years away.

In most arenas, the scoreboards did nothing more than provide the score and the penalty times. Chicago Stadium had a series of small clocks that were supposed to give an indication of penalty times, but to most people, they were incomprehensible. Legendary Canadiens broadcaster Danny

Gallivan never did figure them out, and he complained about them on every trip into Chicago. The scoreboards certainly had no movies, instant replays or cartoons. Some arenas had pipe organs, but in most cases, if the fans wanted sound effects, it was up to them to provide their own. The rinks were noisy and intimate, and they smelled like hockey.

The league was almost totally populated by Canadians, and they all tended to take a rather cavalier approach to conditioning. In that respect, Lafleur stood out. He had an astonishing work ethic.

In the early years, he would regularly stay out after practice with assistant coach Claude Ruel, working hour after hour on developing his skills.

Ruel would stand in the corner with a few dozen pucks while Lafleur circled at centre ice. Then Lafleur would break over the blue line at full speed and Ruel would snap a puck onto his stick. Lafleur would make a feint, fire the puck at the net and head out to centre ice to do it again.

The drill would go on and on. In over the blue line. Make the move. Shoot the puck. Skate back out to centre. All the time, Ruel would be yelling bilingual encouragement. "Go, *mon Guy*. Drive! Drive! *Allez. Allez.* Six seconds. Six seconds. Go. Go." In all Ruel's drills, there were always six seconds left in the game—never five, never seven.

Sometimes, those of us in the media would go into the dressing room after practice, talk to the players, talk to coach Scotty Bowman and start to head off for lunch, only to see that Lafleur was still working on his game.

"Guy was always anxious to be on the ice," recalled Guy Lapointe, one of the star defencemen on that team. "If the game was at 7:30, we'd walk in around 6:15 or 6:30. Flower would already be dressed. Only his jersey would be missing and he'd be walking around the room with his stick in his hand.

"He was always a great guy to be around, a great teammate. If he knew a guy needed a goal for a bonus, he'd always find a way to set him up."

More than most players in the game, Lafleur was aware of the importance of keeping his body in top shape and of giving himself every advantage—at least according to the precepts of the day. He was the first player I heard of who would intentionally shoot wide during warmups in road games just to see how the puck would react when it came off the boards. But away from the rink, he regularly abused that body. He was not only a heavy smoker, he was also much more than just a social drinker.

When the team was on the road, he would often go out on his own, walking the all-but-deserted streets of an American city at night and ending up in some hole-in-the-wall bar to sit by himself, knock back his drinks and stare into space. When the team was at home, he was a regular in a quiet bar at a hotel near Dorval Airport.

More than once, he almost killed himself driving home. On one occasion, his car went off the road and crashed into a fence. A steel pole smashed through the windshield and missed Lafleur's ear by no more than an inch.

On another occasion in 1981, an instance that has never before been made public, he rolled his car when he strayed off the highway. He had a passenger with him, and the hockey world was very lucky not to have lost two of its greatest stars that night. The passenger was Wayne Gretzky.

But perhaps fortune smiles on those who deserve it. The car rolled onto its roof and flipped upright again with no substantial damage. Lafleur drove back onto the highway and went home.

That story stayed out of public circulation for years, because neither Gretzky nor Lafleur wanted it told. But at the Heritage Classic in Edmonton in 2003, Lafleur let it out. However, it still didn't get much notoriety because Lafleur's English isn't as good as his French, and he said that the car "spun." It spun, all right—on its axis.

Yet no matter how late he stayed out the night before, he was always the first player at the rink in the morning and the first player on the ice for practice.

"He always practised hard," recalled Bowman. "He believed the same as Doug Harvey that you could go out at night, but the next day you had to practise hard to get it all out of your system."

Lafleur was a driven man. Being a great player was not good enough for him. He wanted to be incomparable.

As a result, he will never go down as one of the great team players in history. Lafleur had not the slightest desire to set up the winning goal. He had to score it. He wanted nothing more than to have the game rest on his shoulders. Naturally, he wanted the Canadiens to win, but he wanted more than that. He wanted to win their games himself. And for years, he did.

The most memorable of all his goals, the one that Don Cherry will never forget—or live down—is the one that saved the Canadiens from elimination at the hands of the Boston Bruins in 1979.

At that point, Cherry was in his fifth year as coach of the Bruins, and the two teams were bitter rivals, having played each other in the Stanley Cup final the two previous springs. The Canadiens had won on both occasions and were riding a streak of three consecutive Cups. They had four strong lines, lots of depth should injuries occur, a reliable goaltender in Ken Dryden, and what is generally conceded to be the best defence ever.

Bowman was a true taskmaster in those days, and he got results. As Shutt said at the time, "We hated him 364 days a year. On the 365th, we got our Stanley Cup cheque."

He talked the way he coached. His coaching was predicated on a series of quick, decisive actions. And when he talked, it was in sharp, staccato sentences. With the hockey team, he issued clear-cut commands. In conversation, he liked to end his bursts with "eh?"

Let's assume the Canadiens had an upcoming road trip to the west coast. In search of an advance story, you might say to Bowman, "What about the road trip?"

The answer would be something like: "West coast, eh? December. Sam doesn't like home games in December. Can't sell tickets, eh? Too close to Christmas. December. The Kings, eh? They're tough. Good team. Bob Berry. TMR, eh? [Town of Mount Royal, a Montreal suburb.] Vancouver. Always raining. You get up there and it's noon everywhere else. Oakland. Ever try that restaurant in our hotel? Duck specialty, eh? Great duck. They cook if for three days. No grease. After three days, the grease is all gone, eh?"

At that point, he'd spot something that required his attention, and off he'd go, leaving you wondering how you were going to make a story out of those quotes. Obviously, he was a lot different than Cherry.

"There was a lot of animosity between the two teams— and between Scotty and me, too," recalled Cherry, "but we were tougher, and that was the thing that evened it out. We were tougher than them.

"But the one thing I wouldn't allow the players to do is watch the morning skate. The Canadiens put on a morning skate that had you thinking, 'Wow, we've got to play *them* tonight?'"

The bombastic Cherry knew that on paper, his Bruins weren't even close to being a match for Montreal. Dryden had the reputation of being the best goalie in the game. Cherry had a flaky kid, Gilles Gilbert, who hadn't started a playoff game in three years—and had allowed six goals on that occasion. The number one goalie was veteran Gerry Cheevers, who could be great, but sometimes was far from it.

The vaunted Montreal defence was anchored by the players known universally as the Big Three: Larry Robinson, Serge Savard and Guy Lapointe. Cherry had an all-star in Brad Park, but after that, he had to rely on the likes of Gary Doak, Dick Redmond, Mike Milbury and Al Sims.

Up front, each team had good first lines. But the Canadiens were strong throughout. Montreal's fourth line was made up of Bob Gainey, Doug Jarvis and Jimmy

Roberts. For his depth, Cherry had to rely on people like John Wensink, Bob Miller, Stan Jonathan and Peter McNab.

But games aren't played on paper. The Bruins exuded passion, and they were tough in an era when intimidation was a major part of the game. One of Cherry's favourites was Jonathan, a short, stocky scrapper who typified the team. On one memorable night, in a scuffle right in front of the Boston bench, he got the best of Canadiens tough guy Pierre Bouchard, who was about eight inches taller. To Cherry, Jonathan was a bull terrier. That was the ultimate compliment.

Furthermore, the Bruins loved their charismatic coach, who was an absolute master at milking the us-against-the-world approach for all it was worth. He portrayed his players as just a bunch of lunch-pail-carrying working stiffs, battling against all odds to hold their own against the aristocratic Canadiens. He insisted that the league was against the Bruins. The referees were against them. Even his own general manager, Harry Sinden, was against them. And Sinden's assistant, Tom Johnson. And pretty well anybody else in hockey. Don and his loyal foot soldiers were the forces of goodness, trying to fend off all the evil the world could muster.

Even the Canadian customs and immigration officials were part of the nefarious plot. Nowadays, Cherry chortles boisterously as he tells the story.

"We came through the border and the guy said, 'Purpose of your visit?'

"I said, 'To beat the ****ing Montreal Canadiens.' Well, I was over at the side for about half an hour. You know how they go through everything?

"While they're doing this, I noticed a paper on the floor with a nice picture of [Bruins forward] Gregg Sheppard and his kid. So I picked it up and the guy says, 'You can't have that. That's mine.'

"I said, 'Well, I'm taking it.'

"He said, 'You can't have it.' So I reached into my pocket and took out a bunch of change and slapped it down.

"I said, 'Here!' He grabbed it and threw it at me. So I bent down and picked up some and threw it back and it's *zing, zing, zing* all over the place. I'm picking them up and firing them back. He's throwing them at me."

Cherry's acrimony towards Sinden was much more deep-seated. Cherry would regularly criticize the GM to the media, and use Sinden's perceived failings as a spur to his team.

"It got to the point that it was a personal thing," Cherry said.

For his part, Sinden announced publicly that as a result of Cherry's coaching, he didn't expect the Bruins to get past the quarter-final round in 1979.

The series in question was the first playoff round for the Bruins, the second for the Penguins. In that era, twelve teams made the playoffs, but the first-place team in each division earned a bye into the second round. The other eight played a best-of-three series for the right to advance.

By the time the Bruins were ready to go into post-season action, the relationship between general manager and coach had deteriorated so badly that Sinden openly tried to undermine Cherry's authority.

"In our first round against Pittsburgh, Harry called the team off the morning skate," said Cherry. "Can you believe it?

"Anyway, there was a guy whose name was Jim Hamilton and he had scored a bit in the minors and the Pittsburgh Penguins called him up, then sent him down again.

"I would never put the other team's lines on the board the way most coaches do, even against Montreal. If somebody needed to be watched, I had Donny Marcotte to do it. The other guys didn't need to worry about it. The other team could watch us. We weren't going to watch them.

"But Harry had written all the lines on the board and was saying, 'You have to watch this line,' and, 'You have to watch that line.' I was just seething that he would do this to me.

"Then he comes to Hamilton and he says, 'You have to watch this guy. This guy can put the puck in the net.'

"The guys were looking at each other, and once Harry left, they wrote things on the board like 'Are you kidding?' and 'Hamilton who? Check him in Binghamton,' and 'Four straight.'

"And that's what it was. We beat them in four straight.

"But Harry found out about it. The squealer was Tom Johnson. He came in and looked at the board and you could just see him run off to tell Harry. I should have taken it off the board, but at that time I didn't give a damn."

To make matters worse, Cherry's contract was about to expire, and the two sides had been in a protracted dispute over the renewal—if indeed there were going to be one.

When the semifinals opened, three of the four head coaches involved were earning salaries in the $100,000 range. The fourth was Cherry, who earned $60,000, even though his team had the lowest payroll, had the fewest stars and had advanced to the Stanley Cup final the two previous seasons. Cherry had even won the Jack Adams Award as coach of the year. The average player salary at the time was $95,000.

"I knew I was gone," he recalled. "I was only making $60,000 and they didn't want to give me any more. Harry Neale came into the league [with the Vancouver Canucks] and he hadn't won a thing and he had coached in that crap league [the World Hockey Association] and they gave him $100,000."

Sinden hadn't been alone in picking the Penguins over the Bruins. And by the time the semifinals opened, most hockey observers felt that the Bruins were too shallow, too old and too slow to handle the mighty Canadiens, who were by far the league's best team.

But a Montreal-Boston series was always hotly anticipated in Montreal. As far as the Canadiens' fans were concerned, this was the prime rivalry in the game. Fans in Toronto considered the Canadiens to be their fiercest rivals, but that view was not reciprocated in Montreal. When the Bruins came to the Forum, there was always a tingle in the air, no matter which team might be favoured.

Even in the early stages, there were indications that this was to be a memorable series, both on and off the ice. The Canadiens won the first two games at home, and in the press conference after the second, Cherry was asked if he would consider a goaltending change for game three. He allowed that it would be something he might consider.

The questioner then announced that Gilles Gilbert was a better goalie than Gerry Cheevers and that Cherry had erred in using Cheevers.

"And what are your qualifications as a coach?" snapped Cherry. "Who the hell are you, anyway? What paper are you with?"

The questioner wasn't with any paper, he said. He was just a Bruins fan who happened to live near Cherry in North Andover, Massachusetts.

"Get the hell out of here," shouted Cherry. "Security!"

The provision of amenities to visiting teams was never a priority in the Montreal Forum, and naturally enough, no one showed up. Cherry was on his own, which was fine with him.

He marched up to the impostor, grabbed him with both hands, whirled him around and pushed him out into the hallway.

The media loved it. So did Cherry.

"Gee, that felt great," he chuckled. "I wish he'd taken a swing at me. North Andover, indeed! I'll get Blue after him."

No one needed an explanation of Cherry's last statement. His dog, Blue, enjoyed cult status by that time, so much so that Bowman felt the need to tell the media, "I've got a dog, too, you know."

Nobody did know. And nobody really cared. But Bowman insisted that *his* dog, Waldo, be given equal time. "He's even flown on the team charter," said Bowman. "Blue has never done that."

Oh, really? Wow! Stop the presses.

Bowman was far from finished. Waldo was more attractive than Blue, he insisted. He was a white German shepherd, whereas Blue was a bull terrier.

Cherry put an end to the canine controversy by pointing out that Waldo hadn't had his picture in *Sports Illustrated*. Blue had. Therefore, Blue was more famous. End of debate. Cherry turned his attentions elsewhere.

During the previous series against the Maple Leafs, the Canadiens had taken to pouring over the boards and onto the ice to congratulate each other after every goal. In the opener against Boston, they did the same. "My brother phoned me," said Cherry, "and he said they intimidated Toronto the whole series. Every time they'd score, they'd all jump on the ice.

"He said, 'What you should do is throw your whole team on when they do, because there's no rule against it.'"

So Cherry did. The Canadiens scored and their bench emptied. So did the Bruins' bench.

"I threw them all on the ice," said Cherry. "There were forty guys on the ice, pushing and shoving. Gillie Gilbert didn't want to go on—I grabbed him and threw him out there. That's the guy who looks the stupidest—the backup goalie skating around with a towel around his neck. But I said, 'Get out there with the rest of them.'

"They were all out there congratulating Cheevers, and Cheevers was trying to push them away."

Referee Dave Newell was quick to recognize the inherent danger of having the benches empty with one team in a foul mood from having been scored upon. This was an era in which bench-clearing brawls were not uncommon. It wouldn't take much of a spark to create a full-blown donnybrook. He went over to the Boston bench.

"He says, 'You can't do that,'" recounted Cherry. "I said, 'Well, stop *them*, or else after every goal, we're coming out.'"

The next day, an edict was issued from the league office and the Canadiens were told to stay on the bench after their goals.

Trying to dredge some usable quotes out of the Montreal dressing room—on the rare occasions that it was open—was a chore that most media people opted to forgo. Instead, a brief foray to somewhere within the range of Cherry's voice—which, as most people know, is a fairly large area—usually paid dividends.

As early as the second game, Cherry started going after the officials in his statements to the media. The Canadiens came from behind to win 4–2, and as far as Cherry was concerned, Guy Lapointe was offside on Bob Gainey's tying goal.

Cheevers agreed. "If Lapointe wasn't offside, he's awful fast," he said. "He cut right in front of me to screen me when Gainey was still out at the circle taking the shot."

"Oh, doesn't it seem strange?" asked Cherry in the most sarcastic tone he could muster. "All the calls go against us. Oh, well, maybe we'll get all the calls in Boston."

There was a pause. Then, just to make sure that even the dimmest reporter got the point, he added. "Ho, ho, ho."

Bowman, meanwhile, had taken to showing up at the game officials' early-morning skates, magnanimously offering to help the referee and his linesmen better understand all the dirty tactics that those dastardly Bruins were using. And to make sure his advice hadn't slipped their minds by game time, he'd be lurking near the pass door when they arrived at the arena for the game itself.

In the pause between the second and third games, Cherry took the psychological warfare a step further.

"I said, 'If it goes to a sixth game, we'll get screwed because they want Montreal and New York in the next round, not the Boston Bruins, a bunch of scum.'"

This statement was not well received by NHL president John Ziegler, and he wasted no time making Cherry aware of his displeasure.

Cherry recalled, "Ziegler phoned me and he said, 'You know what you're doing? I put up with you because I like you and you're good for the league, but you know what you've just done? You called us dishonest. Now, I'll put up with you calling us stupid and everything, but I won't put up with you calling us dishonest.'

"He said, 'If it was any other coach, I'd have already done something. If you ever say that again, you'll be in serious trouble.' He was going nuts."

Back in Boston for game three, the Bruins rallied with Gilbert in goal. "Maybe it was that guy from North Andover I threw out of the room," conceded Cherry. "Maybe he gave me the idea." But in what turned out to be an ominous development in retrospect, the Bruins got caught with too many men on the ice when Peter McNab went over the boards at an inopportune time.

They also won the fourth game, and this time, the Bruins did appear to get the better of the officiating, taking a lot of liberties with the Canadiens but not being sent off by referee Wally Harris. So now it was the Canadiens' turn to complain.

"It's funny that whenever there's a big brawl in the league," offered Montreal defenceman Serge Savard, "he just happens to be the referee."

After game five, despite a Montreal victory, Canadiens winger Jacques Lemaire joined the chorus. "Cherry sent those guys out there and told them to injure us," he said. "There were high sticks, hacks, all that sort of thing. That's the old NHL at its best.

"I can't understand the refereeing. In the third period, the Bruins didn't take the checks at all. Guys like Stan Jonathan would get hit with a good clean check and retaliate with their sticks and elbows. That's not hockey."

No, but it was the style that Cherry wanted Jonathan to play. In the daily press conferences, Cherry was still referring to Jonathan as his bull terrier. To Cherry, Lemaire was something like a poodle or an Afghan hound.

"You know what a bull terrier does?" asks Cherry. "A bull terrier knows who's boss. She [Blue was a female, so to Cherry, all bull terriers were referred to in the feminine gender] just stops and looks at you with that look that says, 'What are you going to do about it?' No fuss. Just supreme confidence. That's what Jonathan was like."

By this point, the series had developed into a hot story, and each day the papers were filled with claims and counter-claims, usually liberally sprinkled with complaints about the officiating. None of this met with Ziegler's approval. "Can you imagine?" asked Cherry sarcastically. "We were getting too much ink."

Ziegler saw it another way. "He called both Scotty and me in in Boston," recalled Cherry. "He said, 'If you guys keep this up, I'm going to have to do something I don't want to do.' He said, 'This has got to the point that it's ridiculous.'

"So he starts giving us a lecture. He's giving us a lecture, and I look over at Scotty and he's got on a blue suit and he's wearing brown Hush Puppies. Here's Ziegler lecturing us and I'm thinking, 'How the hell can a guy wear brown shoes with a blue suit?' And this is a guy who has won Stanley Cups!"

Ziegler threatened $10,000 fines, a substantial amount to a coach in those days, if the two of them didn't settle down and stick to hockey—and keep their players under control.

That was fine with Bowman. It not only took away some of Cherry's psychological ploys, but it allowed him to justify the media-dodging he had been engaging in in recent days.

"That's why I haven't been talking to you guys much," he said after the Bruins won game six handily to force a one-game showdown. "I haven't got $10,000 I want to throw away. I don't know what you can say or what you can't say. I haven't got the code or the rulebook, so I'm just keeping quiet about it."

As usual, Cherry was giving no consideration whatsoever to avoiding the media.

While being mobbed by the Boston Garden crowd after the Bruins' 5–2 victory, he was relieved of the handkerchief that he had so meticulously inserted into the breast pocket of his black velvet jacket.

"Imagine that," he fumed to the assembled press corps. "That really makes me mad. It matched my tie. Now I know how Elvis felt."

As for the game itself, he said, "We got five goals tonight. There's no reason we can't get five goals up there."

By that point, nobody was ready to argue with anything Cherry said. His Bruins really shouldn't have lasted this long, but their goaltending had been better on some nights, and on every night they played with passion. There were no floaters on Cherry's Bruins, no players out for a skate.

That's not to suggest that the Canadiens were taking a nonchalant approach to the proceedings, but they did have a supreme air of confidence about them. They gave the impression that they felt they had some sort of divine right to the Cup, and that eventually their grace and skill would carry the day.

If that was the case, the day had arrived. There was to be a seventh game, and there was a widespread belief that this was a one-game battle for the Stanley Cup. In the other semifinal series, the New York Rangers had already engineered a stunning upset by defeating their highly favoured crosstown rivals, the New York Islanders, and their chances of pulling off a second major upset were all but nonexistent.

For a hockey fan, there is no more exciting situation than game seven. After battling through six games and coming out even, the two teams must now put everything on the line in one game.

For one of the two, there would be ecstasy and a virtually guaranteed Stanley Cup. For the other, there would be only a gnawing emptiness exacerbated by the realization that all that work, all that pain, all those small triumphs and the three hard-earned victories had amounted to absolutely nothing. The season had ended in failure.

By the time a seventh game comes around, very few players are injury-free, but at this level, there are no excuses. You can get your injury bandaged. You can wear a little extra protection. You can play through the pain. You can even get a needle to take the pain away if you want. But however you do it, you play. Hockey tradition is such that if a player misses game seven, it's for only one reason: he'd do the team more harm than good by playing. How much harm he does to himself is irrelevant.

A seventh game in the Montreal Forum between the Bruins and the Canadiens elevates the whole scenario one step further. These were two fabled clubs, traditional rivals whose animosity for each other went well beyond dislike and was perilously close to hatred.

Each felt that, although losing a seventh game is always unpleasant, losing to this opponent would be downright heartbreaking.

There must have been other things happening in the world at that time. There were probably some political issues that were being hammered out, and if memory serves, spring had finally arrived. But in Montreal, none of these things really mattered. A game seven between the Bruins and Canadiens was the focus of everyone's attention.

The home team had won every game in the series, but the Bruins were determined to change that trend. "We'll just go right at them," said Cherry. "If we get beat, we get beat."

Go right at them they did—and *through* them, on a number of occasions. It was a tough game, with neither team willing to grant a free passage, but it was not violent. By the time two teams of this calibre reach a seventh game, intimidation is not going to be a factor, and both sides knew it. Furthermore, the Bruins knew that they could not afford to give the Montreal power play any more opportunities than were absolutely necessary.

As was often the case in crucial games, Dryden wasn't particularly sharp, and after two periods, the Bruins led 3–1 on two goals by Wayne Cashman, one of the Bruins who had opted for the pain-killing needle before the game, and another by Rick Middleton.

"Middleton and Jean Ratelle played really well for them in that series," recalled Bowman. "And Marcotte and McNab were good checkers. And you know who played really well? Gilles Gilbert. He was very good for them."

The Forum crowd was nervous and quiet. While Montreal fans were as raucous as any in the league when the Canadiens were doing well, they did not lack for knowledge of the game. They knew that their heroes were in trouble. Furthermore, they were definitely not known for being unswervingly loyal. Even though it has evolved into fairly common usage, it was in Montreal that I first heard anyone say, "The fans are solidly behind you, win or tie."

The Canadiens hadn't won three consecutive Stanley Cups by failing to meet challenges, yet it appeared that they weren't going to meet this one. With nine minutes to play, they still trailed 3–1.

Then Ratelle, of all people, was assessed a two-minute roughing penalty by referee Bob Myers. It was a borderline call, and the way Bruins' fans saw it, Ratelle had been guilty of nothing more than retaliation. Gainey had slashed Ratelle, who then pushed Gainey. But as the announcers used to say *ad infinitum* in those days, "They always call the retaliation."

Even so, Ratelle was an unlikely felon. He was a two-time winner of the Lady Byng Trophy who had played the full eighty-game season and earned only twelve penalty minutes.

But there could be no appeal. Ratelle headed for the penalty box and while he was gone, the vaunted Montreal power play lived up to its name.

The first unit couldn't connect, but Bowman was able to engineer a partial line change while Lafleur took the puck behind the Boston net. A fresh Mark Napier darted into the circle, and from behind the goal line, Lafleur fired a diagonal pass onto his stick. Before Gilbert could get all the way across, Napier had buried it and the Canadiens trailed by only one.

The Forum crowd, sensing a comeback, went wild, and

the Canadiens, spurred by their success, unleashed a furious attack. When Dick Redmond hauled down Lemaire, thereby prompting the famous bowing performance by Cherry that opened his "Coach's Corner" segment on *Hockey Night in Canada* for years, Bowman made a crucial move. He sent out the defensive tandem of Savard and Lapointe, but told Savard to go in deep and crowd Gilbert. Up front, he pulled Shutt off the big line and replaced him with Gainey, the principle being that Gainey, like Savard, could create havoc in front of the net.

The strategy worked. With Lemaire stationed on the left point, Lafleur set up Lapointe, who was on the other side. Lapointe blasted a shot that Gilbert never saw—because Savard and Gainey were standing in front of him—and the game was tied.

"I remember they were under pressure because we needed a goal and we were doing everything we could," recalled Lapointe. "Gilles Gilbert was playing tremendous, and they were having a hard time getting out of their end. The puck came back to me, and in situations like that, you just want to put it on the net so you can get a deflection or a rebound or something. But it went right in."

The Bruins were still showing no signs of panic. They were playing a solid positional game and clearing the puck at every opportunity, rather than trying to carry it out of their end and risking a turnover.

But the Canadiens had a well-earned reputation as an offensive powerhouse, and the Montreal fans began to breathe a bit easier. Even though the game was not over, the Bruins were on the ropes, the Canadiens were charging, and surely it was just a matter of time until the next goal.

Indeed it was. But to the dismay of the Forum faithful, it was the Bruins' Middleton who scored it. With only 3:59 to play, he came around from behind the net and beat Dryden with a weak backhander.

Bowman kept the Lafleur line on the ice in the hope of getting the goal back and, as he had done almost throughout the entire series, Cherry countered by sending out Marcotte to shadow Lafleur.

Try as they might over the next ninety seconds, the Canadiens couldn't establish a meaningful attack. In fact, the Bruins had mounted a counterattack and were setting up shop in the Montreal end when the whistle blew.

As is usually the case in situations where there has been no clear-cut infraction, most of the fans were confused. But the Forum had more knowledgeable fans than any other NHL rink, and many had been out of their seats shouting, even while the play continued. When the others saw Myers conferring with linesman John D'Amico, they knew as well: the Bruins had too many men on the ice! With 2:34 remaining, the Canadiens were going on the power play.

"Lafleur never left the ice after we scored," said Cherry, "and as long as Lafleur was on the ice, Marcotte was on the ice. Then Lafleur went off and Donny was at the door and I said, 'Good shift, Donny.'

"I looked over and said, 'Oh, no!' One of the guys jumped on. One guy off and two guys jumped on."

In fact, a third jumped on. McNab, who had been the culprit earlier in the series, did it again, but Cherry was able to grab him by the sweater and reel him back in.

D'Amico, standing near the bench, saw what was happening and looked over at Cherry. Like any good official—and D'Amico is in the Hall of Fame—he wanted to let the players decide the outcome, not the officials.

"He gave us a little while," Cherry said. "If somebody had come close to the bench, he'd have let it go. Hell, if somebody had come close to the bench, I'd have grabbed him."

But the only person close to the bench was D'Amico. Eventually, he made the call, but not before the Bruins had had too many men on the ice for nearly ten seconds.

"They were matching up Marcotte against Lafleur," was Bowman's memory of the incident, "and we kept double-shifting Lafleur. Then there was a mixup and they had eight guys on the ice."

One of the many Bowman aphorisms that he recites in hockey discussions is, "If you're going to get beat, get beat with your best."

And he knew who his best were. Even though they'd just finished a long shift, Bowman gave them a breather by burning his time-out when the penalty was assessed, and then the line of Lafleur, Shutt and Lemaire came back onto the ice.

The Canadiens went to the attack, but when the puck deflected off Lemaire's skate, Brad Park pounced on it and shot it down the ice. Lafleur went back to take the short pass from Dryden and circled in his own end to evade Marcotte, then started up ice. Just over his blue line, he fired a pass to Lemaire at the Boston blue line.

Lemaire carried the puck to the hash marks, then dropped the puck back to Lafleur, who had been flying up the ice. In full stride, Lafleur put everything behind his shot.

And what a shot it was. There was almost no room at all between the far post and Gilbert's leg, but there was enough. Just enough. It was a wicked shot, just off the ice and through that space. There were 74 seconds left in regulation time.

"What a shot he let go," conceded Cherry after the game, offering the ultimate compliment by comparing Lafleur to Bobby Orr. "He's the greatest hockey player in the world now that Himself has retired."

But years later, he's still not convinced that officiating justice was done in that game.

"I still think Lemaire was offside when he received the pass," he said in 2005. "Lemaire was stopped at the blue line. He was straddling the blue line, but when he received the puck, he lifted his leg, which would have put him offside. If you look at that, his leg is up, I still say."

And he wasn't too happy about the penalty to Ratelle that led to Montreal's second goal, the one that started the comeback.

"I'm not saying that the league favoured Montreal," he said, "but you just can't go through all the time getting the breaks they got. They seemed to get every big penalty call."

Even now, the Canadiens hadn't won. But in overtime, they gradually took over. Both Lafleur and Shutt seemed to be about to notch the winner, only to have Gilbert pull off incredible saves to keep the Bruins alive.

Meanwhile, Bowman was still sticking to the premise that if the Bruins were going to win, they were going to have to beat his best.

"Robinson and Savard hardly left the ice in the first ten minutes of overtime," he said. "I had at least one of them on the ice all the time. I think we went down to three defencemen, with the other guys getting an odd shift, but it was mostly Robinson and Savard."

I was working for the Montreal *Gazette* at the time, and that night we had a full complement of writers at the game. I was covering the visiting team, and the logistics of the Montreal Forum were such that the best route from the press box to the visitors' dressing room on the other side of the arena was to walk along the narrow concourse behind the standees at the Boulevard de Maisonneuve end of the building.

But as soon as a game ended, that concourse always became jammed with fans heading for the exits. As the overtime headed past the eight-minute mark, I left for the Boston room. It seemed evident that it was only a matter of time—and not very much time at that—before the Canadiens ended it, and I didn't want to have my access to the Boston room blocked by departing fans.

As a result, I didn't see Yvon Lambert score the winner at 9:33. I was just reaching the end of that concourse.

Lapointe didn't see it, either. "I wasn't there in over-time," he said. "Near the last shift in regulation time, I got hit in the corner and sprained my knee. I was at the hospital. They had taken me there to see how bad my knee was. I couldn't listen to the game and we were in overtime.

"As you could imagine, with it being in Montreal, I was recognized, so I said to the person who was taking care of me, 'If you can find a radio, I'll give you my jersey.'

"I had to give up my jersey, but I got to listen to the game."

But for those of us who missed it live, it's on all the video replays: Savard started the play by cleanly stripping the puck from Middleton, who tried to beat him one on one. He fired it up the middle to Rejean Houle, who redirected it to Mario Tremblay.

Tremblay roared down the right side, past Bruins defenceman Al Sims. But by that time, he was in too deep to have a decent shot, so he slid the puck across the crease. Lambert, who had outraced Park, jammed it past Gilbert from the edge of the crease.

Usually, the third man on that line was Risebrough, but in this case Houle was on the ice. When I asked Risebrough about that in 2005, he explained his absence by saying that a line change was underway and that he was waiting for Houle to come off.

Not so, said Bowman.

"Risebrough was injured," he said. "He had talked us into dressing him, but he had a separated shoulder. We dressed him for the game because he was really a peppy guy, but he didn't play many shifts. He was out there playing with a separated shoulder."

He had also suffered a broken nose in game six. Another example of the overwhelming power that game seven holds over NHLers.

As for the Canadiens' eventual domination, Bowman conceded that overall, he had the better team. "They didn't have the depth," he said. "They had some pretty good front-line players and they had some good role players, but they didn't have enough of them. They didn't have enough guys, that's for sure."

In October 2004, Russ Conway of the *Eagle-Tribune* in Lawrence, Massachusetts, spoke to Middleton and Park about that fateful night in Montreal.

"Just like that, it's over," said Park. "Gone. It doesn't really sink in at first. After three or four days, once you're on your own, that's when it hits. You had it right in your mitts and it's gone. It's something you try not to think about, but you get reminded wherever you go. You never really get over losing a game like that."

Middleton agreed. "Until you go through the experience of living it," he said, "you can never really appreciate how much it hurts to be that close, only to go home with such an empty feeling.

"With us, it was a too-many-men penalty that gave Montreal that extra power play. What are the chances of ever seeing that happen in the last two minutes of a seventh game in the playoffs? It's something you have to deal with, go on and look at it with an attitude that there's always next year."

But there wasn't a next year, at least not one that approximated the year before.

There were far too many epilogues to be written, too many careers that reached their zenith on that fateful night.

Cherry was fired five weeks later, although he still insists that technically he wasn't fired—he was just not rehired. Without him, the Bruins slipped steadily and still haven't won the Stanley Cup that was so tantalizingly close in 1979.

Looking back a quarter of a century later, Bowman was amazed that the Bruins let Cherry go. "If you look at Cherry's record, he won a lot of games for Boston," said Bowman, "and he only coached about five years. I'll bet you he averaged over 45 wins a year."

As is invariably the case in matters of hockey lore, Bowman was right on the mark. Cheery did indeed coach only five years in Boston and he won 231 games, an average of almost 46 a season, an excellent record in an era when the season encompassed only 80 games.

That fateful game wasn't Bowman's last as coach of the Canadiens, but it was close to it. He was behind the

Montreal bench for only five more games before he left the team. Justifiably furious that he was passed over for the general manager's job when Sam Pollock moved on and turned over the reins to Irving Grundman—who had joined the organization in an administrative capacity and whose closest association with sport was the ownership of a bowling alley—Bowman parted ways with the Canadiens within three weeks of winning the Stanley Cup.

Grundman was fired in 1983, and eventually moved into politics as a local councillor. In 2005, he was sentenced to twenty-three months, to be served in the community, for accepting a bribe to change a zoning bylaw. He was also fined $50,000.

Lafleur never rose to such heights again, either. The Canadiens did indeed go on to defeat the Rangers easily that year, even though they lost the first game when they were unable to overcome the psychological letdown that tends to afflict athletes after a highly emotional victory. But it was to be Lafleur's last Stanley Cup, and he was never to earn another trophy.

It was also the end of the Canadiens dynasty. That was their fourth consecutive Cup, but they didn't even come close to a fifth. In 1980, they lost to the Minnesota North Stars in the first round with eight regulars, including Lafleur, out of action.

"If you remember, there was a change in leadership," recalled Risebrough. "Scotty left. Sam left. So there wasn't the leadership at the top that said, 'It's probably time to retool.'

"It was a new group that said, 'What can we hang onto here to see if we can do it again? We want to hang on to it and do it again.'

"But the team wasn't as good by then. At the end of the day, you can look and say that's the last gasp. Or that's the lack of leadership. You can look at all those injuries. But would it have been a lot different? Would we have won the Cup? That wasn't a team that had to just get out of the first round to be successful.

"The fact that we lost that first round to Minnesota with those guys injured was true, but with those guys in, would we have won the Cup?

"In the end of it, if they had made those changes then, guess who would have benefited the most? Guy Lafleur. Guy would have benefited the most because some of those changes needed to be made—probably me, as an example, I should probably have been moved on—so that he could glitter a little longer.

"Every player needed the team, and for Guy, the best days were always when the team was going the best. When that team started to falter a little bit and couldn't live up to the expectations, all the expectations fell on Guy, and that's when I think he became a little bit more outspoken at times and he'd say something in the paper that created friction.

"I do remember saying to myself, 'You know, this guy is under more pressure to perform and the team can't live up to the expectations.' It had won four and it was time for a change."

Cherry went on to coach the Colorado Rockies, missing out on a job with the Toronto Maple Leafs because, once again, his timing was off.

"The truth is I never got fired in Boston," he said. "I got called to the Indian Room, a place in a beautiful country club near Boston. This was a meeting with Paul Mooney, the owner.

"I was more popular than anybody in Boston, more popular than any of the baseball players, and he knew it. He said, 'Look, we don't want to fire you, but just do us a favour. You've got to stop crapping on us, and you've got to stop going to the press so much.'

"How could I make that promise? When [Hall of Fame Boston writer] Fran Rosa calls, I'm supposed to say, 'I'm sorry, Fran, I can't talk to you'?

"They were so good to me, all the writers. They could have hung me a hundred times. I'd be in a fury with the league and calling Ziegler every name in the book—and

Harry too, the same thing—and they always protected me. So what am I going to say? 'Sorry, I can't talk to you'?"

That was exactly what Mooney wanted Cherry to say. When he wouldn't agree to it, he was gone.

At first, he looked to Toronto, where Maple Leafs owner Harold Ballard had not yet evolved into the bitter, vindictive autocrat that he became in later years. At that time, he was no more than a meddling fool with a criminal record for fraud and a reputation for interfering with those he had hired to run his team.

"I never interfere as long as they win," he chortled when I asked him about that trait in May 1979. "There's one way to keep me out of it and that's to put a few wins together. I don't think those two should have any problem doing that."

The two to whom he referred were Cherry and Bowman. He wanted the former to coach the Leafs and the latter to be the general manager.

"I'd like to get both of them," he said. "I think they'd make a tremendous difference to our club."

Cherry was interested right away, but his agent, Alan Eagleson, suggested publicly that his price was too high for Ballard's liking.

"Who is he to say what's too high for me?" snorted Ballard.

Bowman, meanwhile, was in Florida, letting his agent, Jerry Petrie, listen to offers.

Ballard said that he wanted Bowman to hurry and make a decision. "No way," said Bowman on May 30. "I'm going to take all the time I can. The season ended on the 21st so under my contract, I've got fourteen days from the 22nd. That's June 4. After that, I've got six more days. I'm not going to hurry it."

But it seemed that Ballard had the inside track, because he met Bowman's primary condition. "I'm interested in going anywhere I don't have to coach," Bowman said.

On the same day, Ballard said, "I'd like to have him as general manager. If we can have him as manager, he can run the coach. That would be his charge. I'd just look to Scotty for results."

But at the same time, Cherry was negotiating with the Colorado Rockies—and even though he knew Ballard was interested, Rockies GM Ray Miron had made a firm offer while Ballard was still dithering.

It was a matter of the bird in the hand as opposed to two in the very fickle Ballard's bush. Cherry agreed to terms with the Rockies, and once he had done so, Ballard belatedly came through. "I guess I should have made him a firm offer," he lamented.

"He was going to give me $150,000 for a three-year contract," recalled Cherry, "I remember Eagle called and said, 'I got it: a three-year deal at $150,000. You'll be able to visit your mother in Kingston.'

"But I went to Colorado for two years at $135,000 to work with that idiot Ray Miron. What a jerk!"

Why did Cherry do that? After all, the contract hadn't been signed. Why not just back out and take the Toronto deal? "Because I'd given my word," said Cherry.

In 2005, in an interview with Joe O'Connor of the *National Post*, Sinden recalled the break with Cherry.

"Don had made a deal with Ray Miron in Colorado and we knew about it," he said, "and I think it was a better deal for him. Now, I'm not saying I wouldn't have fired Don, because we were at odds with each other.

"It's an unbelievable story with us. We were really good friends in the five years he was here. We did things together. We laughed together. On the road we were great pals. Then, all of a sudden, it fell apart.

"Of course, I have my side of the story, and I always felt the more games Don won, the more dangerous he became. He got mad at any remarks I made about the team, and I was pretty vociferous then.

"And then there was the playoff game in Montreal when there were too many men on the ice. I was mad the entire game because he had a thing going with the

Montreal fans. He'd stand on the bench and yell at them and they'd yell back. And here we were playing the seventh game of a series to go to the Stanley Cup.

"So we get caught with too many men and I blamed him, but in the end, maybe it wasn't his fault.

"So yes, we were mad at each other."

Bowman, meanwhile, was weighing offers from the Buffalo Sabres and Washington Capitals, but as late as June 6, Ballard still wanted him badly.

We were in Nassau, Bahamas, for one of the many merger meetings between the NHL and the WHA, and Ballard, whose hair was rapidly turning orange in the sun, kept scurrying indoors to work on the deal.

"I had hoped to get Don Cherry as coach, and if he hadn't been so quick to go to Colorado, I could have worked something out there," he told me. "I don't want to lose Bowman as well. I'll be very disappointed if he doesn't come. I've been working hard on this for a long time, and it would be very disappointing to me if he didn't accept the offer.

"He could turn this team around. We haven't won a Stanley Cup for years. Sure, we sell out every game, but those people work damned hard for their money. I see the way they look at me sometimes when I'm walking out of the building after a bad game.

"They're thinking, 'Look at that crook. He should be back in Millhaven Penitentiary.' And the way the team plays some nights, maybe they're right. I want the team to win again and I think Scotty's the man to get us back on track."

Bowman might have shared that view, but he didn't want anything to do with Ballard. In his two previous jobs, with the Canadiens and the St. Louis Blues, he'd found himself working for someone whose hockey knowledge he disdained. He wasn't about to make it a hat trick.

"Harold was not a businessman," recalled Bowman. "He wouldn't make an offer. I kept asking him. I was making $90,000 in Montreal, and Buffalo came with an offer of $200,000 for five years. It more than doubled my salary, and I could have made maybe $120,000 at the most in Montreal as a coach.

"Ballard called me and I went to Toronto to meet him, but he never talked about a new contract. He just said, 'We'll take over your contract.'

"The other place that made a good offer, but it was mostly paper, was Washington. I met with Abe Pollin and one of his partners and they offered me 10 per cent of the Washington Capitals. I'm lucky I didn't take it.

"The deal was that I'd get 10 per cent of the assets, but also 10 per cent of the liabilities. I said, 'Well, I can't pay any bills.'

"I wanted to stay close to Canada. In Buffalo, I felt you could go and watch games in the OHA [the Ontario Hockey Association] and you could keep your hockey knowledge up. It was a good offer, so I took it."

The Sabres had also tossed in potential bonuses that could push his annual compensation to $250,000. The package was too good to resist. On June 10, Bowman became their general manager.

Ballard, having seen the writing on the wall, contacted Punch Imlach on June 8 and soon afterwards hired him for the job that Bowman wouldn't take. Imlach thereby embarked on what he liked to refer to as "the worst three years of my long and generally happy life in hockey."

As for Lafleur, he went on to have another 50-goal season—his last—but that was his lowest production since 1974. Then the injuries started to catch up to him, and so did the years of hard living. As his reflexes slowed a bit, he lost that phenomenal ability to thread the puck through the tiniest of holes. Shots of the type that had zipped past Gilbert were now hitting either the post or the goalie himself.

He racked up three consecutive 27-goal seasons, and then popped 30 in 1983–84. But with seventeen games left in that season, his old linemate Lemaire took over as coach of the Canadiens.

Lemaire had always been the defensive force on the line, while Lafleur had provided the offence. The two did not see eye to eye on how the game should be played.

Early in the 1984–85 season, Cherry, who by that time had joined the staff of *Hockey Night in Canada*, travelled to Buffalo with the show's executive director, Ralph Mellanby, to see the Canadiens play the Sabres.

"Lafleur was the best player on both sides in the first period," Cherry recalled, "and he got about two shifts in the second and third period. I leaned over to Mellanby and said, 'He'll be retired by Christmas, because he won't put up with that.'

"It's not that he was struggling. It wasn't that he was scared. Lemaire took his confidence away, and once he took that confidence away, Lafleur was done for the rest of his life."

Bowman wasn't so sure that was the case. "I don't know if he could have played longer than he did," he said. "He played until he was forty and I don't think many guys in those years played much longer. The Rocket played until he was about thirty-eight, but he wasn't really in shape.

"I think thirty-seven was really stretching it at that time. Look at the athletes today. They have personal trainers. They go to gyms all the time. They last longer. But they didn't do that sort of thing at that time."

Nineteen games into the season, Lafleur retired. He sat out the next three seasons as well, but in 1988–89 he made a comeback with the New York Rangers, then played the next two seasons for the Quebec Nordiques.

"Even when he went to New York, he did pretty good," said Cherry, "but his confidence was gone. Lemaire had taken it away. He's the guy that ruined him.

"It wasn't that he was afraid of getting hurt. He lost his confidence; and once a guy loses that, it's over.

"He was a class guy. The only guy on our club that really hated him was Mike Milbury. It was awful what Milbury would do to him—slashing, banging, spearing in front of the net. Any time that Milbury had a chance, he'd get him.

"He would really get crucified. Some of the things Milbury did to him were terrible, but he never complained once. Not once.

"I saw him once, after a cross-check, look out of the corner of his eye to the ref. All he ever did was look at him, but I never saw him complain once. He was the gentleman's gentleman.

"Guy had the same personality as the Rocket. He had a certain nobility about him. When he'd be on the fly and that sweater—they wore light sweaters back then—would be rippling and that hair would be out the back, he was something."

Even though Lafleur made the play that shattered Cherry's Stanley Cup dreams, the respect is still there. In fact, Cherry respects Lafleur so much that he even paid him the ultimate compliment. He compared him to Orr.

"I saw him do things like Bobby," he said. "I remember one time the puck was behind him. He reached back and touched the puck and had the puck go between his legs—on the fly now—and onto his stick. And he did it all in stride.

"Now I know how the guys on the other team used to feel when they saw Bobby. You knew he was going to do something."

"Lafleur was a good team guy," said Bowman. "He never worried about his ice time. He never said much. I think he just accepted the fact that Gainey was always going to be the main guy in a defensive role, and he always fancied himself as an offensive player.

"He never fancied himself as a defensive player. He never killed penalties, but in those days, guys like him didn't kill penalties. But if you were down in a game, he expected to play a lot.

"He was a pretty easy guy to coach because he wasn't worried about his own ice time. He knew that offensively, he was going to go. He had a real flair for the dramatic. He scored a lot of important goals. If you look at the year we lost eight games [1976–77], so many times we'd win a game by one goal and he'd end up being the guy who got the key goal for us."

Cherry has never shirked the blame for having too many men on the ice. Right after *the* game, he said, "Any time you get too many men on the ice, it's the coach's fault."

More recently, he said, "Captain [Edward] John Smith. *Titanic.* It was his fault. And it was my fault. I've always made it perfectly clear. I always blamed myself. I never blamed the guys. You always take the blame like that. You go down with the ship."

But it wasn't Cherry who jumped over the boards at the Forum on that night to remember. It was a young player whom Cherry loved for his enthusiasm and his eagerness to contribute.

The player was devastated by what he had done, and it was no surprise to learn that he was crying uncontrollably after the game. He was always an emotional guy, that Stan Jonathan.

THE GOAL: SEPTEMBER 13, 1984.

Canada Cup sudden-death semifinal.
Scored by Mike Bossy (assisted by John Tonelli and
Paul Coffey) at 12:29 of overtime. Canada 3, USSR 2.

NEW KINGS WERE SITTING ON TOP OF THE HOCKEY HILL IN THE summer of 1984. The young, brash, freewheeling Edmonton Oilers had ended the New York Islanders' run of four consecutive Stanley Cups with a flowing, high-tempo game that was as artistic as it was exciting.

In many quarters, the Oilers' success had not been anticipated. Even though they had broken all the long-standing regular-season offensive records and were a delight to watch, there was no shortage of traditionalists who downplayed their achievements, maintaining that the playoffs would paint a different picture. They insisted that when championships are on the line, defence triumphs over offence every time.

If that were to be the case, then the Islanders would be able to join the ranks of the National Hockey League's truly great dynasties. Only one team in history, the Montreal Canadiens of the fifties, had won five consecutive Stanley Cups—from 1956 to 1960.

Under the artful coaching of Al Arbour, who gave not the slightest thought to offence in his playing days, the Islanders were a defence-first team.

To start their dynasty, they had put an end to the Montreal Canadiens' run of four Stanley Cups, and they did so primarily by checking the opposition into submission and waiting for opportunities.

But the problem with the arbitrary assumption that defence will always beat offence is that hockey games are not all-or-nothing affairs. There are degrees of offence and degrees of defence. Even though the Islanders were defensively oriented and the Oilers loved nothing more than running up the score, neither team was limited to only one facet.

During the Islanders' reign, their top line of Mike Bossy, Bryan Trottier and Clark Gillies was as offensively dangerous as any in the league. It was a perfectly balanced unit, the line that had everything. Trottier was the smooth playmaker, the guy who carried the puck and dished it off when necessary, but was also capable of finishing the job himself. Bossy was the sniper, the finisher, the guy who converted Trottier's passes using one of the fastest releases ever seen in hockey. One instant, the puck would be approaching his stick; the next, it would be in the net. Gillies was the policeman, a rugged, honest winger who made sure that nobody took liberties with his two linemates and who had the ability to convert most of the scoring opportunities that came his way.

But the Islanders' offensive power was not limited merely to the forwards. On the blue line, Denis Potvin was making the kind of plays that only Bobby Orr had made before.

The Islanders were perennial offensive powerhouses; in the 1978–79 season, for example, every one of those stars was among the NHL's top ten scorers. Trottier led the league with 134 points, Bossy had 126, Potvin 101 and Gillies 91.

As if that weren't enough, late in the 1983–84 season, the Islanders added Pat LaFontaine who, despite playing only 15 games, scored 13 goals.

Yet the fact remains that Arbour demanded a defence-first approach. In his playing days, he had built his reputation by blocking shots, not by taking them. In his 712 career games, he scored just 13 times.

Under his tutelage, the Islanders won four consecutive Cups by switching to offence only after the defensive aspect was under control.

That was certainly not the Oilers' style. In that 1983–84 season, they scored 446 goals in 80 games, an NHL record that stands to this day. In fact, the top five goal-scoring seasons in NHL history—every one of which cracked the 400-goal barrier—all belong to the Oilers of the eighties.

But when the time came to play defence in the spring of 1984, they did so, stunning the Islanders in the Nassau County Coliseum in the opener of the Stanley Cup finals with a 1–0 victory.

To the average fan, it would seem that, having watched his team get shut out, Arbour might want to urge them to play a bit more offensively. Not Arbour. That would go against everything he had preached over the years.

"We know what we have to do," he insisted. "We have to be more physical than we were. They had more hits than we did and we have to turn that round."

What the Islanders did turn around for the next game was their offence. They beat the Oilers 6–1.

But that was their final gasp. The series shifted to Edmonton for three games, and the Oilers won all three, limiting the Islanders to two goals on each occasion—a feeble performance by the standards of that era, and proof that when the Oilers wanted to play defensively, they were capable of doing so.

Without a doubt, these were the two dominant franchises in hockey at the time. The Islanders were the gnarled, proven veterans playing a staid, time-honoured style. The Oilers were the brash rebels, changing the face of the game for years to come.

There was no love lost between the rivals, who had battled each other in successive Stanley Cup finals and built up a dislike that bordered on hatred. In 1983 the Islanders had persevered, simply because, unlike the Oilers at that stage, they knew how to win at the highest level. They took the hits. They sacrificed their bodies. They maintained their discipline. When the series finished, they were wounded and hobbling. But they were the champions.

By the time the two teams met again in 1984, the Oilers had become aware of the areas in which they had gone wrong. This time, they were every bit as determined and intense as the Islanders, and by virtue of their superior talent, they prevailed.

So, naturally enough, when it came time that summer to select the members of Team Canada for the 1984 Canada Cup, it was to Edmonton and Long Island that the organizers looked first. Most of hockey's elite could be found in those two locales, and it was upon their shoulders that the reputation of Canadian hockey would rest.

Right from the beginning, there were rumblings of discontent. Even though there was a management committee in place at that point, it was the Oilers' general manager, Glen Sather, who was running the show—so much so that the team's training camp was staged in Banff, which just happened to be Sather's home, and where, it was said, he owned most of the downtown core.

There was some magnificent hockey on display there. Team Canada had thirty-two players in camp, even though only twenty would be allowed to dress for any game once the tournament started. In order to make sure they all stayed healthy, there was an implicit no-hitting rule.

It was certainly a team with potential. The two dominant teams in hockey had contributed most of the roster, but there were also some elite players from other sources. In one case, the organizers had even gone outside the country and brought in Peter Stastny, who, because he was no longer welcome in Czechoslovakia, was willing and eager to play for Canada. Norris Trophy winner Doug Wilson of the Chicago Blackhawks came in, along with Rick Middleton from the Boston Bruins and Michel Goulet from the Quebec Nordiques.

The scenery in Banff is spectacular, and on those beautiful summer days, amid the blue skies and pristine air and majestic mountains, it was not easy for the media people in attendance to force themselves to into a tiny, dimly lit arena near the railroad tracks to watch a hockey practice.

But the compensation was that NHL players of any era can provide fantastic performances when they're not being checked, and in that freewheeling era, the practices provided a magnificent brand of hockey that is rarely ever on view to the public.

Against real opposition, however, Team Canada '84 didn't fare so well. In the exhibition games, the performances were little more than perfunctory, and in the opening stages of the tournament, the Canadians had a hard time rising above mediocrity.

Tournament organizer Alan Eagleson always made sure that Team Canada had the most favourable schedule in events of this nature, and as a result, the Canadians were given the opportunity to ease themselves gently into the tournament with a game against West Germany. They rolled to a 7–2 victory, but observers were unimpressed. A win over such opposition, even a decisive one, had no significance whatsoever.

What did catch the attention of Canadian fans was the result of the next game—a 4–4 tie against Team USA in Montreal. *This* was deemed significant, if not for the intended reasons. The Americans were far from being a powerhouse in those days, even though Trottier had exercised his right as a Native North American and opted to play for them, thereby earning himself a chorus of boos every time he touched the puck in Canada.

Only eight years earlier, in the 1976 Canada Cup, the Americans had been known universally as Team Useless, and as far as Canadians were concerned, the Americans hadn't advanced a great deal since then.

To make matters worse, goaltender Grant Fuhr of the Oilers injured his knee and had to drop out of the tournament, to be replaced by Rejean Lemelin of the Calgary Flames.

Even though Lemelin was a good goalie, he wasn't of Fuhr's calibre. Had he been, he would have been in the training camp with the other Canadian players, not soaking up the sun's rays at his summer home in New Jersey.

The team headed to Vancouver for its game against Sweden in disarray at every level. There were divisions within the dressing room; the concept of using Pete Peeters of the Boston Bruins as the starting goalie seemed to be a concern; and even at the management level, all was not going well.

So Sather staged a coup. He made it clear to the members of the team's management committee, which included Serge Savard of the Montreal Canadiens, Emile Francis of the Hartford Whalers, John Ferguson of the Winnipeg Jets, David Poile of the Washington Capitals and Harry Sinden of the Boston Bruins, that their services were no longer required.

Oh, yes: that committee had also included general manager Bill Torrey of the New York Islanders. He, too, was relieved of his duties.

One of them said, "We were fired," but others tried to salvage their pride and said that Sather had merely made it clear that they were redundant. Many of them were miffed anyway by this time, having felt that Sather had imposed his will on the group and selected an inordinate number of his Oilers.

Either way, it became clear that this was no longer a team run by committee. It was a team run by Glen Cameron Sather, known to one and all as Slats.

"What were we supposed to do?" demanded Sather when he was asked about his newly assumed power. "Meet after every game and talk about line changes? Did they seriously think we could run a team by committee?"

Apparently, they did. After all, when the decisions were being made as to which players to invite to training camp, Sather considered all views. Even then, when asked if the others had managed to persuade him to invite any player who wouldn't have been called on otherwise, Sather was characteristically blunt. "Probably not," he said.

If the off-ice coup was intended to create an immediate improvement in the on-ice situation, it was a failure. Team Canada lost 4–2 to Sweden and was now in serious danger of being humiliated.

Not only were the Canadians not giving the slightest indication that they could win the tournament, they were only a few bad shifts away from disgracing themselves. With a 1–1–1 record, a loss in the next game to Czechoslovakia, the 1976 Canada Cup finalists, would in all probability eliminate the Canadians from further competition and leave them sitting on the sidelines, hanging their heads in shame, when the playoff round began.

Within minutes of the loss to Sweden, Sather swung into action. He made the players sit at their stalls while he blasted them mercilessly for their performance.

"We really needed a situation so that you could really bark at them with some sense of purpose," Sather explained. "We were going through the tournament playing okay, but not really great. Guys were competing, but not really competing. There was no fire until we played that awful game in Vancouver."

Sather made the most of his opportunity to bark. If they weren't prepared to give everything they had, he told the players, then they should go home. And they need not worry about the public perception, he added. There was no need to stick around just to save face. So fervent was his desire to get rid of anyone who wasn't prepared to give his all that he would tell the media the departure had been precipitated by a medical problem.

If you're not going to exert a greater effort than this, Sather told the players, just get the hell out. We don't want you.

"He really laid into us," recalled Kevin Lowe decades later. "I remember he was naming names and he started in on the Islanders guys. I was sitting there and I felt kind of embarrassed that he would do that to those guys. Then he started in on *us* [the Oilers], and it was worse."

Sather had seen the inherent danger of the situation long before it finally manifested itself. "I knew what was going to happen until we started to become a team," he said. "I knew the first day we were in Montreal. I knew there was something building. Bossy came in and was complaining about something and I said, 'Mike, it's not the Islanders; it's not the Oilers. We're playing for Canada. Let's just leave it at that.'"

If there was any favouritism shown towards his own NHL team, Sather said years later, it was unintentional. "We never, ever put a game plan together saying we're going to play all the Oilers together on every power play. That's not the way it worked.

"They could have been out there a lot, but I don't know whether subconsciously you'd do something like that. I can't imagine I would do that because I don't care about that kind of stuff.

"We would talk about that as coaches, and none of us could understand why these guys would worry about that more than they were worrying about winning. Our whole philosophy was to play the best players. If you want to play on the power play, then show me that you deserve to be there."

The players were stung by Sather's wide-ranging condemnation after the Sweden game, but they knew he was right. "We are awful," said Wayne Gretzky. "It's not just one or two guys, it's all twenty. If we play like this again, we won't make the playoffs."

Sather's blast had given the players a wake-up call, but it was defenceman Larry Robinson who threw down the gauntlet to address the real cause of concern: the rift between the Oilers and the Islanders.

Robinson was certainly no stranger to winning, having been one of the stalwarts on the Montreal Canadiens teams that won four consecutive Stanley Cups in the seventies.

In a closed-door meeting with his Team Canada team-mates, Robinson spared no feelings. He knew what the issues were and he aired them.

From the Islanders' point of view, the Oilers were getting preferential treatment. They had more representatives on Team Canada than any other NHL team. The training camp was held in Sather's backyard. The opening game was played in Edmonton, but not a single game was played on Long Island. Their own GM was relieved of his management duties when Sather staged his coup. And the coach, of course, was Sather himself—who, as far as the Islanders were concerned, showed favouritism to his Edmonton players.

The player receiving the most ice time was Gretzky. When Canada was on the power play, it was the Edmonton players who got the lion's share of the ice time.

"We may have lost the Cup to them three months ago," the Islanders moaned to each other in private, "but we won four of the last five, and in the process, we had to have a pretty good power play. We had to come through with great performances under tremendous pressure. We've proved we can do it, but now, we're not getting a chance."

The Oilers, on the other hand, felt that they were merely getting their due. On their first trip to the Stanley Cup final, they had lost to the Islanders. But they had won the rematch the following year and they were the Stanley Cup champions now, not the Islanders. They were the wave of the future, whereas the Islanders represented the past.

They were the ones who had shattered the scoring records and were the hot topic in hockey. They deserved everything they got. They felt that the Islanders were the dirtiest team in hockey, and were simply smart enough to get away with it. Many of the Oilers had scars from injuries inflicted by the Islanders in their battles during their back-to-back Stanley Cup finals and, following established hockey tradition, they had long memories.

Now Robinson was angry, and the players knew that it was not wise to take a cavalier approach to an enraged Robinson. During his playing days, there were a lot of tough guys in the NHL, and fans often argued as to which one was the toughest. Was it Dave "The Hammer" Schultz? John Wensink? Bob "Mad Dog" Kelly? Stan Jonathan? The list went on and on. But among the NHL players themselves, there was no debate. Everyone knew it was Robinson. He didn't fight often, but when he did, the result was conclusive.

Coming from a team that had enjoyed a great deal of success and was forever overcoming the potential for divisiveness between the French and English factions, Robinson knew that for the next few weeks, the team that had to come first in the players' minds was Team Canada, not the Edmonton Oilers or the New York Islanders.

He named names. He pointed fingers. He said that he had worked too hard over the years to sit back while petty feuds put him in the position of being associated with a team that appeared destined to disgrace Canada's proud hockey heritage.

Play as a team, he said, and we'll all be rewarded. Play the way you have been playing and we'll all be vilified. Canadian fans won't say it was the Oilers who let Canada down or it was the Islanders who let Canada down, Robinson warned; they'll say it was you and you and you. Again he pointed his finger.

"It wasn't just the Larry Robinson speech," recalled Gretzky. "That was the big one, but before that, we were going along in our merry way and as players, especially the Oilers guys, we didn't realize or know there was any kind of friction between the Islanders guys and the Oilers guys. We honestly didn't. We were just playing.

"I don't know individually if players felt that way or not, but just because we weren't winning, it all kind of manifested itself and came to a big head.

"Bob Bourne actually called a private meeting with just the Oilers players and the Islanders players and basically put it on the table. He said, 'Listen, we were tremendous enemies when we played against each other, and that's a good thing because we both want to win the Cup and that's what makes us great. Now we've got to put our differences aside.'

"He said basically that we all had to get on the same page. Bob Bourne did that privately in the hotel. It was quite the meeting, because I didn't think there was tension, but obviously there was, and when you're not winning, something's wrong.

"Then the next day, Larry stood up and made his speech. It was a great speech. Of all the Canada Cup teams and Team Canadas I've played on, Larry was the most respected guy ever to be a part of Team Canada. He was the kind of guy who didn't say anything. He was friendly with each player. If you were a young guy, he made sure you felt comfortable. He kept everybody loose in the locker room.

"So when he stood up, we were all kind of in shock, because Larry never did that. That wasn't his deal. And when he did and he made that incredible speech, everyone sort of went, 'Whoa!'"

"That team came together that day in the Hotel Vancouver," recalled Coffey years later. "I'll never forget it. We finished fourth, and four teams made the medal round. Larry Robinson stood up in the pregame meal and with as much feeling as I've ever seen a hockey player have, he said, 'This isn't Team New York Islanders. This isn't Team Edmonton Oilers. This isn't Team Montreal Canadiens. This is Team Canada. This bullshit has got to stop right now.'

"I was about twenty-two or something, and we were all sitting there saying, 'Wow, this is great. Yeah. We're Team Canada.'"

The players looked at each other and suddenly the animosity disappeared. For the first time, there was unanimity of purpose. "The Islanders, for the most part, were a great bunch of guys, too," said Coffey. "They might have been a little bit upset with us because we had beaten them the year before in the finals, but we had nothing but respect for their hockey team. If anything, we wanted to be like them.

"Larry standing up at that meeting we had—that just instantly pulled that team together. I always tell that story. It was phenomenal."

"Right from the beginning, you could see there was a division," recalled defenceman Doug Wilson, "but there was also a group of us—Larry, myself and a couple of others—who were on the outside and trying to enjoy ourselves a little bit and have the team come together. We struggled early in the tournament. There's no doubt about that.

"I give Slats a lot of credit as well. He said, 'Put the heat on me. You guys just go out and play.' I think the players just said, 'To hell with it. We're going to go out there and play and let's be there for each other.' Larry was really the genesis of that.

"There were a lot of subtle things that I saw. You could see Larry looking around, always figuring out a way to break down barriers. It was a heck of a team we had, but it wasn't working on all cylinders until the pressure got built up. Then all of a sudden, all the other stuff goes away. That's what's great about hockey."

The players got the message. So did Sather. When it came time for the game against Czechoslovakia, he started a forward line of three Islanders, rather than what had been his usual choice—the Gretzky line. It was a small gesture, but it adequately served to get the point across.

As the game progressed, duties were more evenly distributed than they had been in the past. The Islanders players got their share of power-play time and were given some of the penalty-killing responsibilities. As a result, the kind of team-work that had not previously been in evidence came to the fore, and Canada rolled to a 7–2 victory.

But there was no time to savour the success. The biggest battle was still ahead.

That victory over Czechoslovakia put the Canadians into the playoffs, but it meant they had to face the power-ful Soviet Union in a sudden-death game. The winner would go on to the best-of-three Canada Cup final series; the loser would go home. It was a matchup that Canadians had been awaiting with breathless anticipation.

The rivalry between these two countries was intense, and in their previous meeting (the 1981 Canada Cup), the Soviets had administered Team Canada an embar-rassing defeat: an 8–1 shellacking, right in the storied Montreal Forum.

The Canadians hadn't been as bad as it might seem in that '81 tournament. In fact, for the most part, they had been very good. They won every exhibition game, breezed through the opening round undefeated, and won their first playoff game. But in the second—the sudden-death final—nothing went well. Reverses of that nature happen every so often, even to the best of teams.

Soviet goaltender Vladislav Tretiak played a magnifi-cent game, and at the halfway mark, the score was 1–1. After two periods, the Soviets were up 3–1 and could thank Tretiak for the fact they weren't trailing. But in the third period, the Canadians opened up the game in the hopes of narrowing the gap, and as a result, the Soviets were able to capitalize.

Now, three years later, the mitigating circumstances had faded from the minds of most fans and only the 8–1 score was remembered with any clarity. And the fact remained that even though the Canadians had looked strong throughout most of the 1981 Canada Cup tourna-ment, they had lost badly in the game that counted.

The Soviets were viewed in hockey circles as the best team in the world, and if Canada intended to assume that mantle, it could only do so in a head-to-head victory. The Canadian hockey establishment believed—perhaps partly as a result of wishful thinking—that the Canadian players had learned a lot since that humiliating occasion, and that with the creative style exemplified by the Oilers, they could beat the Soviets at their own game.

In fact, for the first time in history, it was decided that the Canadian professionals would skate stride for stride with the Soviets. In the past, the idea had been to beat them into submission or restrain them by whatever means possible—if not always legal.

The Soviets were such superb skaters, so disciplined and in such magnificent physical condition, that the concept of Canadians matching them stride for stride had never been given serious consideration. But in 1984, Canadian hockey took a significant step. We're not only going to skate with the Soviets, said Sather, we're going to outskate them.

The Soviets, he knew, could be expected to use five-man units, a quick transition from defence to offence, and spirited forechecking, all the attributes that had made them so powerful over the years.

Team Canada was going to do exactly the same.

These days, that doesn't seem to be such a radical move. Today's coaches are always talking of the transition game, and throughout the late eighties and well into the nineties, aggressive forechecking was the norm for NHL teams.

But it was certainly a radical move in 1984, and as a result of the Canadian national inferiority complex, rooted partly in that infamous 8–1 loss, there were plenty of fans who wondered if Sather wasn't courting another disaster. The Soviets were generally conceded to be the best conditioned, best skating team in the world. They played together eleven months of the year and had excelled at their style for more than a decade. Was it wise to try to beat them at their own game when there was not even a hint of precedent to suggest Team Canada would be able to do so?

Even Sather had his reservations, especially about aggressively forechecking a team as capable as the Soviets. If a couple of forecheckers were to be beaten by a quick outlet pass, the Soviets would be heading the other way with a manpower advantage—always a dangerous situation. But Sather also knew that if you left the Soviets alone and allowed them to set up the play at their leisure and then work their way up ice with their precise passing, they could be every bit as dangerous. It was a calculated gamble, but one that he felt he had to take.

"You have to know whether to go in or pull out," he explained. "You can get in as much trouble letting the man start out as you can by going in and pinching and getting caught."

In the practices, the exhibition games and the early stages of the tournament, the Canadians worked to develop their skills with the well-established Soviet style in mind.

From an offensive point of view, the Canadian plan was to bring the puck down along the boards, then, once in the Soviet zone, crowd the net. It might not be as pretty as the Soviet style, which was built on fast breaks and swirling, free-skating puck-possession attacks, but the Canadian coaches felt it would work.

The Soviets had a tendency in those days to withdraw when pressured in their end. The two defencemen would never be far from the crease, and the two wingers would go no farther than halfway to the blue line. The centre was allowed to exhibit a little more mobility—he would circle around the middle of the zone, looking to pick off a pass or initiate the breakout, a practice today's NHL players refer to as "sharking." You cruise around back and forth like a predator, with no particular destination in mind, just looking for a chance to move in for the kill.

The Soviets knew from experience that the Canadians would shoot from anywhere. They therefore encouraged shots from the point by exerting only minimal pressure on the blue line. Their reasoning was that if the Canadians were going to shoot from somewhere—and they most assuredly were—then they might as well do it from a distance.

The Canadian forwards therefore decided to establish themselves in front of the net—and Soviet defencemen, like defencemen the world over, did not take kindly to this territorial incursion. The result was predictable—a series of classic physical battles on the fringes of the crease, with the Soviets determined to allow goaltender Vladimir Myshkin a clear view of the shot, and the Canadians equally determined to block that view.

The game was an absolute masterpiece of hockey, and the crowd in the sold-out Calgary Saddledome roared its approval. It was everything fans had expected: a thrilling, hard-fought battle between two magnificent teams representing the top two hockey nations, each fiercely proud of its reputation.

Even the coaching staff got caught up in the emotion. "I sat up in the press box and kept track of the good scoring chances," said Team Canada assistant coach Tom Watt. "They had the first four of the game, then we had the next four, and that was it for the first period, 4–4. In the second period, we had ten good chances to their two. After that, I was so excited, I couldn't get them all down."

Late in the third period, despite having dominated the play, Canada trailed 2–1 but was piling on the pressure. The forwards, still determined to establish their position in front of the net, were being flattened by the Soviet defencemen, but were bouncing up and battling back. When the puck finally went in to tie the score, the ice looked like a battlefield strewn with bodies.

"We were putting lots of pressure on them," recalled defenceman Doug Wilson. "We came down and Gretz had the puck in the far corner. It was one of those ones where we had all sorts of pressure on them for two or three minutes and we just couldn't tie the game.

"Then, all of a sudden, Bobby Bourne went to the front of the net and Gretz got it back to me and I fired it onto the net."

But it wasn't a screamer into the top corner. It just trickled in.

"Bobby Bourne created all the traffic and was causing all kinds of trouble in front of the net," said Wilson. "I wasn't really at the point. I was at the top of the circle.

"It wasn't a slap shot, either," he said with a chuckle. "It was a wrist shot. It hit the goalie and went through the goalie. It dropped into the crease and slid in. Bobby Bourne was in a struggle in front of the net and Gretz kind of came around the net and didn't know where the puck was."

It was one of the single most uplifting moments in Canadian hockey history to that point. The game had been a classic battle of thrilling, exciting, high-speed hockey, and although the Canadians had an edge in play, it was beginning to look as if that fact might not be reflected on the scoreboard.

The Calgary Saddledome crowd was not known for its exuberance, but on this occasion the building exploded. The pent-up emotion and frustration that had been building over the course of the evening as the Canadians were repeatedly thwarted were finally released.

The game went into overtime and the stage was set for a result that, one way or the other, would be memorable.

Again, each team tried to impose its will on the other. The Canadians wanted to continue working the puck along the boards—which they had been doing successfully, even though the physical toll had been considerable. The Soviets wanted a turnover and a fast break, the kind of play that *they* had been feeding off for years.

And before long, they got it.

Vladimir Kovin and Mikhail Varnakov broke out of their own end at full speed with only Canadian defenceman Paul Coffey back.

The crowd fell silent. In that era, two Soviet forwards against any defenceman in the world was never a good situation for the defending team. Against Coffey, it looked like certain disaster for Canada.

A national debate had raged a few months earlier, when Coffey's offensive prowess had earned him a spot as one of the finalists in the voting for the Norris Trophy, awarded annually to the league's best defenceman. His many detractors, who took delight in snidely referring to him as "Paul Cough-up," screamed, "He can't play defence. How can the best-defenceman award go to a guy who can't play defence?"

A feeble joke making the rounds suggested that Coffey should quit hockey and become a pastry cook because he was so good at turnovers.

Canada's national newspaper, *The Globe and Mail*, had even assigned a feature story, the theme of which was, Can the Oilers ever win a Stanley Cup with Paul Coffey on defence? The criticism was totally unfair, and Sather provided the conclusion to the *Globe and Mail* story by stating succinctly, "We'll never win a Stanley Cup without him."

Like most innovators, Coffey was misunderstood. The traditionalists had seen the way the stay-at-home defencemen had played over the years and noticed that on occasion, Coffey would make a glaring error as a result of being out of position. But they didn't take into account the fact that he was a prolific scorer and that when he had the puck on his stick—which was often—he was every bit as effective defensively as someone who simply held his position and hoped to block a shot. The other team wasn't going to score without the puck.

Years later, Coffey admitted that at that crucial moment in 1984, outmanned two to one with the game on the line, the thoughts that raced through his mind had to do with his detractors.

"The thing I do remember—and it happened quickly, but I did have time to reflect on it," he said, "was I just said to myself, 'Thank God I'm the one who's back and I'm not caught up the ice, because if I was the one caught up the ice, I'd never hear the end of it.'

"And honestly, in the five seconds those two guys were bearing down on me, that was exactly the thought that went through my head."

But with ignominious defeat staring Canada in the face, Coffey produced what may well have been the greatest defensive play of his career.

"I didn't really know what I was going to do," he admitted afterwards. "The one guy [Kovin] came right at me. Usually, in the NHL, the puck carrier will go off to one side, but he was coming right at me.

"I knew he could only do two things: he could pass or he could shoot. But if he shot, the puck was going to have to go through me to get to the goal because I was standing right there in front of him and I sure wasn't going to move. So really, he could only do one thing. He had to pass."

And when he did, Coffey reacted with lightning quickness. He darted his stick out and didn't merely block the pass, but intercepted it cleanly! Now it was his turn to go on offence.

"That could have been Paul's greatest play," said Sather in 2005. "He made a lot of great plays, but that was certainly a great defensive play."

With the two Russians trapped, the Canadians roared into the Soviet zone and set up the attack. When the puck went into the corner, it resulted in another battle along the boards, one of many in this game. John Tonelli was battling with the Soviet defenders. Bodies banged against bodies and rattled off the boards and glass. Tonelli dug it out and got it back to the point, but the Soviet checkers came out in a hurry, and back it went into the corner. Once more Tonelli was into the fray, and once again the Soviets crunched him against the boards while they tried to dig out the puck.

While all this went on, Bossy was cruising around on the edge of the crease, trying to get to an open area, waiting for a shot he could tip and making sure he was in position to pounce on a rebound should the shot get through.

Back and forth he moved, doing battle all the time with a Soviet checker, usually one of the defenceman. In fact, he was knocked down more than once, but each time he staggered to his feet, and on one occasion, as he passed across the crease, he whacked the stick out of Myshkin's hands.

"Sure, it was interference," Bossy admitted later. "It definitely should have been, but you know the ref is not going to call it in a situation like that. Anyway, when you have a guy draped all over your back, you feel that you can do something. He's taking liberties with you and it's sort of offsetting."

Meanwhile, Tonelli was still persevering in the battle along the boards, this time against the dog-tired Kovin, who had long since switched to defence after the wasted two-on-one.

"Kovin came in and hit me," recalled Tonelli. "The point was wide open. I knew I just had to get it out to Coffey."

He did. Like Kovin, Coffey didn't have an awful lot left by now, but nevertheless, he put everything he had into the shot. As he let it go, Bossy was climbing to his feet, having been knocked down again, but with the instinct of the natural goal scorer that he was, he got his stick up and, fighting off Kovin—who had somehow found the energy to dart to the front of the net when the puck went to the point—deflected the shot as it came in.

Or did he? To this day, there's some doubt about it. Sather is one of those who thinks that the puck went right in off Coffey's stick, that Bossy did not deflect it.

"And he may be right," opined Doug Wilson.

"I don't think Bossy ever touched that shot," said Sather in 2005. "There was such confusion in front of the net. I never said anything publicly. Who knows what it hit? There were guys all over the place when that shot went through. But a couple of guys on the team thought that shot went straight through. I don't think he touched it.

"If you ever look at the replay of that thing, Bossy is in the corner on his knees celebrating and everybody goes to Coff. That's the interesting thing. I didn't care at that point, but after the game a couple of guys mentioned to me they thought Coffey scored the goal."

So we put it to the ultimate arbiter in matters relating to hockey.

"He touched it," said Gretzky. "I saw it."

Coffey agrees with Gretzky. "It didn't really matter, but I'm pretty sure Mike got his stick on it," he said. "I was shooting it for the top left corner, and it went in the top right corner. So it moved across there somehow. I'm pretty sure Bossy touched it."

Either way, no matter how it got there, the puck zipped past Myshkin and the Canadians had won in overtime. A classic game was over and, based upon the balance of play, the better team won. But it almost didn't.

Even though the overtime goal gets most of the spotlight, the victory required contributions of monumental proportions at both ends. Unknown to almost everyone at the time, the Canadians were getting heroics in goal that were in equal proportion to those provided by Coffey and the others.

Starting goaltender Grant Fuhr had been hurt in an earlier game, and the backup, Pete Peeters, played that night, even though he could hardly put any weight on one of his legs.

"Nobody knew it at the time," said Sather, "but Pete Peeters came in and played with a sprained ankle. Grant got hurt two games earlier and Pete came in, and everybody said we couldn't win with him in goal. He played a great game.

"He went horseback riding with Larry Robinson in the mountains and the horse reared up and rolled on his ankle. I didn't know [about] it until ten years later."

Coffey's primary memory of that game had to do with that long shift that culminated in the winning goal. It was typical of that era, he said, but it is no longer a part of the game.

"What Tonelli did and what Kovin did, you just don't see that happening anymore," said Coffey in a 2005 interview. "They took long shifts, but they could do it because they were in great hockey condition.

"It's no slight against today's players—obviously, they're bigger, faster and stronger—but I don't think they're better, and I don't think they're in as good hockey shape as the players were back then.

"Yes, they can bench press the house, and yes, their body fat might be way lower than ours. But I'm not talking about weightlifting. I'm not talking about jumping. I'm not talking about how many sit-ups they can do in thirty seconds. I'm talking about hockey shape—which is on-ice condition.

"Guys now are unfortunately programmed to go for thirty seconds or forty seconds and get off. If you're a good player, a real talented guy, something might not happen in thirty seconds. You need longer.

"I swear to this day that Gretz used to have a built-in clock in his head," continued Coffey. "He always knew how long everybody else was on the ice for, and he knew which defencemen on the other team were going to get tired. That's when he played. He'd jump on them. He'd take advantage of them. He'd chase them down to stop an icing call."

After the exhilarating victory over the Soviets, the final was something of an anticlimax. The Swedes were to provide the opposition, and even though they had beaten Canada earlier in the tournament, there weren't many observers who considered that result to be a true indication of the relative merits of the two teams.

In those days, the Swedes were still fairly timid players by NHL standards. They were skilled enough, and could do well if they didn't have to face any adversity, but against strong physical play or a determined opponent the Swedes usually politely declined to get involved.

"They play hockey the way they handled the world wars," the theory went. "They're neutral."

Even their own coach, Leif Boork, was under no illusions. "The problem with the Swedish team," he said at one point in the tournament, "is that it has too many Swedes on it."

Although the statement represented the thoughts of many hockey observers, Boork was probably playing a mind game, hoping to lull the Canadians into overconfidence.

It was an odd thing to say, but then again, Boork was an odd kind of coach. He was only thirty-five at the time, a short, dumpy, bearded man whose clothes were always rumpled and dishevelled. He looked as if he should be in the press box, not behind the bench.

He had taken over from Anders "The Duck" Parmstrom, the stereotypical nice guy who always finished last—or close enough to it to keep the demanding Swedish press in a state of perpetual unhappiness.

Before that, the coach was Hans Lindberg, universally known as "Virus" because, during his playing days, he always developed a convenient virus when the Swedes were due to play a tough team.

Boork was different, and despite his "too many Swedes" statement, it was under his tutelage that the Swedes started to shed their aura of non-involvement. He demanded a serious commitment, not the usual neutrality, and way back in May, when the Canadian players were either involved in the Stanley Cup playoffs or vacationing after elimination, Boork got all his available players together and started dry-land training.

By July 22, two weeks before Team Canada assembled in Banff, Boork had his entire team on the ice for strenuous practices. After practice, the players were encouraged to hug each other and hold hands. Off the ice, they were expected to do a lot of reading, with the emphasis on philosophy and poetry. It's safe to say that philosophy and poetry were not among the primary diversions of the Canadian players.

And Boork told his players to stand up for themselves, an approach to the game that had not been much in evidence with earlier Swedish teams. Even the normally placid Czechoslovaks and Soviets would suddenly initiate a physical game against the Swedes, knowing full well that after a few stiff body checks had been administered, the Swedes' passion for the game would disappear faster than free beer in the press room.

The Canadians had a tendency to extend the intimidation into the psychological realm. "You want to come over here and take our jobs?" they would say to the Swedish players whenever they were at close quarters. "Well, now you're going to pay the price."

Boork tried to instill confidence in his charges and told them to be proud of their heritage. "It's very important for the Swedish player to play a little more with the heart," he said. "Take a little more air into your lungs so you look a little bigger than you are, especially when you're playing against North Americans."

Hakan Loob, who must have been wearing his skates when the Calgary Flames took the measurements that determined he was 5'9", stunned the hockey media by challenging the Canadians.

"They keep saying that we're taking their jobs and that they're better hockey players," he announced. "Well, let them prove it."

It was Loob who backed up his words by scoring the first goal of the final. But after that, it was all downhill for the Swedes. Canada won the first game 5–2 and the second 6–5.

The Swedes were without one of their better players, Bengt-Ake Gustavsson, who had debated the Swedes-in-the-NHL concept with Team USA's Massachusetts-born goaltender, Tom Barrasso, in a bar and had been so badly punched out that he was unable to play. But even so, the Swedes were never a serious opponent for Canada. Even though the Canadians were by this time down to their third goaltender, Rejean Lemelin, they never looked particularly challenged by the Swedes. For all intents and purposes, the 1984 Canada Cup had been won when Paul Coffey broke up that two-on-one against the Russians.

"I don't think that game ever got enough credit for the type of game it was," said Wilson. "That was one of the last times they had the KLM Line [Vladimir Krutov, Igor Larionov and Sergei Makarov] together on top of their game, and if you watch that game, it was a whale of a game—the tempo and pace of it, the emotions.

"Their eyes . . . you saw it afterwards during the national anthem being played—they were emotionally distraught. You could see the emotions in their eyes. It was quite a game.

"The tempo of that game from the first line to the fourth line was a tempo I had never seen before. The pace was really shocking. There was a lot more flow to this game, and it was as if we were telling the Soviets, 'Okay, we'll play your style,' which we had never done before."

After the game, Larionov and another Soviet player managed to elude their KGB watchdogs and sneak out of the hotel. They ended up on Calgary's famed Electric Avenue with Gretzky and most of the Team Canada players.

"There was Igor and another Russian player, and I don't know his name," recalled Gretzky in a 2005 interview. "There were two Russians and the other one didn't speak any English. He smoked more cigarettes and drank more than any of us. He was an unknown. I think he wore number 31 and he was a right-handed shot. That's all I remember about him.

"They snuck down the back elevator and Charlie Henry [a close friend of Gretzky's father] picked them up. It was a six o'clock game, if I remember rightly, so it was about 9:30 when we picked them up. Igor kept saying he had to be back by midnight."

By this point in his tale, Gretzky was laughing. "Igor we got back by midnight," he said. "The other guy we lost. I don't know if he ever got back. He might still be in living in Calgary for all I know. It's funny now, but we were worried then."

For Gretzky, the evening with Larionov was the beginning of a long friendship.

"He was standing there talking to me," Gretzky said, "and the whole time, I'm thinking, 'This guy is talking to me and the whole time we were playing against him, I was thinking he didn't understand a word I was saying.'

"I would talk to our guys and say, 'Coff, you stand there and I'll get the draw to you,' or say to someone else, 'You go over here and I'll throw it to you up the middle.' The whole time, Igor knew exactly what I was saying.

"The first time I knew he spoke English was when we're standing there having a beer. He started telling me, 'We all want to play in the NHL and maybe one day it will happen.' It was an incredible night because Charlie snuck him out past the KGB.

"He said he would like to defect, but the government wouldn't allow it. But he said, 'One day, we hope we can all play in the NHL.'"

The Canadians urged him to defect, but he insisted that he couldn't. There would be reprisals against his family back in Voskresensk, he said, and he had to put their welfare ahead of his own.

The very fact that the family lived in Voskresensk was proof that such reprimands were indeed a fact of life in the Soviet Union. Larionov's grandfather had been living in Moscow during the Stalin era and casually mentioned to a group of friends that perhaps the country would be better under a leader other than Josef Stalin. That was all. He didn't suggest a coup. He didn't even make his assertion forcefully. He just ruminated publicly. That got the family exiled to Voskresensk, fifty-five miles southeast of Moscow. Had the elder Larionov's "crime" been considered more serious, he'd have gone to Siberia.

Of all the triumphs by Canadian professionals in international play, the 1984 Canada Cup was the one that came the closest to disaster before it was pulled back from the precipice. As a result, the lessons were etched indelibly into the minds of the participants and were called upon for years to come. Not for fourteen years, by which time the lesson apparently had been forgotten, was Team Canada again run by an advisory committee. During the interval, the top man, whoever it might have been, had his hand-picked support staff, whom he relied on for advice, but everyone knew that when the tournament ended, the credit or the blame would fall on only one set of shoulders.

For some reason, the country got away from that principle for the 1998 Olympics in Nagano, Japan. The concept of one-man rule was forsaken for a troika. Canada staggered through a controversy-ridden tournament and finished fourth.

So the nation went back to the method that had been proven successful, selecting Gretzky as the executive director for the 2002 Olympics and then the 2004 World Cup. Drawing on the lessons he had learned back in 1984, Gretzky insisted that his players be mindful of one overriding principle: leave your egos at the door. A player's involvement with his NHL team is part of that ego, and Gretzky remembered only too well how such struggles had almost ruined the 1984 team.

Any organization calling itself Team Canada must live up to both parts of that name. It's not enough to be Canadian; the players must also act as a team. They must feel that they are out there to play for their country, not for themselves or for the further glory of their NHL teams. It's the only real way to be successful.

As strange as it may seem in a nation that loves to brag about its hockey prowess, Canada went a long way towards overcoming its hockey inferiority complex in that 1984 tournament. It's easy to sit back these days and say that Canadian players are as good as any in the world. But in 1984, there was a lot of doubt about that.

The approach that Sather instilled into his 1984 team established the principle that Canada could indeed skate with the Soviets, that Canadian players could indeed match them skill for skill.

The 1981 Canada Cup had been an embarrassment, and so had the 1979 Challenge Cup. The widely held, and not unreasonable, opinion was that Canada could win at that highest level only by negating skills, not by matching them. The Canadian game was seen as one of thuggery and intimidation, not one of speed and finesse, of skill and strategy.

In 1984, that view changed. Ironically, the goal that won that crucial game and contributed so much to Canada's standing in the hockey world has become known in hockey circles as "the Coffey goal," even though it was Bossy, not Coffey, who scored it. But it was Coffey who produced the blend of offence and defence that would later stand the Canadians in such good stead, a blend that they had never before exhibited at this level.

THE GOAL: SEPTEMBER 15, 1987.

Game three of the Canada Cup best-of-three final.
Scored by Mario Lemieux (assisted by Wayne Gretzky)
at 18:34 of the third period. Canada 6, USSR 5.

IT WAS ANYTHING BUT HOCKEY WEATHER WHEN THE TEAM CANADA hopefuls arrived in Montreal for the 1987 Canada Cup training camp.

It had been a hot, steamy August day. Even though temperatures had started to slide a touch as evening fell and the players started arriving at the downtown hotel that was to be their home for a couple of weeks, many were sweating when they entered the lobby.

They would need to get used to the feeling. There would be a lot of sweat before this one was finished.

The coach of this edition of Team Canada was Mike Keenan, known universally as Iron Mike because of his insistence on hard work, rigid discipline and dedication to duty.

"I think it was fairly structured and intense because of what we knew would be the demands of that tournament," recalled Keenan. "We knew that the Soviet Union would be a top team. Look at that team and who they had. We had top players, but it took everything we had to beat them."

For a while, it looked as if the plan was to use most of the National Hockey League to beat them.

The camp opened on August 4 with thirty-five players—Edmonton's Kevin Lowe having been a late medical scratch—as well as four general managers, one head coach, three assistant coaches, one trainer, two assistant trainers, a physiotherapist, a masseur, two team doctors, a team photographer and a gaggle of assorted hangers-on who invariably accompanied Alan Eagleson, the executive director of the NHL Players' Association, in those days.

Within days, three more players were brought in to make scrimmaging easier.

"We actually had more in '91," laughed Keenan in a 2005 interview. "We had a lot more in '91 than we did in '87. But none of the managers were going to be around that much. Eagleson was primarily the point man."

This broad-brush approach would fall out of favour in the 1990s, when it became policy to invite only those players who would be needed, plus a third goalie in case of injury.

"But Eagleson asked them what they wanted to do," said Keenan. "He was the head of the NHL Players' Association at the time and he said, 'Do you want to invite a lot of guys and give more guys a chance to make the team? Or do you just want to invite the group?' A lot of guys said they'd like to have a chance to make the team, so they opened it up."

Right from the first day, it was clear that there was something special about this aggregation.

"I think they came with a very enthusiastic attitude, and an enthusiastic attitude about making the hockey club," said Keenan. "There's a realization among the group that there are some fantastic hockey players here and the in-house competition is extremely high.

"They're very interested in making sure that they demonstrate their best abilities—and acquire their best abilities—through these practices, to make sure that they play well."

There was none of the bickering that had been evident in the early stages of the 1984 Canada Cup. Wayne Gretzky was the captain this time and it was clear that he took his role seriously.

Keenan began his trademark psychological manipulations right away. Even though the team could have used any of the Montreal Forum dressing rooms, Keenan wouldn't let them into the hallowed ground that was the Canadiens room. Players would have to be selected for the team before being accorded that honour. He knew that when the time came, the message would not be lost on these elite players. In the visitors' room, they were guys trying out for the team. In the Montreal room, they would be something special. They would be Team Canada.

"They were not going to be in the big room until they were a team," Keenan explained.

Keenan was not the only one capable of using psychology to pass along a message.

"The first practice was at noon," said Keenan. "It was about one minute to twelve, and I was on the ice and I looked over to that passageway out of the visitors' room. Wayne came out, and there were probably about fifty guys around him trying to get quotes as he was walking to the ice.

"He's very accommodating, as you know, and he had about thirty seconds to get on the ice. He looked up at the clock and stepped on the ice and his eyes lit up.

"I'd never coached Wayne before, but that instant was just an incredibly insightful opportunity for me. I said, 'Oh, wow! This is where he loves to be. This is his solace. Nobody is going to be out here asking him questions.'

"He was so excited. The minute his foot hit the ice, he was like that. It was clear."

Throughout his playing career, Gretzky never failed to support his coaches. Asked about something that went wrong, or some negative aspect of a game, he would discuss it. But he would never, ever criticize his coach.

Even when he had a celebrated run-in with Robbie Ftorek during his stint with the Los Angeles Kings, he didn't waver from that policy. The Kings were losing a game when

Gretzky had a breakaway that he didn't convert. In frustration, he smashed his stick over the crossbar.

Ftorek benched him and explained between periods that he'd done so because he didn't like to see such displays of emotion. "I'm here to teach you guys," he said.

Gretzky, furious at being benched, snapped, "If you want to teach, go to New Haven [the Kings' farm team]. I'm here to win."

Other players gave me chapter and verse on that incident, but to this day, Gretzky has never confirmed it and will never criticize Ftorek. As far as he is concerned, coaches have to be the ultimate authority, and despite the ill feelings that had erupted between his Oilers and Keenan's Philadelphia Flyers during the Stanley Cup final only two months earlier, Gretzky held to this belief.

Although he tried his best not to show it, Keenan was a bit nervous at the time. He was only thirty-eight, had never played in the National Hockey League, and had been coaching in it for only four years. He had no idea how the players would respond to him.

"I blew the whistle to get things started," he said, "and the very first whistle, Wayne came up beside me. He couldn't get any closer than he was. His shoulder was up against mine while I was giving some instructions.

"It was his affirmation of me as a coach. He was telling the rest of them, 'We have to listen to what we're doing here. Everybody has got to be on board.' The very first whistle! The very first practice!"

"Yeah, I did that," said Gretzky years later, "because he was a young guy and nobody knew what to expect out of Mike at that time. Throughout my career, the one thing I really believed in is that although you might agree or disagree with everything the coach says or does, especially when you're a leader or a captain, your best player has to maintain the coach's philosophy.

"I might not agree, but I would never challenge his authority. I don't believe in that.

"Robbie Ftorek—I lived or died by what he believed in, so he can never look back and say 'You challenged the coach' or 'You screwed the coach.' A player is a player, and I really thought that Mike, as a young guy, was nervous. I went and stood beside him and I had Mess go on the other side."

And where, Keenan was asked, was Mario Lemieux?

Keenan laughed. "He was standing in the background. He was in awe."

It was during this Canada Cup series that Lemieux truly became a genuine NHL superstar. He was already more than accomplished as a player. He had been the first-overall draft pick in 1984 and had dazzled the fans with his artistry. In the scoring race the previous season, he had finished tied for third with Mark Messier, behind Gretzky and Jari Kurri.

But he had no idea of what it took to win at the world-class level. In fact, he had no idea what it took to win in the NHL—his Pittsburgh Penguins had missed the playoffs every year of his tenure.

"Wayne was at a point in his career where he was the best," said Keenan, "but I think he needed someone to keep pushing him. His attitude was, 'Okay, Mario, I'm going to teach you everything I know about this for two reasons. And two good reasons. One, if I can teach you and accelerate your ability in six weeks, it's good for Canada, good for the NHL and good for this team. And two, you're going to make me a better player because now I'm going to be thinking "Where's Mario?" for the next ten years.'"

The camp opened to a regimen of four intricately structured practices a day, two for each squad. Swirling high-speed drills that required precision passing left no time for jokes or horseplay. When the players did get to stand around for a moment or two, they were required to check their pulses, an integral aspect of an aerobic workout.

This was uncharted ground for a Team Canada. Even though previous incarnations had shown the ability to knuckle down and get serious when disaster came perilously close, they were never very serious at this stage of the proceedings. The attitude had always run along the lines of, "Hey, we're Canadians. Dry-land training, aerobics, regimentation and plain old hard work are for Europeans and other hockey heretics, not Canadians. Want to go for a beer?"

But right off the bat in 1987, even with a four-week training camp looming ahead of them, there was an immediate sense of purpose, an aura of determination and an attitude of total dedication.

The lesson of 1984, when the team had had to drag itself from the brink of disaster to become a unified group rather than a motley collection of cliques and egos, had not been forgotten.

Certainly there was plenty of fertile ground in which to sow dissent. Keenan's Flyers had succumbed to the Oilers in seven games in the previous Stanley Cup final, and there were those in the Oilers' organization who felt that Keenan had encouraged some of his players to try to injure the Edmonton players. At the end of it, they refused to shake Keenan's hand. Yet the 1987 edition of Team Canada was stacked with Oilers.

And with such a large group in camp fighting for jobs, there was always the possibility of backbiting and undermining. But Keenan worked hard to keep it under control and the Team Canada veterans were aware of the approach that had to be taken.

"There was no conflict with the players," recalled Keenan. "We had Oilers and Flyers and they integrated pretty well. I was pushing them pretty hard.

"The guys who were back from '84 had learned the lesson and they had had success together. They were great people and they knew that their success would depend on each other. They knew as a group what the intricacies of the team—building and bonding—were. And how none of them had to take credit, that it was a team thing."

There was also a realization that the hockey world had evolved significantly during the eighties. The Finns and

Swedes were churning out more elite players than had ever been the case. The Czechoslovaks and Soviets, despite being behind the Iron Curtain and unable to participate in the NHL, were superb players, spurred on by coaches whose approach bordered on fanaticism.

It was never easy to win a tournament at this level, but this one was going to provide the most demanding test ever.

"We can't play our best in the Olympic Games," explained assistant coach Tom Watt. "When you go there or the world championships, you get the guys who are available. This is where we get a chance to have our best."

True enough. The catch was that the other teams had their best as well.

Watt was fully aware of that. "I think it's a mistake if you try to gear your team just to play the Soviets," he said. "The Swedes are highly skilled. They play a very controlled game. And the quality of the Swedish and Czechoslovak goaltending is outstanding.

"The Swedes played tough in the last world championships, too. They're bigger and stronger and not as afraid of the physical game as they were."

The game had evolved to the point that it was increasingly homogeneous. The NHL had learned its lessons from Europe the hard way, and had incorporated many aspects of the European style. Yet at the same time, Canada was widely regarded as a long-standing hockey power, and as a result, some elements of the Canadian game had migrated to Europe.

"I think this is the tournament that will show that whether you play in Sweden, the United States, Canada or Russia, it's all basically the same hockey," said Gretzky.

"All the teams emphasize the same hockey. I think the European teams are starting to play more of the physical game that we play. We're starting to play more of the skating game that they play. We're starting to play more of a puck-movement game that the Soviets play—moving the puck and going into the holes."

It was clear to everyone that the calibre of the opposition was going to be extremely high. It was also clear that the other teams, especially the Soviets, were in superb physical condition. Keenan knew that in the 1984 Canada Cup, Team Canada had, for the first time since the Soviets had risen to prominence, been able to match their skating prowess. But he also knew that this development had not escaped the attention of the Soviets. They had increased the demands of their own training regimens, and if the Canadians were not to fall behind again, they would have to be even better than they were three years ago.

There were rumblings of discontent among the players. Getting ready was one thing, but the tournament was weeks away. Surely they didn't need to work so hard so soon. Accordingly, a delegation was sent to confront Keenan on the matter—Gretzky, Messier and Ray Bourque showed up at Keenan's hotel room one afternoon after practice.

Keenan was chuckling when he recalled it. "It was late afternoon," he said, "They came up to me and said, 'Gee, this is structured. We're working awful hard,' and so on.

"I said, 'We're playing the best team we ever faced and we have to win this thing. I've got no problem backing off you guys,' but I said to Wayne, 'Wayne, what are the expectations of the Canadian public? Of course it's to win the gold medal.'

"I said, 'I'm not putting any demands on you guys with the exceptions of the on-ice practices, none whatsoever, but if you want to back off we can.

"'One thing, though: am I supposed to tell—or are *you* going to tell—the Canadian public we're going to back off a little bit because we've got too much work to do here and you want to kind of take it easy?'

"Wayne said, 'Mike, forget this meeting ever existed.'

"The whole meeting took about two minutes. Wayne said, 'Mike, you're absolutely right. I'm embarrassed I'm here. I'm sorry. See you tomorrow.'

"It flashed on him in about ten seconds: What are we

doing here? The practices had a lot of tempo, but we never practised more than an hour. We're playing the best team we ever faced and we have to win this thing."

When asked about Keenan's recollection, Gretzky said, "That's pretty accurate. We all said the same thing."

But having made their pilgrimage, they had to exact some sort of concession. "We asked him for something," said Gretzky. "We said tomorrow at the skate, you call the practice, but just watch. And that's what he did."

Many hockey writers don't bother to show up for practices. There's a certain sameness to them, and the quotes don't come until the guys leave the ice. If someone gets hurt badly enough for it to be a story, there's always someone around who saw the incident and can provide the details in plenty of time to meet the evening deadline.

But those Team Canada practices were too good to miss. And Keenan, who often joined in the late-night media singalongs in the Montreal bars (there were those who suggested the media version of "Paradise by the Dashboard Light" was better than the recording by Meat Loaf and Ellen Foley) co-operated by holding practices at 4 p.m. Even the most moribund among the media corps could manage to drag themselves out of bed in time to get to the Forum for that hour. After all, there might be a scrimmage, and with these guys going end to end with no checking, few whistles and no TV timeouts, the action was spectacular—especially when you could take your pick of almost any seat in the building.

What set Team Canada '87 apart was that even the drills were riveting. Keenan would have none of the time-worn line rushes. He and his staff had put together a series of drills to prepare the squad for the European opponents they would face in the tournament, especially the Soviets.

One of these started off like a basic three-on-two rush, but as the puck carrier crossed the red line, he would flip the puck to one of the two defencemen rather than to his linemate. This was done to represent an intercepted pass.

The other defenceman had to immediately change direction, and as soon as he did, his partner passed him the puck.

At this point, the forwards mentally changed teams. Now, all five players were on the same team, so the forwards had to wheel and reverse direction to get into position for a lead pass from the defenceman.

There were four provisions to this drill. First, everything had to be done at top speed. Second, the defenders were not allowed to retreat over the blue line. Third, the rushers couldn't give up the puck until they got to the red line. Fourth, the "interception," the change of direction and the head-man pass to start the attack all had to be done before the forwards had crossed the red line.

"Yeah, that was the transition game we were working on there," said Keenan. "And with that kind of talent to work with, I think they really enjoyed what we were doing on the ice, because there were people coming in and saying, 'Hey these practices are better than games.'

"Everybody was flocking in for the practices. That was unbelievable. I can still remember that."

At that stage in the NHL's development, a quick transition game represented a radical departure from the predominant style of play. The standard NHL defenceman would give no thought whatsoever to a quick transition if a pass were intercepted. Instead, he would retreat leisurely into his own zone while considering his options. Sometimes, he would even go all the way behind his own net.

Keenan wanted none of that. If you could intercept the puck and quickly turn the play the other way, you'd probably create an odd-man rush. And an odd-man rush with the kind of forwards Canada had on this team was a high-percentage scoring play.

It was rapidly becoming clear that with this group, the most difficult task of the early stages was not to get them ready for high-level competition, but to make the cuts.

With the one tiny exception of the brief complaint concerning the workload, the camp had run flawlessly. There had been no sign of the usual problems—scheduling foul-ups, public-relations blunders or organizational fiascos.

The lack of involvement of the NHL's New York office probably had a lot to do with that, but whatever the reason, the fact remained that this appeared to be the best Team Canada training camp ever.

But now, the cuts had to be made, and sometimes they can tear a team apart. Organizers must make sure the right people are dismissed, because if that's not the case, it can lead to animosity and even to doubts about the competence of those making the decisions. And to a great extent, that means the coaching staff.

There were a lot of difficult decisions to be made even before the first cut was announced. Should the emphasis be on offence or defence? Could they afford the luxury of a specialist who could kill penalties or take face-offs if that player couldn't have made the team otherwise? Should the selection be made purely on training-camp performance, or should play in the previous season be taken into consideration? And if the latter, how much more weight should be given to playoff performances than to regular-season play?

There were thirty-eight excellent players in camp, many of them revered in their home markets. Steve Yzerman, for instance. To the dismay of fans in Detroit, not to mention his hometown of Ottawa, he was cut. Tony Tanti, the darling of Vancouver Canucks supporters, got the chop as well. Al MacInnis of the Calgary Flames didn't make the grade. Neither did Kirk Muller. Or Dave Poulin ("My own captain in Philadelphia," said Keenan). Boston's Cam Neely got released, thereby causing Don Cherry a few sleepless nights. The rugged Scott Stevens managed to hang on for a long time, but eventually was the last defenceman to be cut.

And there was the cut that outraged Toronto: Wendel Clark, the only bright light on what was then an atrocious Maple Leafs team.

"And I cut Patrick Roy in Montreal," chuckled Keenan. "How dumb am I?"

But all these cuts were made only after a great deal of soul-searching. The coaches and the associate general managers knew how hard every one of these players had worked and how heartbreaking it would be to be told to go home. These were stars; many of them had never been cut from a team before.

"In Patrick's case, we did it purely on what had transpired on the ice," said Keenan. "Kelly Hrudey was the third guy for sure, way ahead of Patrick. Ron Hextall was there, and Grant Fuhr, and they had both played well. Grant was going to be the number one goalie. I told him that, and he had just won the Stanley Cup again. Unless he falters or gets hurt, he's going to be the number one guy.

"The other part of it was I didn't know whether Patrick would have stayed as the third goalie. Kelly was happy to stay as the third goalie, and knowing Patrick, he probably wouldn't have. I've never asked him that, but I felt that he wouldn't, and then we'd have a real controversy. Kelly was happy to be there and just be a part of it so that was a pretty easy determination."

As expected, the players were gracious about their fate. Yzerman, who was part of the '84 Team Canada, smiled ruefully and said, "I don't know if this means I'm getting worse or what." But he added that he wasn't particularly surprised. "This is a better all-around team," he said. "The last time, it wasn't really a team. It was just a bunch of talented players. This time, the guys seem younger and just as talented. Everybody can move the puck around."

But not everyone saw the larger picture as well as Yzerman. "I'm not really sure why I got cut," said Muller. "The frustrating thing is that I only got to play in one game. I think I'm more of a game player than a practice player."

Tanti wasn't really surprised by his fate. "I thought I had a chance," he chuckled, "until the first day of camp.

"But I'm glad I was asked to come out. It was a lot of fun. I'd rather be cut now than just before the tournament."

The cuts gave the first indication that, all other things being equal, this team intended to opt for size. Denis Savard, one of the league's niftiest forwards but also one of its smallest, wasn't even invited. Tanti, Yzerman and Dino Ciccarelli were among the first cuts. Shortly afterwards, another one of Keenan's Philadelphia forwards, Derrick Smith, went as well.

"Personally, for me," said Keenan, "this has the been the toughest thing I have ever had to go through in being a head coach and being involved in these decisions."

With all this preparation, Canadian fans were expecting their team to dominate, even in the unnecessarily long eight-game exhibition schedule. To the delight of the Canadian fans—except those in Toronto who booed them for not having Wendel Clark in the lineup—they started with six consecutive victories, four of them against the United States, the last being an 11–2 blowout.

But when they played the Soviets in their penultimate exhibition game, they received something of a shock. It was another blowout, but this time, the Canadians were on the wrong end of a 9–4 decision.

Naturally, they tried to put the best possible face on it, and Hextall, the number two goalie, tried to shoulder the blame. "I was awful, especially in the third period," he said.

He also spoke of the problems of having so many players battling for spots. "It's tough on goaltenders," he said. "You don't get much work in game situations with four goalies in camp. It's also tough to go out there every night with different guys. Once we get the team together, we'll all be much better."

Perhaps. But not right away.

As was invariably the case, Eagleson had made sure that the schedule provided Canada with a gently rising path. They invariably started against weaker opponents to provide the maximum possible time to get accustomed to playing together before having to face serious opposition.

In view of this, their tournament-opening 4–4 tie against Czechoslovakia was not an overly impressive result. Two days later, they defeated Finland 4–1. Team USA was next on the schedule, and the Americans were planning to make life difficult for the Canadians.

At that point in the hockey history of the two nations, Canada looked upon the Americans as just another step along the way. But to the Americans, this was the game that could make their tournament a success. Most of them resented the fact that the NHL was Canadian-dominated, and their masterful coach, Bob Johnson, didn't have to do a lot to get his team up for the game.

But he did prepare them well. "We're limited in talent, but we play very well as a team," said Rod Langway, a two-time winner of the Norris Trophy as the NHL's best defenceman.

It was the Americans' intention to frustrate the flashy Canadians, to negate their speed as much as possible and to slow the game down as well, initiating as many delays as they could without getting penalized, a tactic that Johnson had used with considerable success when his Calgary Flames played the Edmonton Oilers in the 1986 playoffs.

"We've got a really good system to slow that team down," said forward Curt Fraser. "As long as everyone works well together, it will work well."

One of their tactics, however, left a bit to be desired.

"Wayne was just so incredible," said Keenan, thinking back to that game. "It was in Hamilton, and the building is full and everybody's cheering and he was coming down the ice in the neutral zone on the far side from our bench. He was going down the boards as fast as he can, and all of a sudden, he just makes a ninety-degree turn at the red line, goes right along the red line to the referee and says, 'They've got too many men on the ice.'

"Sure enough, they did. There wasn't one person in the whole building who knew it. But he did. I got the sense that he knew where all his friends were sitting in the building. That was scary, but that's how perceptive he was."

"I saw him do that umpteen times during games with Edmonton," chuckled Paul Coffey years later. "He'd be skating down the ice yelling at the ref. I'd say, 'What the hell is he yelling about?'

"He'd be going down the ice with the puck, shouting, 'Too many men too on the ice; too many men on the ice.'"

Coffey started laughing as he recounted the story that has become embellished over the years, "He'd say, 'I've just gone around five guys. I'm going around my sixth guy. Something is wrong here.'"

The Americans put up a spirited fight that night, but Team Canada persevered 3–2 and was starting to give clear indications that it could indeed win the tournament. Even though the Americans had a solid team with players like Langway, Bryan Trottier, Mark Howe, Ed Olczyk and John Vanbiesbrouck and were playing with passion, the Canadians remained poised, did what needed to be done and came away with the win.

Sweden provided the next test, and the Canadians came through in that one as well. Then it was time for the last game of the round-robin segment, the much-anticipated meeting with the Soviets, a team that still had all the mystique that it had ever had, but no longer the mystery.

It had now been fifteen years since the memorable 1972 Summit Series, and the teams knew each other well. Canada had won some of the head-to-head battles. So had the Soviets. But there was a clear feeling in the hockey community that over that period, Canada's game had evolved at a much greater pace than that of the Soviets, who had continued to do what they had always done. They had produced players of tremendous skill by identifying them when they were pre-teens and subjecting them to intensive, specialized training.

One on one, they could be devastating. But their tactics hadn't changed a lot. They were playing basically the same game in 1987 that they had played in 1972.

It was not their tactical approach that kept them among the elite of the world hockey nations; it was their remarkable individual skills. They had introduced their style to the world more than a decade before, and the NHL had embraced many aspects of it. But the Soviets hadn't really produced any innovations since that time.

"The European, NHL and Soviet styles of hockey have become so similar," said Gretzky. "In the past, you associated the NHL with tight checking, but now it's tight checking with speed. Every team moves the puck quickly. Puck movement and forechecking are a big part of success in the NHL. That's going to make it a lot easier for us to play the Soviets."

In fact, there were already rumours, which proved to be well founded, that the Soviets were on the verge of granting exit visas to some of their players in order to increase the interaction between the world's two leading hockey communities. The idea was that selected Soviets would be able to play in the NHL and learn its ways, but would play for the USSR in international series.

Sure enough, the following season, Sergei Priakin joined the Calgary Flames, becoming the first Soviet to play in the NHL with his nation's blessing.

By 1987, opponents had learned to block the middle against the Soviets and force them outside, where they had less room to operate and were less comfortable. Having done that, opponents could then design their own tactics to make the most of the situation.

In the previous world championships, and in the first game of the round robin, the Swedes had stayed with the Soviets and even defeated them by forcing them outside and leaving them there. They were free to move around the perimeter at will. They weren't dangerous out there.

But on the smaller NHL rinks, that tactic had its short-comings because, even along the boards, the Soviets were only one quick pass away from a scoring opportunity. So the Canadian concept was to force them outside and win the battles along the boards. Even though the European game had become much more physical in the past decade, Canadians felt, with considerable justification, that in the grinding, hard-fought wars along the boards, they were still the best.

This was not the old-style, dirty-play type of game. It was intimidation, all right, but it was intimidation within the rules. This was just the solid, hard-checking, win-the-small-battles approach that had long been the essence of Canadian hockey.

Right from the beginning, Keenan had stressed that the Canadians would have to play a disciplined game, so much so that he warned that anyone who got into a fight, either in training camp or in the tournament itself, would be sent home immediately.

"Our theme has been discipline over aggression," he said. "There certainly wasn't going to be any fighting in the tournament. We told the players, 'We don't need to see that, and you're not going to prove anything to us by fighting because we know who can play and who can't play.'"

The round-robin game against the Soviets was pretty much a bellwether for the championship round. At the end of regulation time, the score was tied, and since there was no overtime at that stage of the tournament, the game ended 3–3.

In the first stage of the tournament, Canada had tied two but gone through undefeated. The Soviets had lost to Sweden but still managed to finish second.

Now, to get the final series that all the Canadian fans wanted to see, the Soviets had to beat their nemesis, Sweden, while Canada had to eliminate the team it had tied in the opening round: Czechoslovakia, led by Dominik Hasek, the acrobatic young goaltender who was still six years away from his first starting NHL job.

Neither had an easy time of it, but in the end, as is so often the case, skill prevailed. The stage was set for the best-of-three Canada Cup final between the defending champions from Canada, and the team that many saw as the best in the world, the Soviet Union.

No one was expecting any great surprises. The Soviets, as already noted, were fairly static in their approach. The Canadians, despite having a different head coach than in 1984, had the same two architects of the game plan: assistant coaches John Muckler and Tom Watt.

"Tom Watt was the coach with the most international experience," said Keenan. "He had coached the national team and he did a super job. He came to us with a report before every game. John Muckler and Tom conversed more about the strategy we would employ, as opposed to myself and the other assistant coach, Jean Perron.

"I was trying to get the acceleration of our game to the ultimate level, at the maximum level. I was trying to get the transition and the speed and then we'd all get together.

"Tom would tell us what the other team was doing and we'd say, 'Well, how are we going to play against that?'"

They were about to face an excellent team, so the game plan had to be complex. But by the time the Canadians went into that series, they knew what they had to do in every part of the rink.

In the Soviet zone, the Canadians intended to crowd the net. People like Messier, Brent Sutter, Rick Tocchet and Kevin Dineen were specialists in that regard—they had been selected with that aspect of their game in mind. These guys were early examples of what would later become a well-defined element in hockey—the power forward. It might seem odd to refer to physically slight players like Dineen and Sutter as power forwards, but they were creating a style that would be perfected by players larger than themselves. They used their muscle, not their guile or finesse, to go to the net. They battled their way through defencemen to get to the crease area, and once there, they refused to be moved. For a time in hockey's history, they also muscled their way through goalies, but eventually, the powers that be cracked down on the practice, altering the rulebook to make it counterproductive.

But even with these archetypal power forwards practising

their craft, the Canadians knew better than to float a prayerful pass into that area in the hope that someone might convert it. The Soviets had looked at the old videotapes, too, and they knew what to expect.

Because their own style was geared to creating high-percentage shots from the front of the net, the Soviets were fully aware of the importance of controlling that territory. They would keep their defencemen deep and they'd have two deep wingers as well—right around the hash marks. The centre would float around in the middle.

Their anticipation was remarkable, and if a pass should be picked off, the forwards would wheel and take off at full speed. A quick pass would give them an odd-man break, always a dangerous situation.

Therefore, the Canadians were putting a lot of reliance on shots from the point. The backchecking Soviet wingers were playing deep, leaving the points open, and any pucks heading towards the net were to come in with speed so that they couldn't be easily intercepted.

The peripheral areas of the ice surface had to be won at all costs. The series was in all likelihood going to be extended to the full three games, and the Canadians wanted to establish the areas along the boards, and behind both nets, as their own. Like all who faced the Soviets, they knew that they had to block the middle and force the play outside. Once it got there, they felt they had a distinct advantage. But to get to that stage, they had to produce disciplined team-wide defence. They had to be where their teammates expected them to be and not get drawn out of position by the Soviets' wizardry with the puck.

One of the astonishing examples of that wizardry was the ability of every Soviet forward to drop the puck into his skates and control it there. In the NHL, a player who did that had invariably lost control, and it was a signal for a defender to close in on him and take the puck away. But to the Soviets, it was just another way of drawing a defender out of position.

"They try to separate your defence from your forwards and create holes on the ice," explained Messier. "As soon as you do that, they just pick you apart. We have to play some good defensive hockey and score on our chances and play with a lot of confidence."

The Canadians also knew that once an attack was going forward, they had to keep it going forward. There were to be no drop passes at the blue line. That was a play the Europeans had introduced and sometimes it could be effective in the NHL. Against the Soviets, with their quick transition game, it courted disaster.

And then there was the most important aspect of all. They had to play tough. It didn't mean that the players should fight or that Gretzky and Lemieux should be throwing body checks. But it meant that battles along the boards had to be won. It meant that the forwards who were supposed to station themselves in front of the net had to do so, even though big Soviet defencemen would be doing all they could to prevent it. It meant the outlet forward, who would be stationed along the boards to start the breakout, had to advance the puck across the blue line, even though he'd often have to absorb a crunching body check to do so.

They had to play the series as if it were a Stanley Cup final. They would be in pain. They would be gasping for breath. They would be so tired that they would want nothing more than to sit on the bench and let someone else take a shift. They would be cut and bruised and aching.

But they had to keep going to the net. They had to keep pushing the Soviets to the outside. The Soviets had created phenomenal hockey players and had schooled them in every aspect of the game. But they had yet to find a way to give them the kind of pride in their game that was evident in the Canadian approach.

The opening game began with a brief feeling-out stretch, but it rapidly evolved into spectacular entertainment, delivering everything a hockey fan could want from a game.

Naturally, a partisan would want his own team to prevail, but purely from the point of view of hockey as a spectacle, this was unbeatable. There were brilliant offensive plays, superb defensive efforts, crunching checks, magnificent saves. It was hockey at its best. And it was all done at full speed. There were no lapses in this game while the fourth-line pluggers handled the puck as if it were a curling rock. These were all superb players and they blazed up and down the ice, shift after shift, period after period.

"That probably was the last of the Russian dynasty," said Bourque. "It was the best hockey I've been a part of. The pace was incredible."

The fans in the Montreal Forum were loving every second of it—well, almost every second. They grumbled a bit when the Soviets took the lead. But many of them had seen the firewagon hockey produced by their Canadiens in the fifties, and this was the same style—up and down the ice with action at each end.

The Canadian forwards were creating plenty of chances, but when play went the other way, their Soviet counterparts were making life extremely difficult for the Canadian defencemen.

"The first two forwards come up to the blue line at full speed," explained Canadian defenceman Doug Crossman. "Then they slow down. So you've got to slow down with them.

"Then one guy comes shooting up the middle. You've already slowed down and you're going backwards and now you've got to try to pick up this guy."

Naturally, they had trouble doing it on a regular basis. If that weren't the case, the Soviets wouldn't have used the tactic so often. The answer for the Canadians was to stick with that trailing forward and make sure he wasn't allowed his full-speed sortie up the middle. But when they did that, the Soviets would use a defenceman as a trailer and get him to jump into the play. The Canadians not only had to play well, they had to be alert and intelligent.

That trailer, whoever he might be, could not be allowed to cruise about unchecked. "Whoever is in position at the right time has to pick him up," explained forward Doug Gilmour, a superb two-way player. "It takes a lot of communication."

Both teams had their brilliant moments in the opening game. The Soviets built a 4–1 lead, but the way the Canadians were playing, it was clear that the game was far from over. Sure enough, the tide turned. Eventually, Canada not only tied the score, but went ahead 5–4 late in the game. It looked as if Canada had pulled off one of the great comebacks in hockey history and the crowd was ecstatic.

Only seconds later, though, the Soviets tied it up, and when regulation time ended, the score was 5–5.

Neither team exhibited any desire to retreat into a defensive shell, and the overtime—what there was of it—was every bit as exciting as the rest of the game.

After only 5:33, Alexander Semak banked a shot off Gretzky's skate and it eluded Fuhr. The Soviets had drawn first blood.

"My dad was really mad," recalled Gretzky years later. "He said, 'Don't you ever do that again!'

"That's really something, when you've just lost a game and your dad is blaming you for it. He said I had stayed on the ice too long in overtime and I was on the ice when they scored the winner."

"I'll never forget it. I'd asked Mike if my dad could go on the charter from Montreal to Hamilton and Mike says, 'Sure.'

"So we're getting on the bus and my dad says, 'How are you feeling?'

"'I'm a little tired,' I said. He said, 'No. I mean how you are feeling?'

"I said, 'What do you mean?'

"This is what his exact words were. He said, 'You lost that game.' That's what he told me.

"I said, 'What?'

"He said, 'You stayed on the ice too long on the fifth goal, the one to tie it. You shouldn't have been out there.'

"I'm thinking, 'Oh, yeah. This is going to be a nice flight.'

"I said, 'I've just got you a ride on the charter and you're telling me that?'"

Earlier in the series, the game's reigning ultrastar got together with his likely successor for a chat.

Gretzky and Lemieux had not spent a lot of time with each other prior to this series. Their teams were in different conferences and they were at different stages of their careers. Gretzky had established himself as the best player in the world, and Lemieux was showing the kind of talent that had resulted in his being anointed the heir apparent.

When the training camp opened, Gretzky was the captain by acclamation. Lemieux was a highly talented kid who had racked up 351 points during his three-year career, despite missing 31 games due to injury. They both were loaded with skill, but Gretzky had the experience. He had won all the major trophies for which he was eligible, as well as three Stanley Cups and a Canada Cup. Lemieux had never made the playoffs and this was his first international experience at this level.

But throughout the tournament, Gretzky worked steadily on bringing Lemieux into the fold. The Edmonton core players in those days had an ability—one that does not accrue to all athletes—to see the larger picture. They saw themselves not only as the champions of the era, but as the torch bearers for the Canadian game of the future. And torches have to be passed. They saw themselves as role models, something many top athletes in other sports refused to do. They had no qualms whatsoever about confronting an elite player who they felt was not living up to his responsibilities to the sport. Many athletes pay lip service to the need to give something back to the game, but the Edmonton players did more than mouth the platitudes. They lived up to what they saw as their responsibilities.

Accordingly, there was no jealousy on the Canadian team. There was no internal battle between the stars to prove who was better.

"Mario was just a kid," recalled Keenan, "and they brought him along. Maybe because of '84 and what they had gone through, there was no delineation, no separation. They were a team.

"They were guiding Mario and bringing him along. He learned quickly, but they had him on the fast track. He was in awe of them when he got there, but he was coming along quickly. You could see it, and his skill set was always so high."

In fact, by that point, Gretzky was fully aware that in some areas, Lemieux's skills were superior to his own.

In the elimination-round game against the Czechs, Gretzky and Lemieux had engineered a two-on-one break and Lemieux passed to Gretzky for the shot. That was the play that precipitated the aforementioned chat.

Gretzky told Lemieux that he shouldn't be passing in those situations. In essence, he said, "I'll make the passes, you take the shots." It was a conversation that would pay magnificent dividends. Lemieux appreciated the down-to-earth approach, and the conversation got rolling, with the two superstars talking about their games. As often happens on such occasions, the talk gradually became more honest and insightful. Eventually, Gretzky told Lemieux how to be successful in hockey.

He didn't presume to tell him how to play the game. But he did offer an opportunity for Lemieux to learn by example.

"All I ever said was, 'Just watch Mess and me. Be the first guy to practice. Practise hard.' It was not so much what we told him. We just said, 'Watch.'

"If Mike said we're going to do twenty-five minutes of skating, we'd say, 'All right, let's go.' Don't say, 'Aww, Jeez.'"

The torch was being passed. Lemieux took the observations to heart, and it is probably more than coincidence that in the subsequent season, he won his first NHL scoring title.

Canada Cup '87 shifted from Montreal to Hamilton for the second game, and, stung by his father's criticism, Gretzky responded with a magnificent performance.

In fact, there are those who say it was the best game of his life. Gretzky is one of them.

Upon his retirement in 1999, he was asked the standard question about the top performance of his career. "That was the second game of the 1987 Canada Cup series," he said. "That was the greatest game I ever played in my life."

He paused for a moment. "Ever."

Then he added, "Second is not even close."

The great ones always rise to the level of their competition. Gretzky was *the* Great One, and the level of competition was sky-high.

"I think at that time, that Russian team was the best team in the world," he said. "The level they were at, they could have beaten any NHL team. You always go against the level of the team you're playing against and that was twenty great players. I didn't get a goal, but it was the best game I ever played."

As he said, the greatest scorer in the game's history didn't score a single goal in that game. He did, however, set up five.

Those who had raved about the speed, excitement and superb hockey they had seen in the first game were astonished. This one was even better.

In the first period alone, Canada created fourteen clear-cut scoring chances. Often, an entire NHL game won't yield that many—even if you count both teams.

That period, veteran hockey watchers agreed, was the best period of hockey a Canadian team had ever played.

But it was a measure of the talent on Team USSR that once again, the score was tied 5–5 after regulation time.

For the fourth consecutive time in a Canada Cup game between the Canadians and the Soviets, overtime would be needed to settle the result.

It was a nail-biter all the way. After scoring almost at will for three periods, the two teams went more than a period and a half without a goal.

There were plenty of chances, and at times it seemed certain that the game was about to end. But Fuhr was spectacular in the Canadian goal and Sergei Mylnikov was every bit as good at the other end.

Keenan had shortened his bench to the point that Gretzky was taking almost every other shift. He was dog-tired, but such was his nature that he refused to ask for a break.

"It was a wonderful experience with Wayne," recalled Keenan in 2005. "He was intuitive and instinctive, and I was quite the same in terms of our interaction with each other. We clicked immediately, and it was weird. I wouldn't even hardly call his name."

Keenan lifted an eyebrow. "He just went like that," he said, "and I could see him out of the corner of my eye. He was saying, 'I'm ready. I'll go again.'"

But every bone in his body was crying for a rest. He was so tired, he told me later, that he could no longer control his bladder. He was sitting on the bench when he felt himself start to urinate. "I didn't have enough energy to stop," he said.

Years later, Gretzky said, "Mike kept going, 'Gretz, are you ready?' I said, 'Mike, I just sat down!'"

But finally, after 30:06 of overtime, he set up Lemieux and there was no return pass. Mario beat Mylnikov, and the series was down to one winner-take-all game.

Gretzky wasn't sure how he'd feel. He was exhausted.

"I was going home with my dad while we were staying in Hamilton and sleeping in Brantford," he said. "We got home at 2:30. We were driving home and my dad says, 'What time do you want to get up?' and it dawned on me.

"I said, 'I can't believe it. I've got to go to practice in the morning. Mike is having us practise.' My dad says, 'I'm going to call him.'"

Gretzky talked him out of it. "Getting up for practice after a game like that was unusual back then," he said in 2005, "but Mike was ahead of his time. Nowadays, the way we analyze sports, it's better for you to get up and just go and do a light workout. You'll feel better the next day than if you sleep in and lie around all day."

By this point, the series had captured the country's imagination. To an entire generation of Canadian hockey fans, the 1972 Summit Series had provided their most memorable international moments. But that was fifteen years before. Mario Lemieux was six years old at the time. A whole new generation of fans had come onto the scene since then, and this was their moment.

"The energy in the room was incredible," Keenan recalled. "I've never felt it before or since in any team I've ever coached. The Stanley Cup team I had in New York in 1994 was a special team, but with that Team Canada, you're talking about the elite of the elite, and the energy in the room was unbelievable.

"It was kind of like you couldn't walk on the floor almost. You were above it. But they were very quiet, very serious.

"Earlier in the week, I'd pushed this jukebox I found down the hallway into the room so the guys could listen to something. They'd only had a little boom box.

"They kept playing two songs for about an hour. Paul Coffey kept going up and pushing the buttons for these two songs over and over.

"There was 'Catch My Fall' by Billy Idol. One line was, 'I'm just a boy but I will win,' and another was, 'It could happen to you so think for yourself.' The refrain was, 'Catch my fall if I should stumble.' And there was the one by Whitney Houston: 'The Greatest Love of All.'

"They had this rhythm going, this energy getting ready." Keenan paused. Then he smiled. "Then we came out and we were getting smoked."

For a while, it appeared that instead of getting a dream game, the new generation of fans would see their worst nightmare. The Soviets scored early and often and quickly built a 3–0 lead.

Keenan laughed about it later, but he wasn't laughing at the time. "I thought, 'If I don't do something in a hurry, I'm going to get in the car and drive north and they'll never hear from me again.'

"We were down 3–0 in a hurry. Eleven minutes in and we were down 3–0!" Worse still, Gretzky was exhausted. In an effort to stem the tide, Keenan had begun double-shifting him early, and his energy was depleted.

"He said, 'I need a break,'" said Keenan. "I could see it anyway. He was gaunt. He had played his best hockey and it was a super-exhilarating pace and he said, 'I need a break.'

"I said, 'You've got it.'

"That's why I changed it up a bit. I said to Sutter and [Rick] Tocchet and Dale Hawerchuk, 'You guys go out and change this whole game plan because these Soviets are used to finesse and skill. They aren't used to people hammering them and grinding them.'

"That's when the grinders went out."

"We were down 3–0 and I looked at him," recalled Gretzky, "and he sat us down a little bit and played a whole bunch of different guys. That was what made that team great. Rick Tocchet scored. Brent Sutter scored. Those guys got us back in the game. People forget we were out of it. I was sitting on the bench thinking, 'We came all the way back in that game two nights ago and now we're going to lose like this?'

"Grant Fuhr shut the door. Tocchet scored. Brent Sutter. Brian Propp was playing great. All of a sudden we're in the game again, and away we went."

Toronto Maple Leafs captain Darryl Sittler battles for position against the Soviets at the Challenge Cup in 1979. Despite sending a roster of stars to New York, Team NHL was badly outgunned and frustrated by the goaltending duo of Vladislav Tretiak and Vladimir Myshkin.

© Mecca/Hockey Hall of Fame

New York Islander stalwart Bryan Trottier in the hotly contested ice in the Soviet zone. Apart from three Swedes, Team NHL was composed entirely of Canadians. Trottier would later suit up for Team USA in the 1984 Canada Cup.

© Mecca/Hockey Hall of Fame

Wearing the "K" for the USSR, Boris Mikhailov enjoys a victory lap with the Challenge Cup. Mikhailov led the series with three goals and surprised many Canadians with his passionate leadership. He later offered Alan Eagleson a wry assessment of Canada's rank in the hockey world.

© Mecca/Hockey Hall of Fame

The irrepressible Don Cherry behind the visitors' bench at the Montreal Forum, May 10, 1979. He had coached his gritty Bruins to game seven of the semi-finals, and was leading with 74 seconds left in regulation time. It was his last game as coach of his beloved Bruins.
© CP

"The Flower" in full flight. Guy Lafleur's goal against the Bruins marked a pivotal moment in many careers, including his own.
© Paul Bereswill/Hockey Hall of Fame

Former Canadiens coach Scotty Bowman announcing his new job as general manager of the Buffalo Sabres. Cherry's nemesis almost ended up in the head office of Harold Ballard's Maple Leafs.
© CP (Doug Bell)

Tournament MVP John Tonelli takes his hand off his stick to let Soviet defenceman Vasili Pervukhin know he's there. Canada's strategy was to control the puck along the boards, and it was Tonelli's tenacious work in the Soviet zone that set up one of the most dramatic goals in Canada Cup history. © Miles Nadal/Hockey Hall of Fame

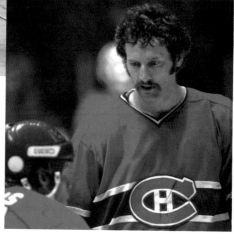

The towering Larry Robinson as a Montreal Canadien. His stern words to his teammates after an embarrassing start to the 1984 Canada Cup tournament were the catalyst for a dramatic improvement. © Mecca/Hockey Hall of Fame

Despite being closely checked by the tireless Vladimir Kovin, Mike Bossy celebrates after scoring what came to be called "the Coffey Goal." © CP/Calgary Herald (Bruce Stotesbury)

Mario Lemieux snaps a Wayne Gretzky pass past Soviet goalie Sergei Mylnikov as defenceman Larry Murphy plays decoy. "Murphy might as well have been my dad," said Gretzky later. "He was never going to see the puck."
© CP (Scott McDonald)

Probably the most lethal duo in hockey history. Lemieux and Gretzky celebrate their 6-5 overtime win to take the 1987 Canada Cup.
© CP (Blaise Edwards)

The bitter holdout and eventual trade of smooth-skating defenceman Paul Coffey threw the 1987-88 Oilers into disarray. When Edmonton met Calgary in the second round of the playoffs, the Flames defence corps was deemed the best in the league. © *London Life–Portnoy/Hockey Hall of Fame*

One of the most impressive one-two punches in hockey history was disappointingly short-lived. Wayne Gretzky's sheer excellence made a trade irresistible to Oilers owner Peter Pocklington. © *O-Pee-Chee/Hockey Hall of Fame*

Wayne Gretzky moves in on Flames goalie Mike Vernon, as the Calgary "Sea of Red" looks on. When Gretzky finally scored in OT on April 21 he told the Saddledome staff to take out the ice. Not only would the Flames not play there again that year, number 99 would never return as an Oiler. © *Paul Bereswill/ Hockey Hall of Fame*

Wayne Gretzky and Eric Lindros at the 1991 Canada Cup. Though Lindros made himself unpopular in some quarters for refusing to play for the Quebec Nordiques, and even for being selected to Team Canada when proven players like Steve Yzerman were sent home, he made the leap from junior hockey to international play with astonishing ease, delivering smart plays and highlight-reel hits on the world's elite.
© *Paul Bereswill/ Hockey Hall of Fame*

Canada's Steve Larmer sets up in front of Team USA's Mike Richter, as Darian Hatcher looks on. Larmer's short-handed goal to win the Canada Cup was the perfect revenge for Gary Suter's hit from behind on Wayne Gretzky.
© *Paul Bereswill/ Hockey Hall of Fame*

The Stars' strategy in the 1999 Stanley Cup final was not difficult to figure out: get under Dominic Hasek's skin at every opportunity. Here the Sabres' goalie is run over by Joe Niewendyk, winner of the Conn Smythe trophy as playoff MVP.
© CP *(Brian Ramirez)*

Brett Hull about to score the goal that won the Cup in 1999. The NHL rule book reads: "If a player has entered the crease prior to the puck...the apparent goal shall not be allowed." Note Hull's left foot.
© CP *(Gene Puskar)*

The excitement of the Stanley Cup playoffs. The Buffalo Sabres wait for the ceremonies at the end of the game some players still dispute. "Everybody is going to remember this as the Stanley Cup that was never won," said Sabres forward Joe Juneau.
© CP *(David Duprey)*

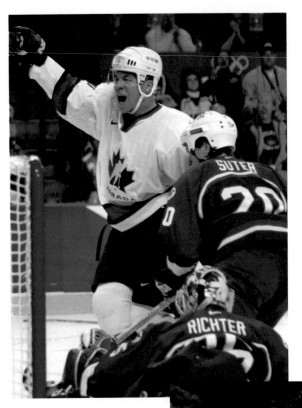

Jarome Iginla celebrates his first goal against the Americans in the gold medal game of then 2002 Olympics, as old enemies of Team Canada, Gary Suter and Mike Richter, hang their heads. A last-minute addition to Team Canada, Iginla played a huge role at the Olympics and went on to win the Art Ross Trophy as NHL scoring leader and the Maurice Richard Trophy as leading goal scorer that season. © CP (Frank Gunn)

In a flashback to 1987, in 2002 the invincible pair of 66 and 99 celebrate the victory that put Canada back on top of the hockey world. © CP (Tom Hanson)

It wasn't just the goals that mattered. The Canadians were starting to assert their authority. Tocchet flattened a couple of Soviets behind their own net. Sutter and Dineen wreaked havoc in front. By the end of the period, the Canadians had started their comeback and were trailing 4–2. "I think that little shift in momentum right there got us back into it," said Keenan, "and the big boys had to finish it off.

"Mario's head was spinning," he added with a laugh. "He didn't know what to do. But he was absorbing this. They just played on their instincts, which you have to let the best players do."

The strategy that had been so meticulously put in place prior to the tournament was paying off. The longer this series went, the more the Canadians were in control of the area along the boards.

It takes a lot of guts to be dominant in that territory, but the Canadians did it in all three games. Going into game three, even the area behind the Soviet goal had been ceded. It had become the property of Team Canada, to be used as the Canadians saw fit.

By the time the late stages of that game rolled around, the score was once again tied 5–5. And no fewer than four of the Canadian goals had their genesis behind the Soviet net.

"That was how we tied the game up," Keenan recalled later. "We played mostly down there in the scrums, and I can still remember Tocchet just drilling a couple of guys down there. He was really mean.

"It was fierce—the infighting in that trench area. That's where they won those battles to come out and stuff the puck in the net. They weren't pretty, but it didn't matter."

The Soviet coaches knew what was happening, but there was nothing they could do about it.

After the game, assistant coach Igor Dimitriev was asked what he had learned about the Canada Cup experience. He said two things stood out. Next time, his charges would have to play better behind their own goal. Also, they would have to learn how to take a hit and carry on with the play.

With the clock creeping down into the final two minutes, Keenan sent out his troops for a crucial face-off in their own end.

"The little bit of a surprise," said Keenan, "was that everybody thought I was going to send Mess out to take the face-off because it was in our zone."

But he didn't. Hawerchuk got the call.

"It was kind of an instinctive thing," Keenan explained. "I had coached Dale in junior in Oshawa and he was doing really well all game in that particular game. Not that Mess wasn't, but Dale was doing exceptionally well. I like to go with the hot hand."

The other two forwards were a pair of guys who had mostly been on separate lines when the team was at full strength. But not now. Not with the title on the line after the three greatest games in hockey history. Hawerchuk was taking the face-off. Gretzky and Lemieux were his support staff.

"I was sitting at the cottage in the summer back in July," recalled Keenan. "I was thinking even then that this would be the matchup in the finals.

"I thought, 'We've got to have something ready for this team we're going to be playing in the finals,' and the thing I thought about was the combination of Wayne and Mario, with Mario playing right wing for Wayne, but I wouldn't show it until the end of the tournament because I didn't want anybody to pre-scout us before that and get an idea of what was coming.

"We had only a few things that would make a difference, and that was one of them."

Sure enough, Hawerchuk won the face-off by shoving it ahead as Lemieux came into the circle. "Mario came across with the big reach and tipped it," said Keenan, "and away they went."

Lemieux squeezed between two Soviet forwards to get that puck, and as the two of them lunged for it, they knocked each other down to give the Canadians an odd-man situation.

As if that weren't enough, Lemieux now took another Soviet out of the action. The defenceman pinched and again Lemieux's long reach came into play. He reached ahead and chipped the puck past the Soviet and off the boards, then eluded the attempted check.

Now the puck was out over the blue line; the Canadians had defenceman Larry Murphy coming up, and Gretzky cutting across the middle from the right side. Lemieux pushed the puck ahead once more and Gretzky gathered it in without breaking stride. He broke across the Soviet blue line on the left side as the other two came up in support. Lemieux was the trailer, coming up the middle as Murphy headed for the far side of the crease.

"Murphy got involved," continued Keenan, "and pulled their defenceman back, and then Wayne made no mistake. He gave it to the right guy."

Lemieux took the perfect pass in the deep slot, cruised in a few feet and snapped a wrist shot that Mylnikov waved at but had no hope of catching. It nestled into the upper corner and Canada was up 6–5 with only 1:26 remaining.

"I was doing my part," laughed Murphy during the ceremonies at his 2005 induction into the Hall of Fame. "I was a decoy. That's what they get for worrying about me. Mario made them pay."

He did indeed. With Hawerchuk delivering a judicious hook to one of the Soviet forwards who was trying to catch up ("We probably could have been called for a penalty," conceded Keenan), Gretzky had moved down the left wing and assessed the situation unfolding in front of him. Then he made the perfect pass.

"Mario did what Gretz had told him," Keenan said. "He had told Mario, 'Don't pass it back to me. You bury it.' Murph was a good decoy, and Mario buried it."

It proved to be the winner, thereby completing Gretzky's triple. "I was in on all three game-winning goals," he said with a laugh. "The first one deflected off my skate and went between Grant Fuhr's legs."

"You know what I remember most?" asked Gretzky a quarter of a century later. "We were playing the Czechs, and Mario and I had a two-on-one. You know me; I made the pass, and Mario passed it back to me and I missed.

"So we go to the bench, and between periods I looked at Mario and I said, 'Mario, don't take this the wrong way.'

"I said, 'I know I have more goals than you, but you're a better goal scorer than I am—you're a natural goal scorer. When I give you the puck, just shoot it. That's why I'm giving it to you. You're stronger. You're bigger. You just shoot it. I'm going to give it to you at the last second to make the play.'

"He said, 'Okay.'

"That's what I remember about that last goal. We got the puck. Larry Murphy might as well have been my dad. He was never going to see the puck. But in fairness to Larry Murphy, not everyone would have done what he did.

"He went to the net. How many times in practice do you say, 'First guy go to the net'? If he doesn't go to the net, there's no play.

"So Larry Murphy, he does exactly what he needs to do. He goes to the net. I give it to Mario and I'm thinking, 'Shoot it. Don't give it back to me.' And actually, when I passed it to him, I went like this—" he pulled his hands up towards his chest "—like I don't have a stick. I don't want it back because I know Mario can shoot the puck better than anybody in hockey. He put it in the perfect spot."

The dressing room that had been so quiet and intense before the game was now a scene of unbridled jubilation.

"That jukebox was still there," said Keenan. "The first thing I saw when I went into the room was Gilmour standing on top of that jukebox dancing—still with his skates on.

"It was an incredible group of guys in terms of how talented they were, yet how respectful they were of each other, and of their team.

"At first, it was, 'Why are we working so hard?' but when we got into it, it was, 'Now we know why we worked so hard.'

"They were quick. They were smart. And they bonded."

For those too young to remember the 1972 Summit Series, it was Canada's finest hour. Even some of the older fans gave the nod to the 1987 triumph. It triggered a hockey euphoria that would remain unmatched for another fifteen years, when yet another generation came onto the scene and thrilled to the gold-medal victory in the Salt Lake City Olympics.

It was a glorious time for Gretzky. He was at his peak and he put on a magnificent display, leading the tournament in scoring and being named its most valuable player—or perhaps after the game two accident, its *moist* valuable player.

And for Lemieux, it marked his successful emergence into the rarefied atmosphere of elite-level hockey, the beginning of a career that would take him to the pinnacles Gretzky had already conquered.

"Mario was still a boy," said Keenan. "He was only twenty-one. He couldn't believe how much he learned about winning. And Wayne said it was the best hockey he ever played."

The Soviet team was the best ever assembled to that date. But with Gretzky and Lemieux leading the way, it wasn't enough to prevent Canada from proving that the 1984 Canada Cup triumph had been more than just a fortuitous circumstance.

Canadian hockey had come all the way back from the depths and humiliation of the 1979 and 1981 confrontations.

Now, even the best the Soviet Union could muster was not enough to beat Canadians at the game they liked to call their own.

THE GOAL: APRIL 21, 1988.

Game two of the Smythe Division final.
Scored (shorthanded) by Wayne Gretzky (assisted by
Jari Kurri and Steve Smith) at 7:54 of overtime.
Edmonton Oilers 5, Calgary Flames 4.

CONSIDERING THAT THE EDMONTON OILERS WERE JUST COMING OFF
their third Stanley Cup win in four years, the 1987 training
camp should have been a happy place.

It wasn't.

The rosy-cheeked boys and wide-eyed kids had grown
up. They had blossomed into aware young men, wise in the
ways of the world, seasoned veterans in a league that tends
to discard most players before they get a chance to attain
that coveted status.

The team's general manager, Glen Sather, was also
their coach—and for most of them, the only NHL coach
and general manager they had ever known. He had been
in place when the Oilers joined the NHL from the World
Hockey Association in 1979 and he was still there.
(Actually, Bryan Watson had coached 18 games in 1980,
but he was fired after accumulating a 4–9–5 record and
became a non-person as far as the Oilers were concerned.
For more than a decade, all references to Watson's tenure
were erased; it was not until the 1990–91 edition of
the NHL's annual *Official Guide and Record Book* was

published that Watson was finally given credit for his coaching tenure).

It's never easy to walk the tightrope of being both a coach and general manager in the NHL. As a coach, you have to instill confidence in your players, praise their abilities and urge them on to even greater heights. But as a general manager, you have to tell them that they're not worth their latest salary demand. You have to demean their contributions to the team, and having done that, you then have to compare them unfavourably to other players who earn the type of salary they are seeking.

For eight years Sather had been a veritable Blondin. He would do battle with the players, then at the end of the negotiations, tell them that there had been nothing personal in his approach. It's just the way the business works at this level, he told them.

His other favourite tactic was to say something along the lines of, "You guys have great potential. You've probably got a magnificent future ahead of you, and the team is one of destiny. But we haven't won anything yet. Once you win, I'll pay you appropriately, but in the meantime, you have to settle for less money."

Hockey contracts tend to run for three years, so by the autumn of 1987, that latter contention didn't carry a lot of weight. Three Stanley Cups in four years is a pretty good argument that potential has been realized in anybody's books. Contracts for players who had won one, two or three Cups were regularly coming up for renewal, and those players hadn't forgotten Sather's promises. Nor had their agents.

All-star defenceman Paul Coffey was in a slightly different situation than most of his teammates. He had signed a five-year deal, and after four years, he didn't want to wait for it to expire. Even though he was legally obligated to play another season for $320,000, he stayed home. He would continue to stay there, he said, until Sather renegotiated and bumped his salary to something in the $800,000 range, a demand he later softened to $600,000 as long as it was all in coin of the realm, and not the bizarre cash-plus-property deal that owner Peter Pocklington had dreamed up.

"It was a MURB in Yellowknife," said Sather in 2005. "A multiple urban residential building. If he'd taken it, today it would be worth ten times what he would have paid for it."

Goaltender Andy Moog, who had been with the Oilers since their second NHL season, was absent as well. His contract had expired and he was unable to come to terms with Sather. He opted instead to play with Canada's national team.

Another long-term Edmonton defenceman, Randy Gregg, a man who always marched to his own drummer, had tired of the Edmonton circus and had also opted to leave the Oilers to play for the national team. It was his intention to participate in the 1988 Winter Olympics, which would be held in Calgary. At the same time, the move would allow him to begin practising medicine, something he wanted to do on the premise that even though he could earn more with the Oilers in the short term, he couldn't earn enough to make it worthwhile to defer his long-term career any further.

All three of those players were hard-core, dyed-in-the-wool Oilers, and not one of them had ever played for another team. But they weren't the only absentees. A couple of players whose Edmonton tenure hadn't been as lengthy, but who had been popular and had made significant contributions to the Oilers' 1987 Cup run, Kent Nilsson and Reijo (Rexy) Ruotsaleinen, had gone back to Europe.

Ruotsaleinen was a gifted skater and a strong offensive defenceman. When he joined Coffey on the blue line, the Oilers' power play was a thing of beauty—not to mention a weapon of awesome proportions. Ruotsaleinen went back to Finland, it was said, because he couldn't find anyone in Edmonton who could keep pace with him in the bars. Given the social proclivities of Finns, he would have no such problem back home (though he was back with the Oilers in 1990).

The story about Nilsson was a bit more prosaic. All his career, he had been known as a man of brilliant talent. In a chat with Gretzky when we were reminiscing about that era, I said, "You know, Gretz, on a pure talent basis, Kent Nilsson might have been more talented than you."

"*Might* have been?" countered Gretzky. "He had a lot more talent than I did." But Nilsson was also a notorious floater. He hated to get hit; forced to choose between coughing up the puck and absorbing a check, Nilsson had no trouble deciding. You want the puck? Here you go. Help yourself.

But when he joined the Oilers late in the previous season, he encountered Mark Messier, a man whose views regarding puck possession and physical play were at the opposite end of the spectrum. The exact words have been lost in time, but a number of players who were there have reported that early in Nilsson's tenure, Messier grabbed him by the throat, put him up against the dressing-room wall and said something along the lines of, "Listen, you little prick. You've spent your entire career floating, but we don't play that way here and you're not going to do it either. Do it just once and you'll be going home to Sweden in a box."

Sather insists that the incident did not occur and that Messier would never threaten a teammate. "I don't believe it," Sather said. "That was not Mark's style. He was more of a quiet leader in those days."

But when the sources were double-checked, they were equally adamant that the incident occurred as reported.

Nilsson had played most of his career in abject terror of his opponents, but this was the first time he had been terrified of a teammate. He was absolutely superb during his tenure with the Oilers, probably because he feared Messier more than the opposition, but when the season ended, he went back to Sweden, never to be seen in the NHL again.

The next fall, in part because of all the departures and the circumstances surrounding them, the sense of rapidly disintegrating camaraderie in the Edmonton dressing room was impossible to ignore.

The Oilers' room had always been a special place. The players on that team in its heyday were easily the most accessible, articulate and accommodating players in any North American professional sport. The only area that was ruled off-limits to the media was the medical room when players were receiving treatment. And even that dictum was waived on occasion if the nature of the player's injury was already widely known and he felt like having a chat.

The Edmonton dressing room, with its Ping-Pong table in the middle, had the aura of a clubhouse for adolescents. The players always seemed to be in a good mood, and even though insults would often fly, it was just part of the fun. No one took any of the shots seriously, and if there was ever any dissension, except for the famed Nilsson-Messier incident, it remained a secret. That probably means there wasn't any dissension. The room was so wide open and the players so honest that keeping a secret would have been awfully difficult.

But that year, the absence of key players, especially Coffey, cast something of a pall over the room. Even Messier wasn't there to take command and right the ship. He too was holding out for a better deal from Sather— but Messier was a notorious practice-hater and to him, all training camp was practice. It was not unusual for Messier to find a way to miss training camp, but no one expected him to reach an impasse with Sather. And sure enough, he didn't.

The atmosphere in the room wasn't bleak, by any means. But the lightness and *joie de vivre* that had always been so evident had dissipated considerably. The laughter wasn't as widespread. The mood wasn't as loose. The jokes weren't as frequent.

"I was a big part of it," admitted Gretzky years later, "because I was close to Coff and I couldn't understand why Slats had traded him, why they couldn't have worked out their differences. I was probably as down as anybody—more down than anybody."

Part of the problem was the fact that Coffey had a valid contract. While the consensus among the Oilers was that he deserved a substantial pay hike, most of them were firm believers in living up to one's obligations. Coffey had signed a contract and agreed to its terms. While they wouldn't say so publicly because he was their close friend, they had to concede privately that Sather made a valid point.

Still, Coffey's absence weighed on them, and for the first time they were forced to be political. Despite being asked about Coffey every day, they couldn't really say what they felt.

It was easy to understand Coffey's stance. The other dominant defencemen in the league at that time, such as Raymond Bourque of the Boston Bruins, Rod Langway of the Washington Capitals and Denis Potvin of the New York Islanders, all earned considerably more than he did. It was also easy to understand Sather's stance. "To me, money is not the issue," he said. "The issue is that he should get here and get his contract signed. We've indicated to him that we're willing to compromise. I've talked to him four times, and each time it has been rejected and each time I've said it would be much better if he came here to play."

When Coffey didn't show up for camp, Sather suspended him and fined him $250 a day.

Sather made no secret of his disdain for Coffey's agent, Gus Badali. It was Badali who accepted the terms of the original five-year contract, he said, just as, in 1979, he had convinced Wayne Gretzky to sign a ludicrous twenty-one-year contract that the Oilers subsequently tore up for no other reason than to be fair to their young star.

It was also Badali who counselled another teenaged client, Mario Lemieux, to refuse to come down from the Montreal Forum seats and put on a Pittsburgh Penguins sweater when he was drafted in June 1984. While it made the point that Lemieux had yet to agree to terms, it was an embarrassment to the league and the Penguins, and was widely condemned throughout hockey. It portrayed Lemieux as a spoiled prima donna even before his NHL career had begun.

"Gus phoned me [a couple of weeks earlier] during the Canada Cup," said Sather during the Coffey controversy. "He said, 'If you don't give Paul a new contract, he's going to stay out.'

"I said, 'Are you telling me that's what he'll do?'

"He said, 'Yes. I'm going to tell him to stay home.'

"I said, 'Just like you told Mario Lemieux not to come down when he was picked first overall? Do you think that's good advice?'

"He said, 'Yep. That's it.'"

Before long, Sather's vitriol spread to Coffey himself. The two had always had a tempestuous relationship, not unlike that of a headstrong father and an equally headstrong son. Coffey was one of the more sensitive Oilers, and when Sather occasionally singled him out for closed-door criticism—as he did with all the Oilers, including Gretzky—Coffey took it to heart. He would dispute Sather's view, saying that he was being unfairly targeted.

Sather's response was, "His attitude has always been to blame someone else. Even when things weren't going well with the team and he wasn't playing well, he'd always blame me. I would accept it and give him what-for and he'd get going.

"But he always wanted to get some attention for himself, so he'd say something stupid in the press. I'd get angry and bring him into the office and we'd have a little father-and-son chat and *whoosh*, off he'd go.

"Right after the Stanley Cup was finished, he was saying, 'They don't want me around here.' Psychologically, why does someone say those things?

"To draw attention to himself," said Sather, quickly answering his own question. "The room is in an eruption, but you're dragging all that attention to yourself.

"In Team Canada, it was the same thing. They just finished getting the Canada Cup and he says, 'I'm not going to camp.' They've just finished the greatest game in history and here he is saying that!"

Sather paused, and in a flash, switched his approach, as he so often did. He always said that he never took the player-management negotiations personally, and only a second after unloading that lengthy broadside upon Coffey, he said, "But I don't care about that. If a guy can play hockey like he does, who cares what he says?"

Team owner Peter Pocklington was nowhere near as tactful. In a telephone conversation with Coffey and Badali, he questioned Coffey's courage and accused him of being afraid to go into the corners.

"I don't remember that one," recalled Coffey in 2005, "but I know it got ugly near the end. If he did say it, I probably didn't listen to him. He called me greedy and all that kind of stuff. It was so stupid.

"As you see now in the National Hockey League today, with the NHL Players' Association fighting the owners, most hockey players, if you back them into a corner, are going to be competitive. Back then, I just said, 'To hell with it. This is stupid.' Then you can't back down. If you go back, you're done."

Pocklington escalated the battle to a level that Coffey had not anticipated, but no matter how far Pocklington wanted to take it, Coffey wasn't going to back down.

"It just started out as just a little thing," he said. "I was going to hold out, then I was going to go back. Then the mud-slinging started with Pocklington thinking he was going to intimidate me. I said, 'To hell with this. This is the same crap I've been listening to for seven years. I'm not going to go through it again.'"

All through training camp, Coffey stuck to his guns. In fact, he hardened his stance, saying that he was no longer interested in a settlement and that he would never play for the Oilers again.

Sometimes, statements of that nature are just rhetoric. In this case, it was true. He never did.

There was a last-ditch effort once the season got underway. All the parties got together in Toronto on October 26, but Coffey was still incensed by Pocklington's attitude and the two sides were unable to come to terms. On November 24, with the impasse clearly insurmountable, Sather traded Coffey to the Pittsburgh Penguins in a seven-player deal. Craig Simpson was the key player the Oilers received in the trade, which marked the beginning of the process that would lead to the total dismantling of the team that had dominated hockey in the 1980s.

"There's a misconception about that whole thing," said Coffey years later. "It had nothing to do with money—nothing to do with money at all. The difference in salary was— I don't know, maybe fifty grand or seventy-five grand, which I might have got in Pittsburgh and not in Edmonton.

"But I had just seen a lot happen on that team. I have nothing but respect for Glen and for what Glen meant to me. And for his accomplishments throughout his time in the game. And for what he did for all of us as players.

"But I had just seen the pendulum swinging and certain guys not getting treated well, and a few things had happened the previous year. For right or wrong reasons, I still think to this day it was a smart move on my part. I had just had enough. It had nothing to do with money."

Sather has suggested that Coffey left because he was too sensitive and didn't like to be prodded. Coffey disputes that.

"Don't get me wrong," he said. "Slats was good for me. He pushed all the right buttons but there were too many other things going on."

Moog and Coffey were gone because of contractual battles, although in Moog's case, money was only a part of it.

"I think the Moog thing was more about playing time than about money," said Sather. "I traded him to the Boston Bruins for Geoff Courtnall and Bill Ranford. That was a heck of a deal for us.

"When we made the deal and got Craig, I understood," recalled Gretzky. "I accepted Craig. I was the captain of the team and I put it all behind me. I understood that Coff did what he had to do and Glen did the best he could do. So now we had a different makeup, a different group."

For the time being at least, Sather's run of success was continuing and the other core players were still in Edmonton. Kevin Lowe, Steve Smith and Charlie Huddy were still on the blue line. Glenn Anderson, Jari Kurri and Mark Messier were still up front supporting Gretzky. Grant Fuhr was still providing heroics in goal.

But it didn't appear to be enough. Down the road in Calgary, general manager Cliff Fletcher had built what turned out to be the real powerhouse team in the league that year.

With longtime coach Bob Johnson having chosen to move on to USA Hockey, Fletcher had brought in Terry Crisp to coach. His abrasive style upset some of the Calgary veterans, who had become accustomed to Johnson's scholarly, gentlemanly approach. But at the same time, Crisp spurred them on to the best regular-season performance in the Flames' history to that point.

As the season dragged on, little went right for the Oilers—by their standards. For many teams, it would have been a good year, but these were the high-flying Edmonton Oilers. They were supposed to do better. For six years, they had been racking up a string of impressive achievements and record-breaking numbers. But not in 1987–88. After six consecutive Smythe Division championships, they finished second to the Flames. For the first time in seven years, they didn't reach the 100-point barrier. Their offensive output was the lowest it had been since 1981—thirty-four goals fewer than the Flames.

And Gretzky didn't even win the scoring title. In his first season, he had accumulated the same number of points as Marcel Dionne, but the title officially went to Dionne on the basis of goals scored. Every year since,

Gretzky had run away with the race, but this time, thanks largely to a knee injury that kept him out of action for a few weeks, he was surpassed by Lemieux.

The Oilers seemed to be on a downhill course, while the Flames were heading in the opposite direction. They were definitely a team on the rise. They still had the core of the squad that had knocked the Oilers out of the playoffs two seasons earlier, and now Joe Nieuwendyk was on his way to winning the 1988 Calder Trophy as the league's best rookie. Hakan Loob was in the process of putting together the only 50-goal season of his career, and on the blue line, the tandem of Al MacInnis and Gary Suter was the best in the game.

To make that defence even stronger, Fletcher had acquired one of the league's most feared defencemen, the wily Brad McCrimmon, the previous summer. Then, just before the trading deadline, he made another major acquisition when he sent young Brett Hull, whose potential he fully realized, to the St. Louis Blues to get Rob Ramage, a solid veteran who had played in four All-Star Games. In short, the Calgary defence, which also included Dana Murzyn and Brian Glynn, was universally acclaimed as the league's best.

The Oilers, on the other hand, were desperately trying to fill the void left by Coffey. Gregg came back after the Olympics, but he had never been much of an offensive threat, and playing a season with amateurs hadn't improved matters. The Oilers' attempts to make do with the likes of Jim Ennis, Ron Shudra, John Miner and Jim Wiemer on the blue line had been a dismal failure.

In the weeks leading up to the playoffs, the most frequently used Edmonton blueline power-play tandem consisted of Huddy and Miner, not a pairing likely to strike fear into the hearts of opponents. Sather's opinion of Miner's contributions became evident in the playoffs, when he scratched him for the duration and replaced him with Esa Tikkanen, a forward.

Even Tikkanen's countryman on the team, Jari Kurri, couldn't offer a ringing vote of confidence for that move. "We don't have a quarterback like Coffey right now," he said. "We have to get some other guys to get the job done back there."

Neither the Flames nor the Oilers had any serious trouble advancing to the much-anticipated head-to-head divisional confrontation. Both breezed past their first-round opponents—the Los Angeles Kings for the Flames and the Winnipeg Jets for the Oilers—in five games.

In hockey circles, much was made of the role reversals undergone by the two teams. It was now the Flames who were stacked with fancy, high-scoring finesse players. The Oilers had evolved into grinders, jamming the net and banging in the rebounds.

In Calgary, where the series was to begin, the anticipation was intense. Flames logos, banners and decals were everywhere. Everyone in the downtown core seemed to be wearing something red and sporting a "Go Flames Go" button. In the local media, the Flames' evident superiority over the Oilers was extolled at great length, so much so that on the morning of the first game, Oilers co-coach John Muckler was standing in the hotel lobby holding a copy of the *Calgary Sun* and laughing.

"Have you seen this?" he asked. "And all this?" waving his arm in the general direction of the Flames banners on the walls. "It makes me wonder why we bothered to come. We don't have a chance."

Muckler didn't believe that for a second—not only because he had faith in his team, but because he knew something that most people didn't.

The Oilers had undergone a radical transformation during their first-round series against the Winnipeg Jets. The fabled Edmonton camaraderie had been re-established.

There is a curious aspect to hockey that sets it apart from all the other sports: the intensity level is the highest when the pay is the lowest. Hockey's Stanley Cup heritage is difficult to explain to those not familiar with the NHL. But when that Cup is out there for the taking, battles are intensified, injuries are ignored and careers are risked—even though the regular paycheques have stopped coming and all that is on the line now is a playoff bonus, a paltry amount compared to a player's salary.

A playoff bonus, that is, and a chance to hoist the Stanley Cup.

All through the regular season, with players coming and going, the Oilers had been caught up in the animosity over salaries.

Whatever the circumstances, Moog, Coffey and some others had gone, and new players had come in to fill the void created by the losses. On a team as close as the Oilers once were, the established players tended to keep to themselves. There were some inadvertent snubs.

But that was during the regular season, when salaries were in the forefront of everyone's mind. At that point, that's what they were playing for. Once the playoffs started, salaries weren't an issue because there weren't any, and the chance to win a Cup became the focus.

It became apparent to old-line Oilers like Lowe, Huddy, Messier, Gretzky and others, that the new arrivals—Craig Simpson, Normand Lacombe, Geoff Courtnall, Keith Acton, Dave Hannan and so on—could make a contribution.

At the same time, a common purpose, a sense of a unified aim, manifested itself, and the newcomers began to realize that they were no longer interlopers in this elite organization. They were an integral part of it.

"It's a two-way street," explained Lowe while his team waited for the Calgary series to begin. "It's not so much that we accept them as it is that they themselves feel more accepted, more a part of it when they contribute to it.

"Some of these guys coming in from other teams have played hard for a number of years and haven't really been rewarded, except for their contracts. But at this time of year, money is secondary. You're playing for the pride of playing. And they feel more a part of it when they're playing."

Simpson, who had come over from the abysmal Penguins in the Coffey trade, knew exactly what Lowe was talking about. You don't just walk on to a team like the Oilers and become a part of the group by putting on the sweater. You have to make a meaningful contribution. And since there was never any serious doubt that the Oilers were going to make the playoffs, no meaningful contribution could be made until the playoffs began.

"You have to earn the respect of all the players," Simpson said. "I went through a period like that when I first got here, and it went on for a while. But now it's the playoffs and you have to prove to the guys that you can handle it. Those two games in Winnipeg really showed that we stick together and that we're a team. Everybody is working towards the same goal."

In each of the two games to which Simpson referred, the Oilers had erased a three-goal deficit. In today's hockey, erasing a one-goal lead is a monumental task. In those days, three-goal leads, while solid, were not insurmountable, especially for a team like the Oilers. For the first time all season, they started to genuinely believe in themselves.

The comments of Lowe and Simpson, delivered in such a straightforward and clinical fashion, sounded more like an analytical critique than what they actually were—an assertion that the old Oilers, with their swagger and verve, were back in business.

After a long, bleak season full of injury, controversy, criticism, naysaying and internecine squabbling, the darkness had suddenly lifted.

Assistant coach Ted Green was the first to comment that the spirit and sense of togetherness that the Oilers exhibited in Winnipeg had not been seen all season.

"I agree with Ted," said Sather when asked about the new attitude. "It hadn't been like that for a long time."

Sather reflected on the larger picture and related it to

the development of the Oilers over the years, leading up to the problems that had afflicted them this season.

"The guys had been together a long time and hadn't had that many changes," he said. "We won Stanley Cups. We won championships. We were all really close friends.

"Then you bring in guys that are younger. They're all good guys, but the older guys are maybe reluctant to accept them right off the bat. Maybe they won't say it, but there's still a kind of reluctance there. It's like a new guy who comes to work in an office. He's not totally accepted until you have a reason to accept him."

The comebacks in Winnipeg provided that reason.

"We noticed it right away," said Lowe. "There was a considerable difference in the way the guys reacted. There was camaraderie."

Suddenly, lying in wait for the Flames, the Oilers were not only on a genuine Stanley Cup quest, they were in their favourite role. As far as the public was concerned, the Flames, who had been the league's powerhouse over the course of the season and had won the Presidents' Trophy, were heavy favourites, especially when the Oilers' struggles and apparent slide into mediocrity were taken into account. That made the Oilers underdogs, a status they relished.

In the first game, they won 3–1 when they shut down the Calgary power play, the league's best that season with a remarkable success rate of 29.5 per cent. But on this night, the Flames were merely one for eight, even though one of those eight chances was a five-minute major. In other words, the Flames were awarded nineteen minutes in power plays—almost a full period—and all they could muster was one goal, and a weak goal that was something of a fluke, at that.

Suddenly, there was concern in Calgary. But not panic—not yet, anyway.

After all, the Flames had lost a game in the previous series as well, but that hadn't stopped them from advancing.

The Calgary fans had faith that the vaunted power play would come through in the next game. The impotence in the opener was just an aberration. Even Edmonton penalty killer Craig MacTavish conceded that point.

"It's like a time bomb," he said. "If you keep giving them opportunities, it's going to go off and kill you. I don't know how many times we can win a game killing off that many penalties against Calgary."

"The rivalry at that point between Calgary and Edmonton got so intense," recalled Gretzky, "it got out of control—not just with the players. The cities got into it. I remember going to Calgary thinking, 'We're in for a dog-fight because they have home-ice advantage.'

"We were down 3–1 in game one. We end up coming back and winning 4–3, and Terry Crisp said it best in the paper. He said, 'I don't know what happened. We out-played them. We dominated them. Gretzky and Kurri were nonexistent and they ended up getting the tying goal and the winner and we lose 4–3,' and he was right. I remember thinking we had a bad game, and we won.

"Now we're in game two and I'm thinking if we can win game two, we're going to beat Calgary. And we really felt that Calgary was the only team in the NHL that could beat us. Teams could beat us once in a while, but over seven games there was no way. Calgary was the only team that had that psychological edge that they could beat us.

"That was when I was engaged to Janet, and it was about 4 o'clock in the afternoon of game two. She said, 'You'll never guess what happened.'

"I said, 'What?'

"She said, 'I'm pregnant.'

"We'd sort of planned it that once we got engaged, that would happen. I went to the rink and I was on a high."

That was not good news for the Flames. Everyone knew that under no circumstances could they afford to lose game two. The Calgary fans were nervous, and justifiably so. They were aware that on paper, their team was better, but the opposition was the hated Oilers, the Flames' nemesis throughout the eighties.

Even the two coaches had been rivals for as long as anyone cared to remember. Sather and Crisp had faced each other as juniors in the 1963 Memorial Cup, when Sather's Edmonton Oil Kings defeated Crisp's Niagara Falls Flyers. Now, twenty-five years later, they were again battling in a crucial postseason game, and it was as close as most people had expected it to be—a high-tempo, end-to-end spectacle featuring one good scoring chance after another.

To the delight of the "Sea of Red"—the Calgary fans all decked out in their red team sweaters—the Flames were in command with a 3–1 lead in the second period. But by the end of that period, the score stood at 3–3 and the crowd was considerably less exuberant.

The Flames were without Nieuwendyk, the star rookie having been injured in the series opener, and although his replacement, John Tonelli, was a capable player, he couldn't even come close to matching Nieuwendyk's scoring skills.

Tonelli was more of a grinder, who had been excellent in that role, as he had shown in the 1984 Canada Cup. But he was nearing the end of his career, and even his skills as a gritty digger weren't what they used to be.

Nieuwendyk's absence left a gaping hole in the Flames' attack. He usually played on the first line with Gary Roberts and Lanny McDonald. McDonald, one of the league's premier snipers, had been traded from Toronto to Colorado on December 20, 1979, after a newspaper story revealed that he and a few teammates had been throwing darts at a picture of Maple Leafs general manager Punch Imlach. He still had a lot left when the Flames traded for him two years later.

Roberts was Nieuwendyk's closest friend. They had grown up in the same area and had been playing hockey, either with or against each other, for as long as they could remember. Roberts was the guy who went to the net and made life difficult for the goalies so that the other two could get a clear shot.

Years later, after McDonald had been replaced on the line by Sergei Makarov, Roberts revealed to Makarov that he would love to have a 50-goal season and promised the crafty Soviet that, should he attain that target, he would name his first son Sergei in appreciation.

Sure enough, Makarov came through. "That's why I never had any more kids," explained Roberts—who had a daughter, Jordan, at the time—with a chuckle. "I sure wasn't going to name my son Sergei."

But at this point in 1988, there was no joking. At times like this, the lesser lights have to come through. At 4:01 of the third period, the Flames got a goal from one of the most unlikely of sources: Tim Hunter, a man known more as a fighter than a scorer.

Crisp did everything he could to make that goal stand up. Every time Mark Messier came on the ice, he'd send out Shayne Churla, Joel Otto and Jim Peplinski, a trio of bruisers who could use their physical attributes to counter the strength of Messier.

Against Gretzky, he used Perry Berezan, a checking specialist, supported by Colin Paterson, another fleet checker, and Joey Mullen, a dangerous sniper. For every important draw, he sent out Otto, considered to be one of the very best face-off men in hockey.

For most of the period, it appeared that the strategy would work. The end-to-end game had evaporated and the Flames were preventing the Oilers from getting any decent chances. But Crisp knew as well as anyone that the Oilers needed only one.

The play that started his Flames on the slippery slope began with Gretzky, deep in his own end—not familiar territory for him in those days—firing a pass up the middle. It was a set play that the Oilers liked to use at times like this. It is also a play that is almost never seen today. Nowadays, the coaches live in such fear of an intercepted pass that anyone who tries to fire one up the middle, rather than bank the puck off the boards, is likely to find himself sitting on the bench for an extended stretch.

On this occasion, Mike Krushelnyski was the target, but he didn't receive the pass. He just stood near the red line to keep the play onside and redirected the puck to a streaking Jari Kurri.

Playing defence for the Flames was Paul Reinhart, who might well have been recognized as one of the greatest defencemen ever to play the game had he not suffered so many injuries. At this time, he was playing only his twentieth game of the season, having been out of action until March 17 with a chronic bad back.

Seeing the puck go towards Krushelnyski on the Oilers' left side, he took one fatal step in that direction. By the time he started to lean the other way, Kurri, in full flight, had streaked past him and left him staggering and falling at the blue line.

Flames forward Hakan Loob was desperately trying to catch Kurri from behind, but he had no hope. Kurri blazed into the right circle and was about halfway between the spot and the hash marks when he ripped a shot that gave Calgary goaltender Mike Vernon no chance.

The Flames had been less than four minutes away from tying the series, but now, game two was about to go into overtime.

In the intermission, the Oilers sat in their dressing room and heard Sather reveal the game plan. "Go out and play to win," he said. "Play to your strengths. Don't lay back worrying about stopping them from scoring."

This was music to the Oilers' ears. Someone—no one remembers who—piped up, "Even shorthanded, Glen?"

"Even shorthanded," said Sather.

You don't have to repeat a command like that to the Oilers. Because of the events that had unfolded during the season, they had been forced to become a more patient, more serious team than had been the case in the past. Nevertheless, in their hearts, they still had that sense of mischief, the desire to scoff at accepted hockey wisdom and win not with their defence but with their offence.

They did not think of themselves as a defensive team. They thought of themselves as the greatest river-hockey team in the history of the game.

Play to win? Wow! Let us out there!

As soon as they stepped onto the ice, with the packed Saddledome crowd hooting with anticipation of a home-team victory, the Oilers were focused on offence, but the Flames were just as determined to shut them down and the goalies weren't really tested. The first genuinely good chance was created by Messier when he came out from the corner and tried to beat Vernon on the short side.

When Vernon made the save, the puck popped up in the air, then flopped down just outside the post. Trying to keep the attack alive, a frustrated Messier hauled down Mullen, who had taken possession.

To the delight of the Calgary crowd, less than six minutes into overtime, the Flames were getting a power play.

But Sather had been asked about the team's strategy should a situation of this nature arise, and he had been unequivocal. It was to play for the win. "Even short-handed."

For the first forty-six seconds, Sather used his dedicated penalty killers, but there was a stoppage of play and he sent out Gretzky and Kurri. "That's why I remember Mess got the penalty," said Gretzky years later, "because I took the face-off. Usually, Mess would have done that."

So, a man short, in overtime of a crucial playoff game, the Oilers went to the attack. It wasn't even a limited, cover-your-butt attack; it was a hell-for-leather, go-for-it-all attack.

A loose puck was chipped out into the neutral zone and, as he so often did, Gretzky pounced on it and came down the left side, floated over the blue line and fed a soft pass across to set up a great chance. His target for the pass was Randy Gregg, but cruising behind as a trailer on the play was Steve Smith.

Smith and Gregg? Aren't they defencemen? They certainly are. If Gretzky's pass had been errant, the Flames could conceivably break back on a five-on-one. And the one in question would be Kurri, a forward. As it happened, Gretzky's pass was perfect, but Gregg's shot went right into Vernon's pads.

The Flames counterattacked, but once again the Oilers forced a face-off, which Gretzky took. Only seconds after his first shorthanded sortie down the left side, there he was again. He had got the puck back to Smith on the face-off, and Smith had dished it off to Kurri, who sent Gretzky away.

But this time, Gretzky was coming down the left side alone. He stepped over the blue line and, only about six feet from the boards, blasted a shot.

"I won the draw, then went down the left side and put the shot over Verny's shoulder," Gretzky recalled. "That was the greatest goal of my career.

"I went to the rink on a high after finding out Janet was pregnant, and the next thing I know, it's 4–4 and it's overtime and I'm coming down the wing and I'm thinking, 'There's no way I'm missing this.'"

"If he has ever shot the puck any better than he shot it there, I haven't seen it," said Muckler afterwards.

"That's as hard as I can hit it," agreed Gretzky. "No question. I can't hit it any harder."

Edmonton goaltender Grant Fuhr was an avid golfer at the time and he chose to use that sport as an analogy. "That shot was 280 right down the middle," he said, comparing it to a picture-perfect drive off the tee.

Vernon had come out to cut down the angle, but there was nothing he could do on this one. The puck rocketed over his left shoulder and into the upper corner. Oilers 5, Flames 4.

Even Crisp had to concede that it was a terrific shot.

"You look up and you see Gretzky coming down the rink," he said. "You think, 'Oh, no! Not again!' But he's cut off and he's got nobody with him. Then he rips that shot. You couldn't put that puck in there with a pea shooter. But he put it in."

Gretzky recognized the magnitude of what he had done. Throughout his career, he had never been one to gloat. But on this occasion, he couldn't help it. He was so enthused that he indulged in a rare display that approached arrogance.

"When I scored," he recalled, "I remember turning the corner, and at that time the Zamboni was right there. I'm yelling, 'Take the ice out!'

"The guy says, 'What?'

"I said, 'You don't have to worry. We're not coming back. You can take the ice out.' That's all I kept saying. I knew once we got back to Edmonton, we weren't going to lose. Had it been 2–0 for us at home, it still could have been a series, but I knew that once we won that second game in Calgary, they weren't going to beat us."

He was right. The devastated Flames crumbled, and the Oilers won the next two at home to sweep the series.

"I always relate things to the situation and the scenario," Gretzky explained. "Calgary was a good team. It was overtime, we were shorthanded. Mike Vernon was playing well. To me, it was the best goal I ever scored."

In those days, Gretzky used a Titan stick, heavy by today's standards but exactly the way he wanted it back then. With that weight behind the puck, he could get the power he wanted, yet the wooden shaft still allowed him to feel the puck on the blade.

In an average game, he would use six sticks, and although they were of the same design, they got shorter as the season progressed. After the first month, he'd saw about half an inch off the shaft. By the second month, he'd have taken an inch off, and so on. By the time the playoffs ended, he was using a stick that was three inches shorter than the one he used at the start of the season.

He felt that at the year went on, he tended to get over the puck more and more; as a result, he needed a shorter stick.

When he blasted the puck past Vernon, the stick was as short as it was going to be, but he gave it full extension. Suddenly, the Oilers' future, which had looked so dim back in training camp, was bright again.

"More than anything, we realize that we've still got the nucleus of a great young hockey team," said Lowe. "There are a lot of good young hockey players and there are a lot of good veterans who are still young, and we see an opportunity to win the Stanley Cup."

Win the Cup they did. After sweeping the league champions, rolling over the remaining obstacles to the Cup wasn't much of a problem.

They beat the Detroit Red Wings in five, then the Boston Bruins in four and a half. That was the year that the lights went out in the decrepit Boston Garden and the fourth game, which was tied 3–3 at the time, was suspended at 16:37 of the second period. Two days later, back in Edmonton, the Oilers won 6–3 for their fourth Cup in five years, and brought one of hockey's golden eras to an end.

But through no fault of Lowe, the rest of his observation proved to be ill-founded. Keeping a very close eye on Gretzky's heroics in the 1988 playoffs was the NHL's most flamboyant owner, Bruce McNall of the Los Angeles Kings. To McNall, Gretzky represented the ideal addition to his team, and when his overtures were not immediately rebuffed by Pocklington—as every Oiler fan would have expected them to be—McNall persevered. Finally, Pocklington capitulated.

On August 9, 1988, Gretzky was traded to the Kings, and "the nucleus of a great young hockey team" to which Lowe had alluded was no more.

Perhaps it's too charitable to say that Gretzky was traded. Really, it was more of a sale. The official deal was this: Gretzky, Krushelnyski and Marty McSorley went to the Kings in return for Jimmy Carson, Martin Gelinas, the Kings' first-round draft picks in 1989, 1991 and 1993, and cash. But as far as Pocklington was concerned, the cash was the key component. Little wonder. When the figure finally became known, it turned out to be no less than $15 million US. To put that figure into perspective, if you had a twenty-man roster of players who earned the average salary of that season, $15 million would have been enough to pay them for almost five years. Or to put it another way, it was roughly the price you'd pay for the services of an average player for a century.

Naturally enough, the trade of a player of Gretzky's calibre rocked the hockey community. Most people had expected that he would never be dealt, and certainly not while he was in his prime. There was a strong sentiment among many fans that NHL president John Ziegler should have stepped in to nullify the deal, much as baseball commissioner Bowie Kuhn did in 1976 when Charlie Finley, owner of the Oakland A's, tried to sell Vida Blue, Rollie Fingers and Joe Rudi.

Anyone who expected such a decisive course of action from Ziegler hadn't been paying very close attention to the way he ran the NHL. A stand of that nature would have been totally out of character. But had he been able to foresee the long-term ramifications of that trade, perhaps even Ziegler would have acted. Long after all the players involved in the deal had moved on to other teams, the impact of that trade continued to be felt. In fact, the aftershocks are felt to this day.

McNall was an ebullient, high-flying executive—so high-flying that he managed to escape the gravitational force of legality and eventually went to prison for fraud. But in 1988, he was still in good shape financially and was determined to make the Kings into a profitable organization.

He was also a truly generous, good-hearted man who wanted to be liked by everyone and wanted to be recognized as a genuinely benevolent employer.

So when Gretzky became the jewel in the Kings' crown, McNall could hardly wait to accord him the kind of salary that was commensurate not only with his ability but also with the circles in which McNall travelled—the Hollywood entertainment industry.

In February 1990, I was covering the Davis Cup tennis tournament in Vancouver. For some reason, I was in my hotel room in the early evening when the telephone rang. It was McNall. He had just come to terms on a new contract with Gretzky, even though Gretzky was in only his second season in Los Angeles, and he wanted me to know about it.

"When Wayne first came here, neither one of us had any idea what he should make," he said. "We did the contract, but I said to him, 'If it turns out that I do a lot better than I anticipated, let's talk again later on.'

"Well, it turns out that his impact has been far greater than we anticipated. We more than doubled my projection. So in the summer, I kept saying to him, 'Wayne, let's get this done.'

"But you know how he is. He said, 'We'll get around to it.' I had to fairly force him to do it."

McNall had tracked me down in Vancouver to let me know that not only was there a new contract in place, but there was a twist.

Upon acquiring Gretzky, McNall had made a promise. Gretzky, he said, would always be the highest-paid player in the league. The initial contract had rewarded Gretzky accordingly, but in late January 1990, the NHL Players' Association released some salary figures and Gretzky's salary was only the second-highest in the league. The Pittsburgh Penguins had wanted to make a long-term commitment to Lemieux and had given him slightly more than Gretzky.

McNall was having none of that. Gretzky was to have earned $1.6 million US plus bonuses. But under the revised terms that would leap-frog him ahead of Lemieux, Gretzky's salary was bumped to $2.72 million. It was an extremely lucrative deal that was to give Gretzky almost $30 million over seven years.

Not all of the money was to be paid up front. Some of it was to be deferred, with the idea being that Gretzky would retire in 1997 and still pull in more than $1 million a year for nine years. But it was fully insured and Gretzky would get the money, even if he were to suffer a debilitating injury. The contract was a display of unprecedented largesse from an NHL owner. But it was something McNall wanted to do.

"It was as close to a non-negotiation as anything could possibly be," said Gretzky's agent, Michael Barnett. "It was truly and totally initiated by Bruce McNall as a form of his following up his word that if he prospered beyond his expectations in the early stages of the contract, he would look at bettering his arrangement with Wayne."

In the 1987–88 season, the average NHL salary had been $180,000. But that figure was a bit misleading because most of the Canadian-based teams still paid their players in Canadian currency; to arrive at its figures, the league used what it referred to as "NHL dollars." If one player earned $200,000 US and another earned $100,000 Canadian, the league would calculate the average at 150,000 NHL dollars, even though the American dollar was worth considerably more than its Canadian counterpart.

In Edmonton, Gretzky's salary had never been the highest in the league. For much of his Edmonton tenure, Gretzky was nowhere near the top of the salary heap, even though he was by far the best player in the game. But when Pocklington sent Gretzky to the Kings and put him in the care of the free-spending McNall, he unleashed a landslide that has yet to be checked.

Agents for players of moderate skill who had been earning something in the range of $200,000 said to the general managers, "Look, I know my player is not Wayne Gretzky, but on the other hand, Gretzky's not ten times better. My player should get a hefty raise."

Unable to find a flaw in that logic, the GMs acceded. Three years after Gretzky got his raise, the average salary had jumped to $379,000, more than double what it had been when he got traded.

In the summer of 1992, Eric Lindros signed his first contract with the Philadelphia Flyers, and because Flyers owner Ed Snider needed to sell corporate boxes in his new arena, he was willing to give Lindros almost anything he wanted. Never one who could be accused of false modesty, Lindros decreed that he was better than Gretzky and should therefore earn more. As a result, Snider agreed to a six-year, $21 million US deal. And that came after the Flyers had paid the Quebec Nordiques $15 million to get him—the same price the Kings had paid in the Gretzky deal.

Waiting in the wings was Lemieux, whose own contract with the Penguins was due for renewal. Lemieux had been dropping hints about asking for a whopping $4 million. But when Lindros got $3.5 million before playing a shift in the league, Lemieux's price went up accordingly: now it was $5 million. The previous spring, Lemieux's *bonus* cheque—exclusive of his salary—was $638,000.

Meanwhile, journeymen continued to see their salaries rise. In Edmonton that year, for example, Dave Manson signed a four-year, $4.6 million deal. Esa Tikkanen had a contract that averaged $950,000. Even McSorley got an offer of $2 million a year, a move that enraged Bruins general manager Harry Sinden.

"There's just no reason to have to play that kind of player that much money," he fumed. "The only two players are Wayne Gretzky and Mario Lemieux that somehow justify those exorbitant salaries. They both filled half-filled buildings. They made hockey in their respective areas.

"They made it a major-league sport in those respective areas and helped their television. They produced income for their teams. The rest of these guys, I mean, it's nonsense."

But what could be done? Sinden shook his head. "I think it's too late," he said.

Young, emerging players wasted no time climbing on the bandwagon. Jaromir Jagr got $1.5 million. Mike Modano accepted a four-year, $6.75 million contract.

In 1993, five years after the big trade, the NHL's average salary cracked the $500,000 barrier, a fact that was directly traceable to the greed of Peter Pocklington when he sold Gretzky to the Los Angeles Kings to capitalize on that playoff success in 1988.

The inflationary spiral that Pocklington and McNall started continued until the NHL owners, trying to find a way to save themselves from their own stupidity, decided that they needed an imposed salary cap and shut down the league in September 2004. By that time, the average salary had risen to more than $1.8 million US.

Perhaps 1988 was the year that the fun started to go out of the game. Perhaps the business aspects and the big money started to take over. But there were other changes as well.

Modern arenas don't go dark anymore, and the NHL's dressing rooms, including the one in Edmonton, are not as open and welcoming as they used to be. It certainly stopped being as much fun for Coffey in that season.

"It was just all so good then," he said in 2005. "It was so much fun.

"I really feel bad for today's players. I don't think they realize how much fun it can be or how much fun it should be. It's too much of a business. The biggest thing I found, in my last couple of years playing and then when I was involved in Phoenix [as a special-teams coach with the Coyotes] is the seriousness. I say to Shane Doan and these young guys, 'Guys, it's all right to laugh. You can smile in the dressing room. It doesn't mean you think any less of the game.'

"The misconception now is that if a hockey player laughs in the dressing room, he doesn't care. What does that have to do with it? It's all right to have fun, and I really think you perform better."

Coffey, who has given thousands of interviews, used that process as an analogy. "It's the same with you," he said. "If you're sitting there talking to a player, if you're loose and you're having fun with the players, you're going to get a better story. And it's the same with a hockey player. He's going to play better if he's loose."

The 1988 Stanley Cup championship was to be Gretzky's last. In fact, the case can be made that the overtime goal against the Flames was the pinnacle of his career.

He was far from finished in 1988. There were still plenty of great moments ahead. He put on some dazzling displays during his subsequent tenure with the Kings. Then the St. Louis Blues. Then the New York Rangers. He went on to set the record as the league's all-time leading scorer. He won more Art Ross trophies. He set dozens of other records, some of which may stand forever. He led the Kings to the Stanley Cup finals in 1993. But there would never be another Stanley Cup for Wayne Gretzky. Never again would he score a goal that defined a Stanley Cup drive.

He came close when his hat trick in game seven of the 1993 conference final against the Toronto Maple Leafs put the Kings into the Stanley Cup final. It was probably the most memorable single game for the Leafs since they last won the Stanley Cup in 1967.

The Leafs had beaten the Detroit Red Wings in seven games, then survived another seven-gamer against the St. Louis Blues and gone up 3–2 against the Kings. But Los Angeles won game six at home (a victory Leaf fans will forever attribute to referee Kerry Fraser's non-call on a Gretzky high stick that cut Doug Gilmour), then went back to Toronto, where Gretzky's magnificent performance put the final nail in their coffin.

Still, there was to be no Stanley Cup for Gretzky that year. The Montreal Canadiens defeated his Kings in five games.

Six years later, in 1999, Gretzky retired, terminating a magnificent career. Those who witnessed his overtime goal against the Flames in 1988 saw that career at its highest point.

THE GOAL: SEPTEMBER 16, 1991.

Game two of the Canada Cup best-of-three final.
Scored shorthanded by Steve Larmer (unassisted) at 12:13
of the third period. Canada 4, United States 2.

HOCKEY PLAYERS WHO HAVE ENJOYED A GREAT DEAL OF SUCCESS IN their careers insist that there's only one thing more difficult than getting to the top.

Staying there.

That was the challenge facing Team Canada as it prepared for the 1991 Canada Cup. After the debacle of the 1979 Challenge Cup and the embarrassment of the 1981 Canada Cup, the nation had elevated its game and won the next two major international competitions—the Canada Cups of 1984 and 1987.

But this time, the task could be expected to be considerably more difficult. The talent pool in Sweden and Finland was improving with each passing year. The Soviet Union and Czechoslovakia were traditional powerhouses. And now, the United States had risen to prominence as well.

This was partly due to the impact of the 1980 "Miracle on Ice" in which the Americans, under the tutelage of Herb Brooks, had pulled off a stunning upset and won the Olympic gold medal. Emerging American stars like Pat LaFontaine, Mike Modano, Craig Janney and others had

watched that Olympic triumph as impressionable youngsters and been caught up in the hockey euphoria.

The American college programs were also improving
and had churned out stars like Chris Chelios, Brett Hull,
Gary Suter, Mike Richter and Brian Leetch.

With only six teams in the Canada Cup tournament,
there were no patsies. A round robin would eliminate two
countries, then the remaining four would engage in a sudden-death semifinal, followed by a best-of-three final for
the survivors.

It was a format that was fraught with danger. The
Canadians were probably safe in assuming they'd get past
the opening round, even though they often started slowly
in tournaments of this nature. But that single-game semifinal would put them in a precarious position, especially if
they didn't finish first and draw the fourth seed. Then they
were assured of playing a tough opponent.

There were also some storm clouds on Canada's horizon.
For one thing, Mario Lemieux wouldn't be available. He had
struggled through the 1991 playoffs and helped lead his
Pittsburgh Penguins to their first Stanley Cup, but he'd had
to miss some action due to a back injury and, despite being
invited, insisted that he wasn't ready to play in September.

Also missing was Mark Messier, perhaps the best team
leader in the history of sport—and definitely the best team
leader in the history of hockey. Messier had been nursing
knee and thumb injuries, and had turned down an invita-
tion to join the team.

Raymond Bourque, as was so often the case when he
was asked to play for Canada, decided that he wanted to
spend time with his family—as if the other players didn't
have families.

Stephane Richer, always something of a free spirit, had
simply refused to participate. John Cullen and Mark
Recchi had also declined invitations. Having played out
their options with their NHL teams, they were free agents,
and as such, weren't covered by insurance. While they

wanted to take part, they couldn't afford the risk of suffering a career-ending injury.

And as early as May, there had been some grumblings about the management team.

Alan Eagleson was under intense pressure as executive director of the National Hockey League Players' Association, and it was widely known that his stewardship of the organization was shortly to come to an end. Three months later, in fact, the United States Federal Bureau of Investigation started seizing records pertaining to his financial dealings with NHL clubs, and Eagleson stepped down the month after that.

But the Canada Cup tournament had been years in the planning, and his virtual lame-duck status with the Players' Association didn't alter the fact that he was the head of Team Canada.

For the most part, the players loathed him. They had serious doubts about his honesty with regard to the handling of the association's finances—doubts that proved to be well founded when Eagleson was sent to jail in 1998 after pleading guilty to numerous counts of racketeering and fraud. Eventually, the disgraced Eagleson would become the only person ever to be stripped of the prestigious Order of Canada, and his plaque would be removed from the Hall of Fame in Toronto.

Furthermore, on a personal level, he tended to be abusive and dictatorial. The Canada Cup tournaments, which were Eagleson's pet projects, were part of a reciprocal international agreement that, beginning in 1977, required Canada's participation in the annual world championship in Europe.

But the world championship was always staged in late April and early May, and at that time of the year, most top-level NHL players were still involved in the playoffs. Those whose teams had been eliminated were often recovering from the bumps and bruises of a long season, and were feeling the effects of the hockey ennui that sets in when the Stanley Cup is no longer available.

Not many players jumped at the chance to board yet another plane and fly across five or more time zones to Europe, and Eagleson's tirades to those who tried to turn him down were legendary in hockey circles.

He was notorious for invective directed not only towards the player in question, but also towards anyone who answered the phone, be it the player's wife or one of his parents. Threats of recrimination were commonplace, and it's safe to say that many of his constituents were afraid of him.

By the late summer of 1991, he was on his way out, but a lot of players were distressed to learn that he was still running Team Canada.

There were also those who expressed a degree of unhappiness about the return of Iron Mike Keenan as coach.

In the four years since he had coached Team Canada to victory in the 1987 Canada Cup, Keenan had become even more demanding of his players. He was no longer a young coach trying to force his innovative methods on a recalcitrant league. Now, he was a proven winner and an even sterner taskmaster.

There was no doubt that Keenan would handle the reins of Team Canada 1991. Eagleson was his agent and it was still Eagleson who called all the key shots. But in his NHL incarnation, Keenan had moved on from the Philadelphia Flyers to the Chicago Blackhawks, and his near-fanatical approach to conditioning worried a number of potential Team Canada players.

For eight consecutive days in January, Keenan had put his Chicago players through a regimen that started with a gruelling forty-five-minute skate, followed by half an hour on the exercise bike and a full weight-training cycle. Even on game days, the routine was not altered.

"There were four of us on that 1991 team who were playing for Mike in Chicago," recalled Steve Larmer. "Brent Sutter, Eddie Belfour, Dirk Graham and myself. We knew what to expect, more so than the others.

"I remember the day of the first game and the game-day skate. Mike's pre-game skate was what they all are today—but not in those days. It was a shortened version of a full practice with a lot of intensity. I remember a lot of the players saying, 'What the hell is going on here? Doesn't he realize we have a game tonight?'"

"I said, 'In Chicago, this is what we always do.'"

Still, demanding or not, Keenan's methods were successful. He had brought the Blackhawks back to prominence, a status that they were never able to regain after he left, and whether Eagleson was in disfavour or not, he was well within his rights to name Keenan the coach.

Some of the Team Canada candidates may have had their misgivings, but even so, despite the few exceptions mentioned above, the vast majority of Canadian players felt that the demands imposed by Keenan were a small price to pay for the chance to wear the coveted Team Canada sweater.

Not only did the legendary Canadian hockey mystique, with its inherent sense of duty, come into play, but Wayne Gretzky had made it clear that no matter what difficulties might arise, he intended to be a part of Team Canada. If it was good enough for Gretzky, the most revered player in this extremely peer-conscious sport, then it was good enough for almost everybody else.

So even though there was some grumbling, the organizers had so many prospective players that they opened camp with more than twice the number they would need—fifty-six to be precise.

"There's always that Catch-22," explained Keenan. "Do you invite them all and get them upset by cutting them, or do you get them upset by not inviting them?"

In a situation like this, you would think that Canada would consider only players with an established track record. Not so. One of the candidates in camp was an eighteen-year-old kid who hadn't played a single second in the National Hockey League: Eric Lindros.

His inclusion was the source of a great national debate, and it was duly noted that Mario Lemieux had been eighteen when the 1984 Canada Cup team was selected, but hadn't been considered. While many said that a player who had never progressed past junior hockey had no place in a Team Canada camp, many others said that if Gretzky was "The Great One," Lindros was "The Next One" and deserved a chance to show what he could do.

To the impartial fan, the latter view seemed by far the more reasonable. After all, if Lindros wasn't good enough to make the team, all the organizers had to do was cut him. There would be plenty of others who would share the same fate.

But Lindros rubbed many hockey purists the wrong way, and they were opposed to making any further concessions to him. He had started his NHL career by alienating a large segment of the hockey world when he refused to play for the team that drafted him two months earlier, the Quebec Nordiques.

To the traditionalists, this was an outrageous stance. But to Lindros and his family, the NHL and the Nordiques were to blame. The family had repeatedly said that if Eric were drafted by the Nordiques, who had the first selection in the June draft in Buffalo, he would not play for them. A few days prior to the draft, there was an unprecedented meeting to discuss the matter.

Lindros was there, as were his parents, Bonnie and Carl, and his agent at the time, Rick Curran. Three members of the Nordiques hierarchy attended: president Marcel Aubut; general manager Pierre Pagé; and director of corporate and community affairs, former Montreal Canadiens superstar Guy Lafleur.

And astonishingly enough, in view of the fact that the central character in the scenario had yet to have any involvement whatsoever with his league, NHL president John Ziegler also took part.

The Lindros family did not want Eric to play in Quebec,

and the Lindros family was used to getting its way. Throughout Eric's junior hockey career, the family had dictated the terms of his involvement. As a sixteen-year-old, he had been drafted to play junior hockey by the Sault Ste. Marie Greyhounds of the Ontario Hockey League. But he not only refused to attend the draft, he refused to report to the Greyhounds. Ostensibly, the reason was that he didn't want to have to play so far away from his hometown of Toronto. But shortly afterwards, he moved to Detroit to play Tier II junior hockey for Detroit Compuware.

The Greyhounds appeared to be stuck, since an OHA rule prohibited a team from trading its first-overall pick. But the OHA changed the rule to allow such a trade under certain conditions—and conveniently enough, those conditions just happened to allow Lindros to be moved.

He went to the Oshawa Generals and had a distinguished junior career, twice playing for the national team that won the world junior championship.

When he was ready to enter the professional ranks, the family saw no reason why they should not continue to chart their own course. Bonnie Lindros had even accosted the legendary Scotty Bowman outside an arena one day to ask his advice on how Eric could make sure that he got to play in a city of his choice. Bowman, appalled by Bonnie's brashness, said that he had no advice to offer and beat a hasty retreat, subsequently telling everybody he met about the encounter.

But the Nordiques were equally resolute. Lindros was the best player in the draft, they said, and therefore they would draft him, no matter how he and his parents felt about the matter. When they were true to their word, Lindros staged his own draft-day protest. He shook hands with Pagé, but refused to don a Nordiques jersey.

As a result, when the August opening of the Team Canada training camp rolled around, the hottest topic in Canadian hockey circles was where Eric Lindros would eventually begin his NHL career.

Even after the Nordiques drafted him, he did not change his stance. He had repeatedly sworn that he would never play for them. But he was only too happy to play for Team Canada—or at least try out for the team.

"We had all the coaches in for a meeting," recalled Keenan, "but I can't remember who brought his name up. Maybe it was Eagleson, but Eagleson wasn't representing him, so it probably wasn't. Maybe it was me."

As the Team Canada training camp progressed, the Lindros saga remained in the spotlight. He was playing well, throwing his weight around—so much so that he even suffered a mild concussion. Yet he also excelled in the other areas of the game. He carried the puck. He made the plays. He looked right at home, playing more like a twenty-eight-year-old than an eighteen-year-old. It appeared that, despite the odds, he would still be around after the final cuts had been made.

"He was impressive," recalled Keenan. "He caused quite a stir. We played an exhibition game in Ottawa and we had to sneak him out the back door and across the football field. He had a pretty big game, but we did that because there was so much media hype and so many media waiting for us that it would have held us up, so we went out that way. He was all excited like a giddy young guy. He was only eighteen."

But before the decision was reached on his status, a more urgent matter required the attention of the coaching staff—Keenan and his four assistants, Tom Watt, Pat Burns, Tom Webster and Brian Sutter. With only four days left before the opening game of the round robin, there were nagging concerns. Despite all the talent, the team simply was not coming together the way it should. Similarly, despite the presence of Gretzky, the offence was not all it should have been.

There was nothing clearly tangible about it, but the coaches knew something was wrong. They felt that the team needed offence and focus, and they were fairly sure that they knew how to solve both problems in one move. They called in Gretzky for his advice, and he agreed on all fronts. Yes, he recognized the problems, and yes, he knew the answer.

Call Messier and see if he'd change his mind.

"If he's feeling capable and he's feeling healthy," said Keenan, "we'd be happy to have him."

So it was agreed. Messier was to be courted. Now the question became: who would make the call? All eyes turned to Gretzky.

As the summer had progressed, Messier had undertaken a therapeutic program that included regular skating sessions, so he probably wasn't too far away from game shape. There was always the danger that the distress call to Messier could be perceived as something of a slap in the face to all the players who had gone through the grind of the training camp, but Keenan tried to downplay that aspect.

"It's not a last-minute sense of urgency," he explained, "because I have a great deal of respect for the guys who are here, but you have to consider that guys like Messier are special athletes."

So Gretzky made the call to his buddy, and Messier, notorious for his dislike of training camps of any sort, rolled into camp on August 29, two days before the Canadians were due to open the round robin against Finland. He was happy to be there, and almost as happy to have been able to make the team without attending a camp.

Immediately, the old guard took notice of the upcoming generation. "The first drill, the first practice that Mess was there, I was standing near the boards," said Keenan. "I don't know what Lindros had done, but something happened and Mess came over and stood beside me and said, 'Well, that prick's a player.'" That was quite a compliment, coming as it did from the stereotypical power forward, a man to whom Lindros was expected to be a successor.

But the next day, all of the hockey world, especially Team USA, received a staggering blow. That morning, the

American coach, Bob Johnson—known universally as Badger Bob because of his years as coach of the University of Wisconsin Badgers—had undergone surgery to remove a brain tumour. The news came as a shock not only to the American players, but also to Canadians who had crossed paths with the irrepressible Johnson.

"I was devastated," said Paul Coffey, who had earned his fourth Stanley Cup ring playing for Johnson's Penguins a little more than two months earlier. "I heard about it last night and I couldn't sleep. I've never met a better man in hockey in my life."

Al MacInnis, who had developed into one of the NHL's top defencemen under Johnson's tutelage when the two were in the Calgary Flames organization, said, "He was certainly, without a doubt, a big influence on my career. One of my fond memories is that after I'd been in the league about four years, he said, in front of a bunch of guys, 'That Al MacInnis, he made the commitment.'

"He'd tell stories about Gary Roberts and myself. He'd say, 'They were in such awful shape and look at them now.'

"The first time he saw me in Pittsburgh this year, he shouted, 'Look at that MacInnis, a million-dollar man.' I always got a great kick out of him. That's the way he was. He was always full of life and enthusiasm and [the attitude that] there's always tomorrow to look forward to. And he's right.

"We'd be on the bus and he'd see people working on the street and he'd shout, 'Look at that guy on that jack-hammer. He'll be on that jackhammer eight hours today and you guys are complaining about a two-hour practice.'"

"When you first meet him," said Coffey, "you almost think it's an act. He can't be that positive. But when you spend seven or eight months with him, that's him. He's for real. He's one of the main reasons we won the Stanley Cup. He made us believe in ourselves. Over the course of time, he makes you believers. That's what's going to be on his side now. He's so positive."

Unfortunately, this was a battle that even Johnson's optimism couldn't win. He remained in hospital for the duration of the Canada Cup tournament, and although he sent a steady stream of notes of encouragement and advice to Team USA, the coaching duties had to be turned over to his assistant, Tim Taylor.

When the tournament started, the Americans, who loved Johnson, tried to use his departure as motivation. They dedicated their efforts to him and said they would do everything in their power to win their first Canada Cup for him.

They certainly started the tournament in emotional fashion, roaring to a 5–0 lead against Sweden before settling for a 6–3 win.

Even so, the Canadians were still the odds-on favourites to win. If everyone stayed healthy, this was easily the most powerful team ever assembled. A number of players, including goaltender Bill Ranford and defenceman Steve Smith, were at the peaks of their careers. Gretzky was the best player in the world and Messier was the best power forward. Specialists like Rick Tocchet, Brent Sutter and Dirk Graham dotted the lineup. The defence corps, with the likes of Al MacInnis, Eric Desjardins and Paul Coffey, seemed unassailable.

Even so, Team Canada's start was much less impressive than that of the Americans. In their opening game, the Canadians had to settle for a 2–2 tie against Finland and, as is so often the case, the nation's fickle hockey fans made no secret of their disdain for such an unimpressive beginning. Some of the spectators at Toronto's Maple Leaf Gardens actually booed Team Canada's efforts, even though they would have been better advised to applaud Finnish goalie Markus Ketterer. He was by far the best player on the Finnish side and was the real reason that the Finns were able to force a tie.

From coast to coast afterwards, there was no shortage of people who wanted to talk about Team Canada. But very few of them wanted to say anything positive. The Canadians didn't try hard, they said. They lacked motivation. They didn't have enough offence. They were outcoached. They used the wrong lineup. They were too cocky. They didn't skate well enough. They didn't want to make a serious commitment. And on and on.

The love affair with the national team that had blossomed during the 1987 Canada Cup had apparently run its course, and it did no good to remind fans that in that tournament, as in this one, Canada had started with a tie against a perceived mediocre team—Czechoslovakia on the earlier occasion.

To make matters worse, the Finnish coach decided to put the boots in. Usually, coaches are extremely guarded when talking about their opposite number. But Pentti Matikainen apparently hadn't been apprised of the unwritten rule.

"I was surprised that we could do what we wanted and they didn't change their style at all," he announced after the game. He said that in his brilliance, he had anticipated an early charge by the Canadians and had reacted accordingly, going with short shifts in the early stages. "We knew we were a better skating team than them," he continued. As if that weren't enough, he pointed out that he had outcoached Keenan in another area. "I thought that they would try to change to get our weak players against their strong players," he said, "but they didn't."

To those who were veterans of these international tournaments, it seemed somewhat unlikely that Keenan knew less about coaching than a Finn. It seemed even more unlikely that all four of Keenan's assistants, each a successful head coach in the NHL, got just as stupid just as quickly. Perhaps Keenan was biding his time and saving his best for the later stages of the tournament. It was also possible that the players who were selected for the team after the lengthy and demanding training camp had breathed a sigh of relief and subconsciously relaxed.

Whatever the case may have been, the Canadian fans were not mollified. A tie against the Finns simply was not acceptable.

It wasn't particularly acceptable to the players, either. And it certainly wasn't acceptable to Gretzky, who was playing brilliantly even though the final 50-goal season of his career was already behind him. He had evolved into his super-playmaker phase, and although he had scored "only" 41 goals for the Los Angeles Kings in the previous season, he had assisted on 122 to lead the league in that department.

Canada's next game was against the Americans, and Gretzky was brilliant, floating passes perfectly onto sticks and setting up goal after goal. By the midway point in the game, the Canadians had run up a 5–0 lead.

At that point, the Americans, who had seemed to be in awe, came to life somewhat and played a more physical game, but it was far too late to make a comeback. Canada breezed to a 6–3 victory and the nation breathed easily again.

But the next day, Keenan stirred up the malcontents once more when he cut Steve Yzerman rather than have him sit in the press box as an extra player. Even though it was a move that was dictated by the circumstances, Yzerman was extremely popular with Canadian hockey fans and was one of only two players on the team who was coming off a 50-goal season.

But this was a transition period for Yzerman. He was starting to slow down ever so slightly, and at that point in his career he hadn't evolved into what he later became—the best two-way player in the game. He was still a superb performer, but two other forwards, Lindros and Theoren Fleury, had been remarkably strong in camp. Based purely on performance over the past few weeks, Yzerman was the one who had to be left out of the lineup.

He handled it with his usual consummate class. "The story here shouldn't be that a player was released," he said, "or that a player is upset or that the coaches don't like this or that player.

"The story should be that Canada is preparing to win the Canada Cup again. They had an impressive win over the United States and I don't think the story should pertain to one player's happiness or unhappiness.

"It's a situation that all adults and professional athletes have to deal with. You enjoy the good times, but unfortunately, there's a down, and you've got to accept that. I'm prepared to do that."

Yzerman's many fans weren't as charitable, and once again, it was left to Gretzky and friends to win back their confidence.

Sweden provided the opposition and Gretzky provided the show. He set up three of Canada's goals in the 4–1 victory, each with a brilliant pass.

The first came when he anticipated a clearing attempt by Swedish goalie Tommy Soderstrom and intercepted it. In a flash, he fired the puck out to Steve Larmer, who had just crossed the blue line and was in the deep slot. Larmer one-timed it and the Canadians were in front. It was a superb play because it came on a line change, and Gretzky was deep in the Swedish end chasing the puck. "I just came off the bench," marvelled Larmer. "I don't know how he knew I was there."

That uncanny ability to know what was going on around him was always one of the attributes that set Gretzky apart. He put the puck right on Larmer's tape.

"It was an incredible experience playing with Wayne," recalled Larmer in 2005. "Guys were fighting to play with him, just because you don't want to let anybody down.

"Playing with him, you try to figure where he's going to put the puck. I always tried to go to an open area because you know that's where he's going to put the puck. You're trying not to overthink, but you remember how you used try to defend against him. He doesn't pass the puck hard. He kind of lays it out into an area for somebody to skate into."

Then it was Paul Coffey's turn, this time on a two-on-one break with Gretzky.

"I was trying to remember all the way down the ice, 'How did we do it four years ago?'" said Coffey, who had been Gretzky's teammate during their years in Edmonton. "It was only about five seconds, but I was trying to remember. Some guys on a two-on-one will go slow. He goes slow.

"So I thought, 'I'll come in a little late and then I'll go quick to the net.' And that's what I did.

"I was trying to remember how I used to do it, not how he used to do it. He can do pretty well anything. But that's what we used to do. If I go quick, right to the net, even if he doesn't give it to me, he'll have a pretty good shot."

As it happened, Gretzky set Coffey up perfectly. "I told him his daughter Paulina could have put that one in," laughed Coffey.

It wasn't quite that easy. Soderstrom reacted quickly and Coffey needed to put the puck up. But Coffey was a great scorer in his own right and he did what needed to be done.

The next one was a classic Gretzky play—the kind that hockey fans saw so many times over the years. He pounced on an outlet pass in the neutral zone, went over the blue line and curled, waiting for something to happen.

Dirk Graham came roaring up the middle, and Gretzky fed him the puck to send him in alone. The clock hadn't even reached the seven-minute mark, but already Canada led 3–0.

Like every hockey player, Gretzky enjoyed getting goals. But he enjoyed setting them up even more.

"Ever since I played junior, I always felt that if I was going to play professional hockey, I had to do something out of the ordinary," he explained. "At the time, I was being knocked for my speed and my size, but I always felt that if I could help other people put the puck in the net, then I'd have the opportunity to play professionally.

"I worked a lot in practice on passing. Every day. Backhand passes. Forehand passes. Over sticks. Over gloves. Still today, I do a lot of passing in practice. Still over sticks and gloves.

"Maybe just as important is the way I feel. I guess some guys don't have this feeling, but I've always had this feeling that I'm just as happy, and sometimes more happy, to see other guys score than if I score myself."

Those little saucer passes required a delicate touch, but Gretzky had it. "Say you're passing in a three-foot radius," explained Coffey. "He can get the puck up and down in that three feet. Other guys might take the three feet just to get it up."

"He's phenomenal," agreed Messier. "Amazing. Whatever kind of pass it takes, he'll make."

Yet despite the brilliance of Gretzky and goaltender Bill Ranford, there were still concerns about Team Canada's overall performance, the primary one being a lack of consistency. It was there in the game against Sweden, just as it had been there throughout the tournament. In the second period, Sweden had been in complete control, and the high-powered Canadian attack had managed to muster only one shot on goal. But at other times, the Canadians played with supreme confidence and showed a full arsenal. They could score. They could play defence. And, led by some highlight-reel bodychecks from Lindros, they could be dominant in the physical aspect as well.

First Ulf Samuelsson made the mistake of going shoulder to shoulder with Lindros in a battle for the puck. Lindros sent Samuelsson flying into the corner. The big Swede emerged with a separated shoulder.

Canada's next victim was Czechoslovakia. Lindros's next victim was Martin Rucinsky. Again, it was a thundering, but clean, open-ice check. Rucinsky was carrying the puck up the left side when Lindros bore down on him like a runaway truck. This time, the result was a broken collarbone.

The game was played in Montreal, and to the delight of the Forum fans, Canada got off to another fast start, taking a 2–0 lead before Czechs had even managed to get a shot on Ranford. Before the game was ten minutes old, the Canadians were up 4–0.

They did it against quality goaltending. In the nets for the Czechs (and curiously wearing sweater number 2) was Dominik Hasek, who went on to win no fewer than six Vezina Trophies and an Olympic gold medal.

As they tended to do after they had rolled up a big lead, the Canadians eased off, and when the final siren sounded, the score was 6–2.

Again, Gretzky was dominant. The Canadians had played only four games to this point, but for the third time, he was selected as player of the game. On the other occasion, he was the runner-up.

Despite the momentum that was building for Team Canada, there was a risk that the focus could be lost in Quebec City, where the Soviet Union was to provide the opposition—and where the Lindros circus was in full three-ring mode.

Everybody in Quebec loves to talk about hockey, and all the fans were excited about the Canada Cup. But a discussion of that subject couldn't begin until *l'affaire Lindros* had been exhausted. If Lindros had given any indication that the hype was overblown, the controversy might have died down somewhat. But he was getting better as the series progressed and was clearly a world-class player, even though he was still a teenager. The concept of losing a player of this calibre for no reason that they could comprehend infuriated the Quebec fans.

The Lindros controversy had been a major story in Montreal, where the Canadians had played the Czechs. But in Quebec, it was raised to another level altogether. While most of the Quebec fans were angry, some took it personally. They saw his decision as anti-French and some went so far as to issue threats against Lindros and his family.

It was a very serious matter at the time, but talking about it fourteen years later, Gretzky was laughing.

"Did Mike ever tell you what he did in Quebec?" he asked.

I don't know. What was it?

"We were practising in Montreal and busing to Quebec City. After practice, Mike calls me over and he says, 'Gretz, listen. I think this would be really good for everyone.'

"I said, 'What?'

"He said, 'I'm going to have you room with Eric.'

"I said, 'In Quebec?'

"He said, 'Yeah.'

"I said, 'Why should I have to be blown up with him?'

"He said, 'No, no. It will calm everybody down if you and him are roommates. I'm going to tell everyone.'

"I said, 'Mike, you can't tell anybody. I don't want them blowing up my room.' I said, 'Mike, honestly, you don't understand. They hate this kid. I'll protect him. I'll calm everybody down, but don't tell everybody we're roommates.' I was scared to death."

Usually, the Team Canada dressing room was open to the media as soon as the practice ended, but on this occasion, it remained closed until Lindros had departed the premises. The media crush would have been too much.

Gretzky wandered out of the room first, and for perhaps the first time in his pro career, he occasioned little interest. He drew a group of only five or six people.

But the subsequent appearance of Lindros started a stampede. Security guards had to usher him down the hall, with the media pack nipping at his heels, into a separate room for a full-blown press conference.

And what new development in the impasse had prompted this pandemonium? Absolutely nothing. There were no new developments. He still had no intention of playing for the Nordiques.

The Canadians needed only a tie against the USSR to clinch first place in the round robin, and that's all they got. The ice was awful, not surprising since the Quebec Colisee was an ancient building and the weather in early September was warm. Perhaps the distraction of the Lindros controversy had something to do with their performance as well.

The Soviets could probably have played better, but they were having problems of their own. Their country was in turmoil; the so-called Evil Empire was falling apart. As a harbinger of the collapse of the Soviet Union, the Berlin Wall had recently come tumbling down, and to many of the Soviet players, there were more important matters to worry about than hockey.

The Soviets played fairly well, as was often the case when they faced the Canadians, but once again, Gretzky and Ranford were the stars and propelled Canada to the result they needed.

The Soviets, meanwhile, had been eliminated from further play before the game began, having staggered to a fifth-place finish. There would be no rematch of those great playoff-round games in the Canada Cups of 1984 and 1987.

Soviet coach Viktor Tikhonov had plenty of excuses. In addition to the turmoil caused by the political situation, he had been without some of his stars—including the entire KLM Line of Igor Larionov, Sergei Makarov and Vladimir Krutov. Valeri Kamensky was recuperating from a broken leg, and goaltender Arturs Irbe had withheld his services as a form of protest.

Irbe is a Latvian, and during the spring 1991 uprising, some of his countrymen had been killed by Soviet soldiers. When he refused to play for the USSR, which he viewed as an invading force, he had been threatened with arrest. He collected his family together and tried to head for North America. On the first try, they were refused permission to leave, but in subsequent weeks, a degree of political stability was established and he moved to San Jose to join the NHL's Sharks.

None of this went over well with Tikhonov. The Soviets would again become a hockey power, he said, "if the NHL stops stealing our players."

Canada's round-robin record was 3–0–2. The Americans had won four while losing one, so they too had eight points. But that loss had been at the hands of the Canadians, and under the pre-arranged tiebreaking system, Canada earned the coveted top spot. That gave them a semifinal game against Sweden, while the Americans would have to play the surprisingly tenacious Finns.

By this time, Johnson, his condition worsening, had been moved to a hospital in Colorado Springs. Yet astonishingly, he still managed to send messages of encouragement and support to the team.

The inspired Americans played an excellent, disciplined game against the Finns. There was only one penalty and it was assessed to Finland's Kari Eloranta. With no power plays to kill, the Americans were able to control the game and roll to a 7–3 victory.

Canada established the same margin of victory, but the Canadian defence was starting to make its impact felt by now, and the Swedes fell 4–0.

All through the first period and well into the second, it appeared that Tommy Soderstrom might be able to singlehandedly lead his team to an upset. He stopped a screaming Larmer slap shot with his head. He got a break when a Shayne Corson shot went off the inside of his pad, then both goalposts, before being cleared out of harm's way.

Canada outshot the Swedes 18–5 in that first period, but were not rewarded for their efforts. When the teams went to their dressing rooms for the first intermission, there was no score.

But midway through the second, Gretzky made the most of a breakaway, beating Soderstrom on a backhand. It appeared that the floodgates might open, but Soderstrom continued to hold his ground.

The death blow for the Swedes came when Dale Hawerchuk jammed the puck into the net in the dying seconds of the period. In the third, the Canadians had little trouble, adding goals by Brent Sutter and Graham to earn their spot in the final.

In the view of most fans, if the Canadians couldn't play the Soviets for the Canada Cup, a matchup against the United States was the next best thing. After all, Team USA had come a long way since its first Canada Cup experience in 1976, when it was generally referred to as Team Useless.

On the roster back then were Alan Hangsleben, Joe Noris, Fred Ahern, Mike Polich, Danny Bolduc and a number of equally unacclaimed NHL fringe players, supplemented by a few World Hockey Association journeymen.

Want some more names? How about Dean Talafous, Mike Curran, Harvey Bennett and Mike Christie?

But by 1991, Team USA had blossomed into a genuine world-class squad with guys like Pat LaFontaine, Chris Chelios, Rod Langway, Gary Suter and so many others who were, or would become, NHL All-Stars—and even, in some cases, Hall of Famers.

And there was nothing they would rather do than beat Canada, something that no American team had ever done at this level. For that matter, there was a long history of Canadian domination over the Americans at almost any level you'd care to name.

There was also a perceived caste system in the NHL in those days, which created the sense south of the border that the Canadians treated them like second-class citizens. Not long before the Canada Cup began, the internecine rivalry between the Canadians and Americans on the Boston Bruins had become a serious detriment to the team's success.

As one Team USA player put it prior to the Canada Cup showdown, "We want to get the right to sit in the front of the bus."

There was also a sociological difference between the Canadians and Americans. In that era, most of the Americans came to the NHL via the college route, while Canadians tended to be graduates of junior hockey, a system that made an extended education difficult. Canadians often saw the Americans as coddled, pretentious snobs. Americans often saw the Canadians as rough, uncultured rednecks.

The American players had another incentive. They knew that the prognosis for Johnson was not good. They wanted to win it for the Badger, fearing that Johnson would never again have a chance to see an American team be victorious.

The Canadians were under no delusions as to what they could expect. "I can tell you right now," said Canadian forward Rick Tocchet, "that every American guy in that room wants to beat us so bad they can taste it.

"I hate to say it, but they probably want it more than the Russians did in '87, they want it so bad."

"There are a lot of bragging rights at stake," agreed another Canadian forward, Brendan Shanahan. "The guys involved in this series are going to hear about it for the next eighty games, maybe even right through to the next Canada Cup. This is going to be played like a Stanley Cup."

And it was. Emotions were high and the battles along the boards were of an intensity that had not been seen in the tournament to this point.

The European teams tended to avoid physical play, and as a result, both Canada and the United States, with the exception of the recurrent aggression provided by Lindros, had adapted to that style. The two teams had finished first and second without a game plan requiring physical intimidation, so why tempt fate—or European referees—by laying on the body?

But when they met in the final, it was a different story. The hitting was of the solid NHL variety, and the game provided the best of both worlds for the spectators—end-to-end action with plenty of physical contact. But in typical NHL fashion, there were also a lot of cheap shots, and as a result, a lot of power plays.

The Canadians scored first when Eric Desjardins finished off a stretch of intense pressure that had seen Mike

Richter make great saves on Messier and Luc Robitaille.

In the second period, Gretzky went to work again, reeling in the rebound of an Al MacInnis shot on the edge of the circle, then timing his pass to Larmer perfectly.

Richter had to get himself square to face Gretzky, and as he did so, Larmer cut in towards the far corner of the crease. Gretzky laid the puck on his stick and Larmer had only to redirect it into a vacant net to make it 2–0.

As the midway mark of the second period neared, Gretzky was on the attack again, chasing a dump-in down the right boards. As he moved towards the corner, he slowed to avoid a check from Chris Chelios, danced around him, then went after the puck. Chelios's defence partner, Gary Suter, came across to cover up, and as Gretzky reached for the puck in the corner, Suter flattened him from behind.

The crowd was in a state of shock. Gretzky had been hit about three feet from the glass. He had gone into the boards head-first and was clearly hurt. He staggered up, leaving one glove where he had fallen and dropping the other as he wobbled towards the bench. At the top of the circle, he fell to his knees.

No penalty was called by referee Don Koharski on the play. The Canadians were stunned. Throughout the tournament, they had been carried by the play of Gretzky and Ranford. Now Gretzky was gone, and judging by the way he had made his departure, his return did not appear to be imminent.

"The trainer went over the boards," recalled Keenan, "and he came back and said he's finished for tonight. 'I don't know after tonight,' he said, 'but he won't be back this game.'"

It was a difficult time for the Canadians, but Keenan's first memory when asked about the incident years later was in a lighter vein. "I remember a funny story about that," he said. "I'm standing behind the bench and I hear this, 'Psst. Psst.'

"I'm thinking, 'Who's that? What's going on?'"

"I look over and it's Coffey. He gives me a head signal to come on down. So I go over there and he says out loud, 'You can double-shift me now.'"

"I said, 'Okay, I will.' And I did."

"He did," confirmed Coffey years later. "He played the crap out of me.

"At that point we were playing seven defencemen. Any time I played on a team with seven defencemen, it was tough. For a guy like me—I can't play short shifts. I've got to get a lot of ice time to be productive. The whole bench loosened up, and started yelling, 'Yeah, let's go; let's go.'

"Mike was good to play for because he gave you a chance to prove yourself. He wanted you to stand up to him and prove to him that you have it."

"Coff had been around Wayne and he knew how to handle it," said Keenan. "Probably it was good for the bench because the rest of them heard it. Instead of everybody saying, 'Oh, my God, we've lost Wayne,' they were more relaxed. All these years after, I'm still laughing about it.

"But I did double-shift him. I called his bluff and everybody on the bench started to laugh. He said. 'Geez, I was only kidding.'"

Even so, with Gretzky gone, the Americans knew their chances were increased appreciably. To literally add insult to injury, Suter beat Ranford through the five-hole before the period ended to make the score 2–1.

The Canadians were reeling. Their momentum had disappeared. Their star player was gone. The Americans were down only one goal and charging hard. But the Canadians managed to make it out of the period without further damage, and once they were settled in the room, Messier took charge.

A situation like this highlighted the reason that he had been brought into camp at the last minute. Based on his play in the early going, he should have been one of the first cuts. But he stayed around throughout the camp and was kept on, even when Yzerman was let go.

The coaching staff had a fairly simple premise in mind. If a player possesses one overriding skill, one attribute in which he excels far more than any other player, then he had to be on the roster.

Messier's skill was that no one in the history of hockey had ever been able to lift a team the way he did when it mattered the most. This was one of those times.

You'll never get Messier to talk about it. I've tried and tried over the years without any success. Usually, he just grinned and dodged the question. Once, he even apologized. I don't remember his exact words, but they were something along the lines of, "I know what you're trying to get at, Al, but I just can't bring myself to talk about that."

Fortunately for those who want to know such things, his club-motivating speeches are, by definition, delivered to a number of people. And most of the recipients are less reticent than Messier to discuss their content.

Sometimes, the speeches are powerful, to the point of being downright threatening. Sometimes they appeal to pride. Sometimes, hockey heritage and nationalism enter into the equation. But there's always one constant. Always, those famous Messier eyes stare at you, glare at you, bore into you. The recipients know, beyond even the slightest doubt, that their future, perhaps even their health, will be a whole lot rosier if they heed his exhortations.

"It's like those stockbroker ads," explained Ranford. "When Mark speaks, everybody listens.

"That's a mark of the respect that people have for him. There are not too many guys who have as much Canada Cup, world championship and playoff experience as Mark does, so when he has something to say, everybody listens to him."

There was one man who could match Messier's experience, but he was in the training room at the time, getting his back injury treated. So Messier took charge.

Judging by the reports of those who heard it, the speech went along these lines: "We can't worry about the fact that

Gretz is out. There's not a thing we can do about it, so we just have to go out there and play as if he had never been a part of the team. We can't let it get us down. In fact, we have to make it pick us up. Everybody. Everybody has to pick up his game a notch. We're in front and we intend to stay there. They knocked out our star, but we want to make damn sure that they're not rewarded for it."

Messier looked around the room. Was everybody clear on the concept? They were.

So then Messier went out and scored the goal that restored Canada's two-goal lead, beating Richter with a wrist shot from the circle. Brent Sutter added another, not that it mattered much by that point, and the Canadians had won the opener, 4–1.

Keenan was full of praise for Messier. "He's the man responsible for picking this team up tonight," he said. "He's the man who took charge in the locker room between periods. He's the man who showed the intensity and the leadership on the ice and the composure on the bench.

"I can't say enough about him. I have a great deal of respect for him as a person and as an athlete. His leadership qualities are going to be dispersed among the group because they have so much respect for him.

"He felt a great deal of passion for Wayne. He knows how much Wayne wants to play in this tournament, wants to be on the ice."

"When somebody like that goes down, there are always opportunities for other people to step up and fill the void," recalled Larmer. "We knew that no single person could ever fill those shoes, but we felt that if collectively, we all picked it up a step, then the fact that Gretz was not playing might be something that we could overcome."

Over in the American room, Suter was under siege. The media descended on him in full force, and to his credit, he didn't run and hide.

Suter was a genuinely funny guy, and he once admitted to me that he used to lie awake at nights, trying to think up good quotes to give the media. Unfortunately, they were sometimes too good, as far as the Calgary Flames' management was concerned, and he was told to be bland like everyone else.

At that point in his career, he was not seen as a dirty player. He and MacInnis formed the best power-play point tandem in the NHL, and although he was involved in an occasional scrap and threw the odd solid body check, he never seemed to be trying to hurt anybody.

Seven years later, he cross-checked Paul Kariya in the jaw after a goal, and his reputation, among Canadians at least, was to take a nosedive, particularly when it became clear that the concussion Kariya suffered would keep him out of the Nagano Olympics.

Ironically, in the summer of 1991, the NHL had passed a rule regarding the kind of check that Suter unloaded on Gretzky. In the future, it would warrant a major penalty. But the NHL season hadn't started yet and the new rule hadn't kicked in.

"It was a legal hit," Suter insisted over and over again, clearly astonished by the media reaction to his check. "If it had been anyone else in the world, we wouldn't be talking now. I guess that's the stature he has."

The pointed questions continued to rain down on Suter. "It's unbelievable," he said, still clearly shocked. "It's a game of hits. Any other player but him . . . I don't think it was a cheap shot."

The Canadians didn't see it that way. Suter's buddy MacInnis tried to defend him, saying he didn't think he had intended to hurt Gretzky. But even MacInnis had to admit, "It didn't look pretty on TV, that's for sure."

"It was definitely a hit from behind," recalled Larmer in 2005. "And I just don't know there was a whole lot of hitting from behind back then. I don't think that Wayne was really expecting something like that. Today it seems that it happens frequently, but for that time, it was a dirty hit.

"There was almost a level of respect—that when somebody was in a vulnerable position you didn't hit him to hurt him. It was more to hit and get in the way and take people out of the play, not out of the game."

"It was an illegal hit, no question about it," fumed Keenan.

Either way, Gretzky was out of action for the duration, and the possibility of an American comeback was now very real indeed. Team USA was a high-quality aggregation, and without Gretzky, who had been nothing short of magnificent throughout the tournament, the Canadians were at best a toss-up to prevail.

But that certainly wasn't the message that Messier delivered to them before the next game. Gretzky's absence just gave them one more obstacle to overcome, Messier said, but there was no reason they couldn't do so. That's what obstacles are for—to be conquered.

Gretzky, who was known more for leading by example than through speeches, also spoke to the team and echoed the sentiment. "You guys are great players," he told them. "You can win it without me." He told them that it was just the end of his Canada Cup 1991 participation, not the end of his career, and that if there were another Canada Cup in 1995, he fully intended to be a part of it.

On the ice, Messier once again led by example, opening the scoring with a blistering wrist shot into the upper corner on Richter's stick side. When Larmer fought off a check from Chelios and slid the puck past Richter to make it 2–0, the Canadians seemed to be in control.

But the Americans were a gritty group. They could easily have folded at that point and gone through the motions. Some of the European teams would have done so.

Instead, the Americans fought back in the second period, scoring first on a power-play goal by Jeremy Roenick and then tying the game on a goal by Kevin Miller.

Now, the Canadians' position was precarious, to say the least. Even though they held a one-game advantage in the series, the Americans were coming on, and without Gretzky, the Canadian game wasn't all that it should be. If the

Americans managed to pull this one out, there was no reason to think they couldn't win the deciding game as well.

Gretzky was in the building and watching with a glum look on his face, but he couldn't help them from a suite, and if the series went to a deciding game, he wasn't going to be back for that one, either.

Everyone was feeling the pressure, and sometimes, situations like this are harder for the coaches to handle than the players. If you're on the ice, you can take a role in the developments, but if you're behind the bench, all you can do is hope that others come through for you.

"That was group of pretty intense coaches," recalled Larmer. "Tom Watt and Tom Webster weren't too bad, but there was Mike himself and Pat Burns and Brian Sutter. We wanted to win that game and the momentum was changing a little. We really didn't want to let it get to a third game."

Between the second and third periods came another one of those moments that all the participants remember for years afterwards. "All hell was breaking loose," said Larmer. "The coaches came into the room and they were getting loud and uptight. They were shouting at everybody."

That's when Larmer's friend and teammate, Dirk Graham, took over.

"It was really funny, looking back on it," Larmer said. "Dirk stood up told them, 'If you don't have anything positive to say, or good to say, then get the hell out of the dressing room. We don't need you in here. We'll get this all settled down.' And that's what happened.

"The coaches left. Some different guys had things to say, things like, 'We're here because we're good. We've got twenty minutes left. Let's just go out and do it.'"

"Dirk would say something like that," said Keenan. "He was the captain in Chicago and he was always very protective of the players. I had a great relationship with him. He would do something like that just to buffer the whole situation if he thought it was necessary, then he'd turn around and wink at me."

When the third period started, the Canadians tried valiantly to apply some pressure—and succeeded. But without Gretzky, the finishing touch wasn't there. The puck just wasn't bouncing their way.

Robitaille, in a sequence that was representative of the Canadian game at that stage, was set up in front for a high-percentage chance—the kind he capitalized upon throughout his career. But on this occasion, he fell as he was shooting and the puck skidded off the heel of his stick and went wide of the net.

Midway through the third period, with the score still 2–2, Canadian defenceman Steve Smith was penalized. It was a golden opportunity for the Americans, who always looked dangerous with the man advantage and had already scored one power-play goal.

From his vantage point high above the ice, Gretzky looked on, clearly nervous.

With the situation being so critical, Keenan had sent out his best penalty-killing forwards, Graham and Larmer. "They were the premier penalty killers in Chicago," he recalled, "and we were the best penalty-killing team in the league at the time. Those two guys were great soldiers for us."

The Americans worked the puck around the Canadian zone crisply, waiting for an opportunity to develop near the slot, but for the time being, there was nothing there.

Chelios should have been manning the left point, but to keep the pressure on, he had chased the puck towards the corner, so winger Brett Hull went back to cover his post.

When Chelios encountered traffic in the corner, he made the sensible play of sending the puck back to Hull on the point. As Graham closed on him, Hull snapped a pass across to Suter on the other point.

It was quick enough. And it was in the right general direction. But it was a touch off the mark, right into Suter's skates.

Suter had to turn towards Hull to get it, and when he did, Larmer, always lightning fast at times like this, pounced.

He swept past Suter, not only relieving him of possession, but knocking the puck ahead as he did so.

It was a clean breakaway!

Larmer was one of those salt-of-the-earth guys that everybody liked. He had a deadpan, self-deprecating sense of humour and a remarkably even temperament. "It's a great life I have," he told me one time. "I get up in the morning aching all over, stagger through a morning skate, play a game at night and have a bunch of guys try to beat the crap out of me, then go to bed and wake up in the morning aching all over."

He was as steady a player as the NHL has ever seen. For an eight-year stretch when he was in his prime, he played all 80 games every season, never amassing fewer than 75 points and never more than 90. He never scored 50 goals, but he never scored fewer than 30, either. There was always a suspicion that he could have produced a lot more.

"Yeah, but if you do that, then they expect you to do it next year," he explained.

When I told him I was doing a book about important goals in hockey history, his lightning-quick response was, "Then why do you want to talk to me?"

This is the guy who was roaring down the ice with the puck on his stick in 1991. There was no way Hull was going to exert himself unduly, and Suter was far behind. Larmer knew he had plenty of time.

"I had too much time," he recalled. "I was thinking, 'Oh, my God.' It was from the red line in. The way I skated, there was still a chance they could catch me."

He approached Richter from left to right, and Richter had to move with him. But there is simply no way that any goalie can make that move and keep his legs together. As the five-hole opened up, Larmer backhanded the puck through it and into the net.

Is that what he was trying to do?

"It worked," said Larmer.

But did he plan to make that move on Richter?

"I don't know what the plan was," Larmer said. "I was never one to deke a goalie. For most of my goals, even when I had breakaways, I would just shoot. I don't know what was in my head at that time. For me to deke a goalie like that—or even try something like that—was actually pretty surprising to me."

For the Canadian fans, nothing could have been sweeter. Not only had Team Canada demoralized the Americans with a shorthanded goal, but they were back in front with time running out. And to top it all off, the guy who had been victimized on the turnover was Suter.

After that, it was just a matter of keeping the Americans off the board—an area in which the Canadians excelled. With a minute to go, Taylor tried the standard desperation move of pulling Richter, but with forty-two seconds left, Graham took a pass from Messier and put the puck into an empty net.

Team Canada had won 4–2 and for the third consecutive time, Canadian players hoisted the Canada Cup trophy.

Despite the loss, this was a watershed moment for the Americans. They were now regarded as legitimate occupants of that rarefied atmosphere at the top of the hockey world. They still hadn't defeated the Canadians in a best-on-best tournament, but they were steadily improving, and it seemed likely that one day in the not too distant future, their ultimate goal would be met. And five years later, it was.

Lindros also used the 1991 Canada Cup to prove that he was capable of playing the game at any level—except the level that required him to wear a Nordiques sweater.

The team offered him a ten-year, $50 million deal—in an era when the average NHL annual salary was $230,000—but he turned it down.

Undeterred, Marcel Aubut made repeated overtures to the Lindros family, and even travelled to Albertville, France, in 1992 to see if the Olympic spirit had done anything to ease the Lindros resolve. It hadn't. Lindros came home with a silver medal. Aubut came home with nothing.

Finally, a year after they drafted Lindros, the Nordiques accepted their fate and put him on the trading block. Even that move turned into a fiasco, as both the Philadelphia Flyers and New York Rangers claimed to have been promised Lindros in trade. An independent arbitrator was called in and he awarded Lindros to the Flyers. In retrospect, the Flyers should have let the Rangers have him.

Lindros's services cost the Flyers Mike Ricci, Peter Forsberg, Kerry Huffman, Steve Duchesne, Ron Hextall, future considerations (Chris Simon), their first 1993 draft pick (Jocelyn Thibault), their first 1994 pick (Nolan Baumgartner) and $15 million US.

As of this writing, the Flyers have yet to win another Stanley Cup. The Nordiques, however, moved to Colorado in 1995 and won the Stanley Cup that season. They won again in 2001.

Lindros had one brief fling with greatness and won the Hart Trophy as the league's most valuable player in the lockout-shortened 1995 season. But the concussion he suffered during the exhibition phase of the 1991 Canada Cup was not his first, and it was far from his last. Since the impact of concussions is cumulative, each one he suffered during his pro career took a greater toll than the one before.

Thanks to the injuries he incurred as a result of his rugged style, and especially the concussions to which he proved highly susceptible, he never came close to attaining the superstar status that had been anticipated for him after his Canada Cup debut.

As for Messier, his brilliant performance in the Canada Cup only increased his value—and his asking price, to a level that the Edmonton Oilers refused to meet. As a result, Messier never played for them again. The New York Rangers were only too happy to pick up the tab for Messier, however, and they negotiated a trade with the Oilers, then signed Messier to a five-year, $13-million deal that made him the second-highest-paid player in the league behind Gretzky. In the midst of the negotiations, Rangers GM Neil

Smith promised his Edmonton counterpart, Glen Sather, that if his team won the Stanley Cup with Messier, he'd kiss Sather's posterior in the front window of Macy's department store in Manhattan.

In 1994, Messier teamed up with Keenan again, and the Rangers won their first Stanley Cup in fifty-four years. "I knew what Mess was made of," said Keenan. "He showed it in that '91 Canada Cup. You saw what I said about him. I think that's a pretty good endorsement of his skills from a coach, don't you?"

In the Rangers' Stanley Cup run, Messier's leadership again was instrumental. In game six of the semifinal series against the New Jersey Devils, he guaranteed a win and made sure it happened by scoring a hat trick to overcome a 2–0 New Jersey lead.

In game seven, when Valeri Zelepukin tied the score for the Devils with only 7.7 seconds left in the third period, Messier addressed his teammates throughout the entire intermission. By the time they returned to the ice for the overtime, there wasn't a hint of gloom or depression. Messier had convinced them that the game—and the subsequent trip to the Stanley Cup finals—was as good as theirs.

He was proven right when Stephane Matteau scored the winner in the second overtime.

Neil Smith, by the way, reneged on his pledge to pucker up at Macy's—a fact that Sather has never let him forget.

For Keenan, the Canada Cup victory was another step to the top of the coaching hierarchy. He went straight from the Canada Cup celebration to the Blackhawks' training camp and took them to the Stanley Cup final—their first appearance since 1973.

The 'Hawks fired him the following year, but that was due more to the dysfunctional nature of the team's front office than any failing on Keenan's part. It turned out to be a blessing in disguise that allowed him to be reunited with Messier for his date with destiny in New York.

For Gretzky, the 1991 Canada Cup was a turning point of a different sort, the beginning of one of the worst stretches of his career.

A month after the triumph, Wayne's father, Walter Gretzky, suffered a brain aneurysm. Although he eventually recovered, it was a laborious process and a trying time for the entire Gretzky family.

As a result of the injury inflicted by Suter's hit, Gretzky's back continued to bother him, and although he returned to play for the Kings in the regular season, he was a shell of his former self.

"That was the beginning of all my back troubles," he said years later. "It was an accident. People want to get mad at Gary Suter, but it was my own fault. I was killing the penalty and I kind of turned a funny way and he hit me. I kind of wrenched my back.

"I couldn't move for three days and I said to Mike, 'Mike, we're up one game to none and I can't play tomorrow night. Hopefully I can play game three.' Fortunately, we didn't have to do it. Stevie Larmer played out of his mind and scored the winner. He might have been the best player in the tournament."

Gretzky persevered through the 1991–92 season, playing seventy-four games, but for much of the time, he was in agony. He knew that he wasn't playing well, and he was so unhappy that he even mused publicly about the possibility of retiring after the season. But his hope was that such a radical approach would not be necessary and, once he was able to get away from the rink, the pain would ease and the injury would heal. It did nothing of the sort. In fact, it got so bad that he feared not only for his hockey career, but for his mobility.

By September 1992, he had to check into a hospital to be administered intravenous painkillers. Around the same time, Gretzky's doctor attended a major conference of back specialists in Seattle. He took along Gretzky's medical data to show his colleagues, and as a result, many of the top specialists in North America became familiar with Gretzky's ailment. Eventually, with a proper diagnosis in place, Gretzky gave in to the inevitable and underwent an operation that caused him to miss the first thirty-seven games of the 1992–93 season.

The fears about Bob Johnson proved to be well founded. In September, the two teams he had coached to Stanley Cup victories, the Penguins and Flames, faced each other in an exhibition game in Denver. Johnson insisted on seeing the game, and he made the one-hour trip from Colorado Springs by ambulance. He was in a wheelchair and couldn't speak, and when he met his former players, many of them were reduced to tears.

"He was in rough shape," said Flames goaltender Mike Vernon. "It was tough, not just for himself but for his family and the people who surrounded him. He's the type of person who would keep fighting and keep fighting, but this was just something he couldn't beat."

Johnson died on November 26.

And although Canada had risen to top of the hockey world by virtue of that stirring, undermanned triumph in 1991, that was the end of their Canada Cup run.

In fact, it was the end of the Canada Cup. With Eagleson deposed and eventually going to jail in 1998, his creation, the Canada Cup series, was dropped.

In reality, this was only a cosmetic change. The World Cup of Hockey that superseded it was basically the same tournament with a different name.

But the Canadians didn't win the first World Cup in 1996. The Americans, continuing their rise to prominence, beat them in the best-of-three final.

The 1998 Olympics gave Canada a chance to recoup lost glory, but that turned out to be an even bigger disaster than the World Cup. In the semifinal, Canada and the Czech Republic played the full game and an overtime period without being able to determine a winner. In the ensuing shootout, Canadian coach Marc Crawford astonishingly managed to put together a list of five shooters that did not include Gretzky. Not one of his five choices scored. Robert Reichel banked one in off the post for the Czechs and they advanced to the gold-medal game, which they won.

It was a format that the Canadians, who grew up with the unlimited overtime of the Stanley Cup playoffs, found hard to accept. "We didn't lose that game," snarled one of the entourage. "We lost the sideshow."

Canada, unable to get excited about a bronze-medal consolation game, lost to Finland and finished fourth.

When the Canadians won the 1991 Canada Cup without losing a single game, there appeared to be no end in sight to their dominance.

But in fact, it was not until the next century—at the 2002 Olympics—that they were able to rise to that level again.

THE GOAL: JUNE 19–20, 1999.

Game six of the Stanley Cup final.
Scored by Brett Hull (assisted by Mike Modano and
Jere Lehtinen) at 14:51 of the third overtime period.
Dallas Stars 2, Buffalo Sabres 1.

IN JUNE OF 1998, THE NATIONAL HOCKEY LEAGUE'S GENERAL
managers were once again desperate to put some scoring
back into their game. To that end, they devised a few rule
changes that they submitted to the board of governors for
the usual rubber stamp.

There was no doubt that something needed to be done.
In most sports, the pendulum between offence and defence
swings back and forth, but in hockey, it had swung to
defence and stayed there. Low scores were the norm.
Superstars were being prevented from exhibiting their skills
by marginal players who didn't care whether or not there
was a puck on the ice. Play away from the puck became a
priority. Coaches employed systems based on restraint and
intimidation, then took great delight in bragging during
postgame press conferences about having limited the number of odd-man rushes—blithely ignoring the fact that the
spectators had paid to see the exact opposite.

In the United States, fans were starting to look elsewhere for their entertainment. The litany of failed soccer
leagues in North America is ample proof that that sport is

not yet popular on this continent, but the NHL had managed to create soccer on ice.

Beautiful goals, which had been common in the eighties, were as rare as tax reductions. For that matter, goals of any variety were rare. A score of 0–0 was far more likely than 7–5, and when a goal finally was scored, it was often a carom off a leg or a trickler emanating from a goalmouth pile-up.

Fans in every NHL city were screaming for more scoring, more excitement and more opportunities for the stars to display their skills. To accommodate them, the general managers debated a host of possibilities before finally producing some concrete proposals.

With the encouragement of Brian Burke, who was the NHL's executive vice president and director of hockey operations at that time, they decided to move the goal line out two feet from the end boards in the misguided belief that by doing so, they would somehow produce an increase in scoring. The theory was that if players were given more room to perform their magic behind the net, they would be able to set up goals from there.

Naturally, when the goal line was moved out, the blue line was also moved out. It would have made no sense to reduce the distance from the blue line to the goal line. Instead, the general managers were making each offensive zone two feet longer, so the reward, they theorized, would be more offence.

They conveniently ignored the fact that only two players in the history of the game, Mario Lemieux and Wayne Gretzky, had ever shown any great artistry behind the net, and both of them had retired (no offence to Doug Gilmour).

Granted, Lemieux would make a comeback of sorts in 2000, but the general managers weren't to know that at the time they were tinkering with the rules.

Years later, Colin Campbell, who succeeded Burke as the league's "hockey man," reflected on that rule change.

"When I first came here," he said, "they had just moved the blue lines out and the goal line out. They figured it would give people more room behind the net to be like Gretzky. But halfway through the season, Teemu Selanne and Paul Kariya said to me, 'You know what? We get ten fewer breakaways a season because that extra two feet was just what we needed.'

"Sometimes you don't think about these things when you're changing the rules."

The move further defied logic when you consider that in 1990, the nets had been moved out one foot without creating any noticeable impact upon the league's scoring statistics. Why would a further two feet make any difference?

Burke also overlooked one other crucial point. The staging area for most scoring plays is the neutral zone. By moving the nets out and shrinking the length of the neutral zone by four feet—six feet with the earlier rule change taken into consideration—the rule-makers played right into the hands of coaches who loved to inflict the neutral-zone trap upon their opponents. As the name implies, the neutral zone is the area in which the trap is sprung, and once that zone was made smaller, offensive-minded players had less room to manoeuvre and therefore less chance of avoiding the trap.

Although some NHL coaches employ variations, the basic trap is fairly simple and based upon positioning. The three defending forwards, the forecheckers, station themselves so that the puck carrier's movement towards a given side of the rink is blocked. They create a funnel that forces him inexorably towards the boards. The trap had evolved gradually over the years, and is generally agreed to have had its roots in a system that Scott Bowman put in place with the Montreal Canadiens dynasty of the seventies. But all Bowman did was require one of his wingers to drop back a bit to make sure that odd-man breaks were less frequent than had traditionally been the case.

When the Islanders took over from the Canadiens as the top team in the league, coach Al Arbour refined the concept considerably and demanded even more defensive responsibility from his forwards. Throughout the history of hockey, the duties of forwards had been almost totally offensive in nature. Now, the inexorable shift towards defence was underway.

But it was not until Roger Neilson became the head coach of the New York Rangers in the early nineties that the trap was raised to an art form. Neilson was a fine man, knowledgeable and humorous. But he probably did more to destroy the entertainment value of hockey than any man in history. To Neilson, a perfect game was one in which his team allowed no goals. Whether or not his own team scored was irrelevant.

When Neilson was between coaching jobs at one point in his career, he worked as an analyst for *Hockey Night in Canada*. Without exception, every highlight he reviewed focused on a defensive lapse that he found unacceptable.

A trapping team—and that described almost every team in the NHL by 1999—stresses defence first from its players. If they lose control of the puck while they're on the attack, they get out of the zone in a hurry. Then they position themselves so their opponents cannot move the puck up the middle of the ice.

Soon, the puck-carrying team runs out of room and has only two choices. The first is to try to move along the boards, but once the puck-carrier gets into that area and mobility is by definition reduced, the defenders collapse on him and prevent any further advance.

His other option is to dump the puck into the attacking zone. But at that point, the trapping defenders block the opponents' access, thereby giving their defencemen time to get to the puck. And the process starts again.

It makes for an awful spectacle, but it is what hockey had become in the nineties.

When the general managers voted in favour of shrinking

the neutral zone, it was their intention to increase scoring and thereby take some of the trapping out of the game. After all, if you're down by two goals, the trap does nothing to help your cause.

But the rule change affected the game in a different manner altogether. By shrinking the neutral zone, the general managers made it even more difficult to avoid the trap and much easier to inflict it.

At that same 1998 meeting, they once again debated a rule that did more than any other to detract from the spectacle that hockey can be: the old offside rule.

A few years earlier, in 1986, they had managed to breathe some fresh air into it by instituting the "tag-up" rule, and for the most part, the fans loved the variation because it kept the game flowing. It allowed play to continue even if a player had preceded the puck over the blue line. Instead of immediately whistling the play dead, linesmen were instructed to raise an arm to signal a delayed offside. The player or players who had entered the zone too quickly could come out over the blue line and "tag up," just as a baseball player must go back to the base and tag up if he wants to advance after a fly ball has been caught.

But in the mid-nineties, the general managers who had instituted the tag-up rule eliminated it, largely because some of their number felt that it inhibited the development of defencemen.

By 1998, those same GMs were starting to waver, and there was a great deal of discussion, some of it exceptionally heated, about bringing back the tag-up rule. This discussion continued with equal fervour every year until 2005, when the rule was finally reinstated. At the same time the league moved the goal line back two fet closer to its original position.

But in 1998, with the newly introduced larger offensive zones in place, the tag-up rule would have been an excellent addition. When it had been in effect before, goalies often negated its impact by pouncing on a loose puck and turning the play the other way. But with the boards two feet further back from the net, that tactic, though still possible, was a lot more difficult to implement. Furthermore, the talent level of NHL players was increasing steadily, and by 1998, every player, even if he was an enforcer, was a strong skater. The forwards were so fast that they would often have been able to clear the zone and get back to the attack before a defender had a chance to make a play.

But at that point, the return of the tag-up rule was not to be. Instead of acting, the GMs merely discussed the matter and chose to leave the basic offside rule unchanged.

They did, however, decide to experiment with a two-referee system for the 1998–99 season, with an eye to instituting an all-encompassing two-referee system down the road.

And then, almost as an afterthought, they tossed in another pair of rule changes that didn't seem to be of major concern at the time, but were to have a devastating effect upon the game.

One of them reconfigured the crease. As a result of some earlier tinkering, the old rectangular crease—eight feet wide and four feet deep—had been surrounded by a semicircle to create a crease that was twelve feet wide at its base (and therefore, for the benefit of geometrically challenged readers, extending six feet out at its deepest point).

In that 1998 meeting, the general managers decided to lop off the edges of that semicircle so that even though the crease reverted to an eight-foot width, it still had an arc beginning at the top of the old crease, four feet from the goal line. At the same time, the general managers chose to allow the video judges to decide whether a review of a goal was in order. Previously, that decision had been the purview of the referee alone.

Even though these rule changes didn't seem to be significant to the casual viewer, the rule-makers looked at them in a different light. It was their intention to impose a radical change on the game.

Together, the new rules were an indication that a severe crackdown on crease infringement was about to be unleashed on an unsuspecting league, and for that matter, an unsuspecting public.

A first glance at the rules would do nothing to further that impression. The decision to chop the side off the old semicircular crease might seem to be a move towards leniency, nothing more than an attempt to give crease-trespassing attackers more leeway. But that was not the case. It was done so that there could be no excuse for entering the crease. Players could no longer plead that with a twelve-foot crease, their transgression into the outer regions had no bearing on the play.

Now, the rule was to be clear: the crease is smaller and if you've got as much as a toenail in it, any apparent goal will be disallowed.

And just in case the referee—or referees, as the case might be—didn't witness the transgression, the video judge up in the press box was given the authority to intercede.

As the season progressed, the farcical nature of these changes became increasingly apparent, and as a result, hockey fans started to have the mindset of football fans. Just as football fans don't cheer for a touchdown until they've scanned the field for flags, so hockey fans learned to restrain their enthusiasm until it was clear that no one was putting the goal on hold pending the completion of a video review.

It was not uncommon for a goal to be disallowed because a player's skate was barely touching one edge of the crease at the instant of a scoring play being created and consummated on the other side. Even though the offending player had touched neither the puck nor the goaltender, and even though the scoring play was not affected in the least by his presence in the crease, the goal would be disallowed.

All season long, there were warnings that if this type of rule enforcement were to continue, the league would likely find itself in an extremely embarrassing situation.

Regularly on the evening sports-highlights shows, goals that had been disallowed because of an irrelevant toe in the crease were shown and ridiculed. And although fans in the rinks cheered lustily when a visiting team's goal was waved off, they booed with equal fervour when an apparent goal by the home team suffered a similar fate.

In a way, the players had brought it upon themselves, and the need for some sort of crease crackdown had been clear. As Colin Campbell said in justifying the rules, "Our goalies are getting killed."

Indeed they were. While they were watching a play in one area, they were repeatedly being bowled over by players who "accidentally" ran them from another direction. Players who made it to the NHL because of their strong skating ability somehow lost that skill when nudged by a defenceman near the crease. They'd go flying into the goalie and, on occasion, cause serious injury.

It could do irreparable damage to a team's hopes. The St. Louis Blues, with Wayne Gretzky, Craig MacTavish, Charlie Huddy and a number of other capable veterans, felt they had a good chance to win the Stanley Cup in 1996—until Toronto's Nick Kypreos crunched their goaltender, Grant Fuhr, in the opening round of the playoffs.

Fuhr injured his knee and was out until the following season. Even without him, the Blues pushed the Detroit Red Wings to the second overtime of the seventh game in the following series.

"I think it's absurd that Nick Kypreos got only a one-game suspension and Grant Fuhr's season was ended," fumed Blues coach Mike Keenan. "I find it unexplainable and inexcusable."

Because of such incidents, no one disputed the need for the league to put an end to the goalie-running that had become commonplace. But this was not the way to do it. The more sensible method—the one that the league eventually adopted—was to penalize any player who came into contact with a goalie whether a goal was scored on the play or not. Before long, players learned to respect the sanctity of the crease. Furthermore, a common-sense approach of no harm, no foul was instituted.

But with those 1998 rule changes, the NHL tried to create an increased level of respect by means of video goal reviews, and all season long the controversies raged.

By mid-March 1999, forced to respond to a dispute over a disallowed goal in a game between the Montreal Canadiens and the Toronto Maple Leafs, the NHL's director of officiating, Bryan Lewis, admitted that he and his colleagues were in the process of putting together a lengthy memo detailing the interpretation of the crease-infraction rules.

This was to be the latest inclusion in the Case Book. The NHL's official rule book is the basis for referees' decisions, but it is the Case Book that tells them how to interpret a rule.

For instance, if a player has fallen to his knees and is hit in the face by an opponent's stick, should a high-sticking penalty be assessed, even though the stick wasn't high? The rule book doesn't answer that question—and many like it— but the Case Book does. Yes, it's a two-minute penalty for high sticking, or four minutes if the infraction draws blood.

For years, only referees had Case Books, and their contents were a tightly guarded secret. But by March 1999, the video judges had a version of the Case Book as well. And theirs was getting steadily thicker. A stream of memos full of crease-rule interpretations had been sent to them throughout the season, and each one had to be retained, added to its predecessors and memorized for future use.

The memo to which Lewis referred on this occasion was to form the latest addition and was no fewer than three pages long. It covered, Lewis said, "all the situations that could or should or may possibly happen."

In reference to the disallowed goal in the Montreal-Toronto game, Lewis said that the video goal judge had to ask himself only one question: "Where was the player when the puck entered the crease?"

Lewis then went on to explain the general responsibilities of the goal judge in cases of disputed goals.

"In our language, there's no debate in this," he said. "What we say to our video goal judge is, 'Bring the tape up and stop it with the puck on the crease line. Where is the foot? He's in the crease?' Therefore we don't care what happens after that. It's not going to be a goal."

If only it were that simple.

Such was the climate in the NHL as the 1999 regular season wound down: the league was almost totally devoid of scoring; goals of beauty were far outnumbered by goals disallowed by video reviews; coaches concerned themselves only with defence on the premise that the offence would take care of itself; and the trap had been developed to such a degree of sophistication that teams regularly got fewer shots in a period than the Edmonton Oilers of a decade earlier had routinely achieved on a single power play.

As if that weren't bad enough, once the playoffs started, the coaches invariably decided to crank up the defensive aspects of their game yet another notch. No coach ever went into the playoffs saying, "We've really got to get our offence in gear." It was always, "At this time of year, a mistake can kill you. We've got to redouble our efforts defensively."

This virtual eradication of offence was not an overnight trend. For the first few years after becoming commissioner on February 1, 1993, Gary Bettman insisted that he was dedicated to increasing the scoring throughout the league. When it didn't happen, he started to resort to statistics. He had the numbers to show that scoring wasn't dropping as fast as it once had. (Of course it wasn't. The closer a temperature gets to absolute zero, the more slowly it gets there). He then tried the old diversion tactic, insisting that scoring didn't matter. What was important, he said, was the fact that the league had so many close games. Again, that was to be expected. If a game had only three goals, it wasn't going to be a blowout, was it?

The offensive slide continued relentlessly to the point that, in the three seasons immediately prior to the 2004 owners' lockout, the once-common 50-goal plateau was reached only twice by an NHL player, and in two of those years, not a single player managed to muster 100 points. In 2003–04, no player scored more than 41 goals. By then, even Bettman had stopped trying to defend the predominance of defence in his league. Instead, he tried to convince everyone that the game was still exciting—a view that apparently was not shared by the American populace. TV ratings in the United States dropped steadily and precipitously in those years, a decline that started to become evident in 1999 when two of the least entertaining teams in the NHL hooked up in what should have been the league's annual showcase.

It was the Dallas Stars against the Buffalo Sabres, the former a defensively obsessed team that played its home games on what was probably the worst ice in the NHL. Even if coach Ken Hitchcock had wanted his players to open it up—which he didn't—it would have been all but impossible on that chipped, rutted slush.

Temperatures in Dallas during the playoffs were often in excess of 100° Fahrenheit, and even the Dallas players couldn't excuse the ice conditions.

"Sickening, isn't it?" Mike Modano asked rhetorically when I mentioned the matter to him during the Eastern Conference finals.

The Sabres, meanwhile, were also a defensively obsessed team. But at least Dallas had a couple of identifiable offensive stars.

The Sabres didn't. They relied on their goaltender, Dominik Hasek, to keep them in games. In the first playoff round that year, for instance, they swept the Ottawa Senators. Even though one of the games went well into the second overtime, Hasek allowed a total of six goals in the entire series.

At the same time, as a further indication of the scoring malaise that had blanketed the league like a Bay of Fundy fog, the Toronto Maple Leafs and Philadelphia Flyers were dragging themselves through the lowest-scoring six-game playoff series in the eighty-two-year history of the NHL. The Leafs scored nine goals, yet won the series 4–2.

By comparison, in a six-game series between the Oilers and Chicago Blackhawks in 1985, the two teams combined to produce sixty-nine goals.

Meanwhile, in a blow to fans who fervently hoped for the return of some sort of offensive orientation to hockey, the Stars were getting out of the first round by breezing past the Edmonton Oilers in four games. The Oilers, the only team that had never resorted to building its defence around the trap, managed to score only six goals in four games, nowhere near enough to defeat the skill-killing Stars.

Having had plenty of time to rest before the next round, the Stars were able to dispose of the St. Louis Blues in six games, while in the East, the Sabres just as quickly got past the Boston Bruins.

It was the next round that raised a few eyebrows. The Sabres were not expected to defeat the Maple Leafs, who had looked powerful in defeating the Pittsburgh Penguins. But all of a sudden, the Toronto defensive system, which had been so sound in the opening rounds, fell apart. Buffalo scored twenty-one goals in the five games they needed to eliminate the Leafs—a whopping total for the hockey of that era.

The Stars, on the other hand, were in a battle against the Colorado Avalanche—a perennial powerhouse, but occasionally unpredictable.

The odds-on favourites to win the Cup that year had been the Detroit Red Wings, the two-time defending champions. The Wings swept the Anaheim Mighty Ducks and handily disposed of the Avalanche in the first two games, thereby running their playoff winning streak to eleven games over two seasons. The question then being asked in hockey circles was not whether the Wings would win the Cup, but whether they'd do it in sixteen straight.

As it happened, they never won another game. The

Avalanche turned its game around, looked extremely impressive in taking the next four in a row from Detroit and moved on to face the Stars.

As usual, disallowed goals and video reviews were a part of almost every game, but they had become so commonplace by that time that they were hardly noticed.

Still, the series was one of the most tedious in recent history. Colorado had some genuine offensive stars in Joe Sakic, Peter Forsberg, Milan Hedjuk, Sandis Ozolinsh and others, but the Stars slowed the games to a crawl.

In Dallas, the ice helped. In the opening game, before he knew better, Sakic made a nifty one-on-one move that would have hit all the highlight reels had it worked. It was a little pirouette that saw Sakic go one way and the Dallas defender go another.

The puck, however, went nowhere. It was left behind in the Reunion Arena slush.

"I just wanted to stop it and bring it back and shoot it," explained Sakic. "The puck just kind of stopped on me. I don't really know what happened."

Actually, he *did* know what happened. But the NHL had sent out an edict to the players telling them not to complain about the ice.

"The puck," Sakic said, "was bouncing a little bit but . . . Well, that's all I can really say."

The ice in Dallas was so bad that it was almost impossible to make two consecutive decent passes. So the Stars had long ago given up trying to bother.

Who could blame them? Why not use a system that relies on picking up errant passes in the neutral zone— i.e., the trap—when other teams tried to defy the odds? Why not dump the puck into the offensive zone at every opportunity rather than make a pass, which is, by definition, a low-percentage play?

Hitchcock was so adamant that this tactic had to be used religiously that he and Brett Hull argued about it on a regular basis.

Only Wayne Gretzky had scored more goals in a season than the eighty-six Hull notched in 1990–91, but Hitchcock demanded that Hull put defence first. One morning in practice, when the players were taking shots, Hull put puck after puck into the seats. Hitchcock ignored him.

Then they started two-on-one breaks. Hull dumped the puck into the corner. Hitchcock ignored him. The next time around, Hull did it again. Hitchcock blew his whistle furiously and charged at Hull, demanding to know what he thought he was doing.

"Dumping it into the corner," snapped Hull. "That's all you ever want us to do. I'm just doing what you want."

"Get off the ice," screamed Hitchcock.

Hull shrugged and left. He didn't want to be out there practising defensive hockey anyway.

Against the Stars, the Avalanche had trouble adapting to the slow, grinding style. But the two teams split the first two in Dallas (the second one seeing a disallowed goal because Pat Verbeek, trying to get out of the way, momentarily put his foot in the crease) and then the next two in Denver.

Then came the game everyone had been anticipating: a poor performance by Stars goalie Ed Belfour, who held the dubious distinction of being the goalie who had played the most playoff games in NHL history without winning a Stanley Cup.

Belfour was known for his mercurial temperament and for brooding about bad goals to the point that he would let in a few more. Team trainers who have had the responsibility of catering to his whims over the years say that it is a seemingly endless task. He is fussy about his equipment to the point of paranoia and, no matter what concessions are made, never seems to be satisfied.

He can be brilliant, but he can also be very poor, and on this occasion, the Stars lost 7–5 and needed to win the next two to win the series.

So they did what they do best. They shut down the

powerful Avalanche, allowing only one goal in each game, and they advanced to the final.

Although neither game was thrilling, to put it mildly, the second was downright excruciating. A game seven should be exciting, but the only excitement in this case was provided by the situation, not by the spectacle.

The Stars got a fortuitous goal early in the game and then proceeded to bleed the game of any entertainment value it might have possessed. They froze the puck against the boards. They flipped it over the glass. Belfour held it at every opportunity. They set up their neutral-zone trap, broke up plays and dumped the puck. Then they did it again.

"That's their style of play," said Avalanche coach Bob Hartley afterwards. "As soon as they get a lead, they really collapse well in the neutral zone, and that's where their experience and their size come to be a positive factor."

"They're tough to play when they get a lead," said Sakic. "They play a checking, checking game. Against them, you can't open up."

Said Colorado forward Claude Lemieux, "They're a club that likes to sit and wait. The puck bounced their way in the first period; then they came out in the second period really dedicated to sitting on that lead."

Once again, the Stars had won on defence. They had allowed sixteen goals, but seven of them had come on Belfour's bad night. Other than that, their goals-against average had been 1.50.

It was clear therefore that the 1999 Stanley Cup final was not going to be a freewheeling affair. The Stars and Sabres were two of the most accomplished trap teams in hockey, and on their priority lists, any form of offence was well down—after about ten forms of defence.

Neither team was likely to take a chance, and neither was likely to make a dazzling play. This was to be a dump-and-chase final, and the team that emerged victorious would be the one that produced the most unified effort.

"Who cares?" asked Verbeek when the observation was put to him. "Who cares what they say? We're just happy to be here."

The fans, apparently, didn't enter into either team's priorities.

As for the type of game that could be expected, Verbeek was prophetic. The result, he said, would be determined on the edge of the crease.

"For us, the key is the second and third shots and getting to the net," he said. "Our team is not built on shooting and scoring off the first shot. Look at the last series. We scored on our second and third shots. We get rebounds. That's how we get our goals."

As long as Belfour continued to play as well as Hasek, which had been the case so far, the Sabres and Stars were almost mirror images of each other. This was not a final that would conform to any of the standard confrontations—age against youth, offence against goaltending, rich against poor. It was simply a contest of nuances of the same defensively oriented game. There would be almost no centre-ice play at all. The only team in the league more adept than the Stars at blocking the middle was the Sabres.

Six years later, the Stars' captain and premier checker, Guy Carbonneau, reflected on that series. And naturally, he spoke only of the defence.

"We knew that we could beat Buffalo," he said, "and we had to be aggressive but smart.

"Hitch was always promoting a defensive system, but he always wanted to have pressure from the back of the puck carrier as well.

"I wouldn't say we were like Tampa in 2004 where they had two or three guys forcing and the defenceman pinching, but we always tried to put pressure on with at least one guy.

"If that didn't work, you'd try something else and we'd go with two guys. It all depends on what makes you feel comfortable and who you're playing against."

"I don't think that they're a team built on a goaltender," said Hitchcock of his upcoming foes. "They're a team that's built on a really sound combination of team play.

"I think that for us, the strength obviously starts in goal, but it also filters right through the middle of the ice. We said after the last time we played in Buffalo in the regular season, that was the strongest group of centre-ice men that we had played against all year. We never had the puck much and it was a very difficult game for us to have played in."

Both Hitchcock and Sabres coach Lindy Ruff were integral parts of their team's success. Each was making his first trip to the Stanley Cup final and each demanded strict attention to detail. Each liked to think he could make the difference in a game—which was probably true—and each saw himself as an innovator. It came as no surprise, therefore, that these two matched wits all through the opening game.

Hitchcock, for instance, had spent two days dropping broad hints that Derek Plante would be in his opening-night lineup. It made sense. The Stars had picked him up from the Sabres at the trading deadline and his knowledge of his former teammates could be useful.

When the game started, Plante was nowhere to be seen. But Jonathan Sim, who had played only one game in the previous series against Colorado, was dressed.

Hitchcock had also done a fair degree of bragging about the fact that the Stars were an unrepentant and unrelenting four-line team. "Our system is based on pressure and position," he had said on a number of occasions. "It's based on twelve forwards and six defencemen. We can't play this way with three lines. We need four lines."

So he started his third line. Then came the first line. Then the second. Then the first again. Then the second once more. All the while, the crucial fourth line warmed the bench.

Ruff, meanwhile, was pulling a few little tricks of his own. He repeatedly tried to get away with a late line change, especially as the game progressed and the Sabres started taking a string of penalties. He wanted to give his penalty killers a rest without using a timeout, and the tactic did provide a little relief.

Realizing that the ice was awful and could not be relied upon to react properly, Ruff occasionally had his centres intentionally lose a face-off in the Dallas end. The Sabres were such a good forechecking team that they didn't mind chasing the puck into the corner to try to get possession, rather than hope it would slide evenly back to the point from a face-off.

And so it went. The coaches were doing their best and had provided decent game plans, but on that ice, it sometimes looked more like short-track speed skating than hockey, as normally sure-footed players suddenly had their feet fly out from underneath them. If another player was in range, he too would be taken out in a domino effect.

Eventually, the Sabres won in overtime on Jason Woolley's shot from the point, but once again, there was a controversy over a disallowed goal.

"The play that bothered me the most," said Ruff, "was the goal that wasn't called." The Sabres appeared to have scored, but Vaclav Varada had bumped Belfour in the crease and the goal was waved off.

Before the next game, Bettman dropped into town for his annual Stanley Cup state-of-the-game press conference.

The matter of the crease rule came up, and Bettman's observations proved to be just as prophetic as those made by Verbeek a couple of days earlier. He admitted first of all that the much-maligned crease rule was in the process of being reconsidered. The rule was being properly applied, he insisted, but there was a question as to its usefulness.

Bettman said that he personally was leaning towards a radical change in the rule for two reasons. First, he felt that "it is taking too much of the energy and excitement out of the building. When a goal is scored, people are worried about whether or not they can cheer."

Secondly, he said, "We have been taking some very skil-
ful plays that have resulted in goals and disallowed them
because of things that had nothing to do with the play."
Still, nothing could be done until after the season.

In the series opener, the Stars had outplayed the Sabres
but lost. Hitchcock knew the reason. Hasek, as was so
often the case, had been brilliant.

Prior to the first game, Hitchcock made his backup
goaltender, Roman Turek, lie on his side in the crease with
his pads stacked, just the way Hasek did. Then the Dallas
players tried to shoot the puck over his body and into the
net. The idea was that the Stars would get used to Hasek's
tactics and therefore might have some success. They didn't
have enough.

So, for game two, Hasek was clearly the Stars' target.
The theory was that they would be subtle about it. There is
no more certain way to earn a penalty or to arouse the
opponents' ire than to run a goaltender.

But Hasek liked to roam and he didn't like to be
touched. The Stars planned to jostle him at every opportunity—not to hurt him, but to aggravate him, which was
easily done. They also intended to employ the timeworn
tactic of standing near the crease and allowing themselves
to be pushed into Hasek.

Apparently, not all of the message got through. Brian
Skrudland checked Hasek from behind in the corner and
got penalized for it. But the purpose had been served:
Hasek was enraged.

Not long afterwards, when Joe Nieuwendyk was heading to the net and got bumped, he managed to go hard into
Hasek, knocking him back into his goal.

The Sabres weren't too happy about that, either. But
when Modano tripped Hasek at the end of the first
period, the Sabres fought back, and a few skirmishes
broke out, with Nieuwendyk and Brian Holzinger coming to blows—the first fight in a Stanley Cup final in
three years.

"Modano slew-footed him," complained Ruff afterwards. "You are not even allowed to do that to a defenceman. It was definitely a cheap shot by Modano."

It was also a 4–2 win for the Stars—not an inordinately high score, but nevertheless the highest the fans were to see in the finals that year.

By this time, it was mid-June, and even though the series moved to Buffalo, the outside temperatures were so high that the ice wasn't much better than it had been in Dallas.

The devotion to defence on the part of both teams, coupled with sticky ice, led to predictable results: a 2–1 victory for each team, both of which produced astonishingly high readings on the boredom meter.

Instead of improving as it went on, this series was getting worse. It was velodrome hockey, the centre of the surface having been rendered a vast wasteland, devoid of activity. Players increasingly ignored the puck to bang each other into the boards.

Potential scoring chances were not pursued for fear that they might lead to a turnover. If there was the slightest doubt about the success of a clearing attempt, the puck was simply launched into the seats. Similarly, the goalies were skating yards to freeze the puck, even when no opponent was within shouting range.

The series had ground its way to the halfway mark and could hardly have been more evenly matched. The Stars were exhibiting a distinct advantage in time of possession, much of it attained in the Buffalo end. But they were facing the one situation they had hoped to avoid. They needed a contribution from the aspect of the game that they had so studiously ignored—offence.

The puck was bouncing erratically in both arenas; Hull and Benoit Hogue, two of Dallas's better offensive players, were hurt; and Hasek was giving them fits.

Without his linemate Hull, Modano was not as effective, so Ruff reassigned his top defensive line of Varada, Michael Peca and Dixon Ward to Nieuwendyk's line.

Nieuwendyk had scored both goals in the 2–1 Dallas victory. In the next game, with Peca on his tail, his line didn't get a sniff.

The Stars were in a singularly unpleasant position. An offensive team can often ratchet up its defensive game with relative ease. But when a defensive-minded team is asked to produce more scoring, it tends to be impossible.

The Stars found the perfect solution: shut out the opposition. That way you don't need much scoring—which was just as well, because they didn't get it. Hull and Hogue were back in the lineup, but even that didn't help.

The first period featured no scoring, but early in the second, Buffalo's Curtis Brown was sent off for interference—no easy feat considering the way these games were being played.

The penalty came at a crucial time. Because the ice had just been resurfaced, it was almost playable, and the Stars made the most of it. Modano set up Darryl Sydor for the winner.

There were more than thirty-seven minutes left to play, but it was immediately clear that the Stars looked upon that one goal as sufficient. And they were right. They shut down the Sabres for the rest of the night and added an insurance goal late in the third. Now they were heading back to Buffalo, one win away from the Cup.

It was June 19, far too late in the year to either produce or maintain good ice, so when the Stars opened a 1–0 lead only 8:09 into the game, they did what they had done in the previous game: they sat on the lead.

In fact, they sat on it a bit too comfortably. Again and again, Belfour had to make some fine saves as the Stars opted for the curious tactic of collapsing into their own end and icing the puck whenever they had a chance.

The lead held throughout the first period and for most of the second. But the problem with playing that type of game is that it takes only one bad bounce to negate all the hard work. As the second period wound down, Buffalo's

Stu Barnes took a shot that, as usual, a Dallas defenceman tried to block. The defenceman in this case was Sydor, and the puck bounced off his body and past Belfour, tying the score.

The game dragged on through the third period.

Through the first overtime.

Through the second overtime.

It was far from exciting hockey. In fact, it was downright tedious. In the press box, the journalists were amusing themselves by checking off the list of overtime games that the league public-relations staff had distributed. The game became the sixth-longest in NHL playoff history. Then the fifth-longest. Then the fourth. Then the third. Then the second.

Wait a minute! Is that a genuine scoring chance down there?

Modano had taken a shot on Hasek, and Hull had moved in for the rebound. He got a shot away, but Hasek blocked that one as well. But when the rebound went into Hull's skates, he kicked the puck back onto his stick and put it into the net.

The red light went on. The Stars poured off the bench and mobbed Hull. The dejected Sabres headed for centre ice to form a line for the traditional post-series handshakes. The Zamboni gate opened and out came the table with the Stanley Cup for the presentation.

At 14:51 of the third overtime, early in the morning of June 20, the Dallas Stars had won the Stanley Cup. Bettman came out to present the Cup to Carbonneau, and the Conn Smythe Trophy (for the most valuable player in the playoffs) to Nieuwendyk.

The Stars were experiencing the euphoria that hockey players derive from winning the Cup. Earlier in the series, Dallas forward Dave Reid explained that he had been close to touching the Stanley Cup when he saw it on display in the Hall of Fame, but decided not to do so.

"It's not a big deal to go up and touch it," he said. "Raising it over your head is a different matter."

As the Stars took turns raising the Cup over their heads, the journalists left their press-box seats and started to head for the elevator to go downstairs. But on the way, some of them stopped at TV monitors to watch replays of the goal. Wait a minute! Isn't Hull's foot in the crease?

They recalled Bryan Lewis's explanation way back in March: "Bring the tape up and stop it with the puck on the crease line. Where is the foot? He's in the crease? Therefore we don't care what happens after that. It's not going to be a goal."

Most people in the building were oblivious to this. The Stars were still celebrating on the ice, mingling out there with the photographers, cameramen, TV interviewers, security people and a few NHL personnel. The Sabres had left the ice. Most of the Buffalo fans had left the building.

But Ruff, aware of the situation, had gone up to Bettman and protested that the goal should be reviewed. Bettman ignored him. When Ruff got to the Buffalo room, he was distraught. "This is a nightmare," he was saying. "All I wanted was a review. Everybody saw it."

The Stars finally left the ice and trooped into their dressing room, cheering and whooping. They popped the champagne corks, sprayed the stuff all over each other and slapped each other on the back. They were blissfully unaware of what was going on down the hall.

"I don't think anybody thought about it," said Carbonneau years later. "We won. We scored the goal, jumped on the ice and celebrated and went back in the room.

"Maybe, oh, I don't know, I'd have to say almost an hour after we scored the goal, somebody came in the room and started what we thought was a rumour at the time that Lindy Ruff was still in his room and was upset at the NHL.

"That's how we found out."

Doug Armstrong, then assistant to Dallas general manager Bob Gainey and later his successor, found out sooner.

"It was probably about fifteen minutes afterwards," he said. "You celebrate, then you have to walk down the stairs, but by that time there was a lot of commotion, and I didn't think they were going to go back on it."

"The one thing I recall from that," he said in 2005, "is that the day before, we were in a GMs meeting, and I went because assistant GMs were allowed to be there.

"We went through the whole thing, and they said if a player controls the puck in the crease with his foot in the crease, it's a good goal.

"So what defines 'control?' When Hull kicked it from his skate to his stick, that was control. On our side, that wasn't that big of an issue. But I remember we went through the whole thing and it was clear as day that if you have control, you're allowed to have a foot in the crease, even if the puck is outside the crease.

"Hull kicked it from his skate to his stick. He had control."

Ruff had a totally different interpretation of the sequence, and at the post-game press conference, instead of the usual rehash of the series, the disputed goal dominated the proceedings.

"I wanted Bettman to answer the question," Ruff said. "Why is that not reviewed? And really, he just turned his back on me. He almost looked to me like he knew this might be a tainted goal and there was no answer for it.

"I just wanted an explanation. Just tell me: 'Listen, it is a good goal,' or 'It is not a good goal.' There was no answer. No review. There was no answer."

Instead, Bettman threw Lewis to the journalistic wolves and let him hold a hastily arranged press conference.

"The rule was absolutely, correctly applied," Bettman said later. "Everyone understands it was the right call."

Well, not everyone. Most of the Sabres were operating under the belief that the goal had not been reviewed. "I don't understand what the video judge is doing," fumed Hasek. "Maybe he was in the bathroom. Maybe he was sleeping. Maybe he doesn't know the rule."

Not so, said Lewis, who started off by insisting that every goal scored that year had been reviewed and this one was no exception. Then he moved on to the infamous crease rule itself.

"A couple of things I'd like to point out in terms of rules," he said. "The debate would be this: Are there reasons that a guy can have his foot in the crease and score a goal? Absolutely."

Yes, but according to what Lewis himself had said in March, not if the foot went in before the puck.

But Lewis moved on to the specific case of Hull's goal. "Having looked at it," he said, "the determination by those in the goal judges' location upstairs, including myself, was in fact that Hull played the puck. Hull had possession and control of the puck. The rebound off the goalie does not change anything. It is his puck then to shoot and score, albeit a foot may or may not be in the crease."

Lewis went on to say that this was not a new interpretation. "The terminology 'possession and control' has always been there," he said.

It may have always been somewhere—in the Case Book, for instance—but it wasn't in the rule book. Here's the relevant Rule 78 (b) from the official NHL rule book of 1998–99:

> *Unless the puck is in the goal crease area, a player of the attacking side may not enter nor stand in the goal crease. If a player has entered the crease prior to the puck, and subsequently the puck should enter the net while such conditions prevail, the apparent goal shall not be allowed.*

That seemed pretty clear. Hull's goal should have been disallowed.

It was Lewis's contention, however, that his March memo to the league's video judges had discussed plays of this nature. The interpretation was that when Hull made the first shot, he was in control of the puck. Sounds reasonable so far.

Hasek blocked it with his glove, but he didn't control it. The puck went back into Hull's skates where he kicked it to his stick, then shot it. Therefore, because Hasek had never had control, Hull was deemed to have control throughout. And a player who is in control of the puck has the right to enter the crease.

"A puck that rebounds off the goalie, the goalpost or an opposing player, is not deemed to be a change of possession," Lewis said. "And therefore, Hull would be deemed to be in possession or control of the puck, allowed to shoot and score a goal, even though the one foot would be in the crease in advance of the puck."

This is the explanation Lewis had passed along to Ruff, but Ruff was having none of it. He said that Lewis had told him that Hull "had it under control in the crease and he stickhandled to his forehand and shot it in."

Ruff disagreed. "Well, that wasn't the case," he insisted. "It went off Dom's glove, [Brian] Holzinger's skate and went outside the crease. His foot is in the crease when he scored the goal."

While that may be true, it still doesn't change Lewis's interpretation. Holzinger didn't have possession any more than Hasek did, so if the ruling was "control and possession," then the goal would stand.

But many people on both sides of the argument felt—and still feel to this day—that even if Lewis and the others in the booth had ruled against the goal, the celebration had gone so far that it would simply have been too embarrassing to call it back.

The result would be shown on blooper reels for years to come, much like the famous incident when the Stanford University band poured onto the field with a football game still in progress.

"That was their worst nightmare right there," said Ruff. "They knew that they ran the risk of an overtime goal determining a series. Stanley Cup pandemonium sets in and they can't go back to review it. That is my opinion. They just can't take it back."

"It was a gutless move," said Sabres forward Joe Juneau. "If we had scored a goal like that, it would have been called back. Because it was a goal that gave them the Stanley Cup, everybody jumped on the ice and they were afraid to make the call."

Lewis denied that this was the case and was asked directly if he would have stopped the celebration if he believed the goal should not have been allowed.

"Absolutely," he said, going on to point out there had been "many, many occasions when the players are celebrating or cheering and we just say, 'Whoa, there! It is not a goal. It doesn't count.'"

The play was being reviewed while the on-ice jubilation continued, said Lewis. "If you notice—and I can't tell you how long it took—the officials stood at the penalty bench. They don't leave that area until they have been given a signal by us."

It should have been a fairy-tale ending. Hull had suffered a torn medial collateral ligament in game three of the final and had missed the rest of that game and all of game four. But, heavily bandaged and having taken a series of pain-killing injections, he played in game five and scored the Stanley Cup winner in triple overtime of game six.

It is the stuff of which hockey lore is made, almost akin to Bobby Baun scoring a playoff winner on a broken leg.

Instead, the focus was on the crease rule and its interpretations. And it was a total embarrassment to the league.

But the era of the insidious crease rule and the invasive video judges ended that night in Buffalo. A few days later, Bettman announced that the league would no longer use video replays to routinely determine the validity of goals.

As *The National Hockey League Official Guide and Record Book* noted the revision in its point-form explanation of rule changes implemented for the 1999–2000 season:

> *Crease rule revised to implement a "no harm, no foul,*
> *no video review" standard. An attacking player's*
> *position, whether inside or outside the crease, does not,*
> *in itself, determine whether a goal should be allowed or*
> *disallowed. The on-ice judgment of the referee(s)—*
> *instead of video review—will determine if a goal is*
> *"good" or not.*

The NHL's video era was finished. And unlamented. Perhaps there was a lesson to be learned there; perhaps it isn't true that all uses of technology enhance the game. Or, to put it more broadly, not all the changes that had come into the game were for the better.

A few years later, when the general managers frantically tried to get some scoring back into the game, they started by eliminating some of the changes that had occurred over the years—forcing the goalies to revert to more traditional, less cumbersome equipment, for instance, and bringing back the tag-up rule.

Perhaps the Stars would have won the 1999 Stanley Cup anyway, even if Hull's goal had been disallowed. They were certainly outplaying the Sabres. But stranger turnarounds have happened in sport.

In Dallas, Hull's goal is seen as a Stanley Cup winner. In Buffalo, that goal is regarded as tainted, and Sabres fans still believe that their Cup dream was stolen from them that night.

Juneau expressed the view that is the overwhelming consensus in the Buffalo area.

"Everybody is going to remember this as the Stanley Cup that was never won. It was given away. The goal was not a legal goal. It's cheating, you know? It's not a loss. The game is not over. It's just not. They just decided to end it."

THE GOAL: FEBRUARY 24, 2002.

Olympic gold-medal game.
Scored by Jarome Iginla (assisted by Steve Yzerman
and Joe Sakic) at 16:01 of the third period.
Canada 5, United States 2.

IF YOU WATCHED THE OPENING CEREMONIES OF THE 2002 WINTER Olympics in Salt Lake City, Utah, you might have got the impression that Canada hadn't bothered to enter a men's hockey team.

The Canadian delegation that marched proudly into the stadium was one of the largest in the parade, with plenty of athletes accompanied by office managers, photographers, media attachés, administrative agents, therapists, editors and so on. But there wasn't a single representative of the men's hockey team. Not one.

The players couldn't be there. Their schedule was so tight that they were still honouring their National Hockey League commitments. The only members of the team who were on site were two of the assistant coaches, Ken Hitchcock and Wayne Fleming. They had entered the opening ceremonies lottery to try to earn the right to march with the others, but neither of their tickets had been drawn.

The COA—which officially stands for Canadian Olympic Association, but according to media lore is actually short for Can't Organize Anything—had found itself with fifty-five extra spots in the opening ceremonies parade because a number of athletes had yet to arrive. So the association staged a lottery to find support staffers to fill those spots, and Fleming and Hitchcock missed out.

To the casual observer, logic would dictate that as coaches, they should have automatically had spots ahead of the bureaucrats. But as elite Canadian athletes such as Ken Read, Marnie McBean, Donovan Bailey and others had pointed out over the years, logic and the COA do not have a long and happy history of coexistence.

About five minutes before the entourage was due to enter the stadium, someone in the COA recognized the inherent stupidity of the situation and offered Hitchcock a spot. He politely declined. He was gracious enough to say afterwards that it didn't matter that he was excluded, but others on the staff of the Canadian Hockey Association saw it as a calculated insult, a direct snub of the men's hockey team because it was perceived as "professional" while the COA likes to think of itself as being devoted to what passes for Olympic amateurism.

"It's typical," growled one member of the Canadian Hockey group. "They use us for their fund-raising and to build support for the Olympics because they know men's hockey is what people care about in our country. But when it comes to doing something for us, they deliver a slap in the face."

And so Canada's 2002 Olympic hockey quest was off to an inauspicious beginning. Whatever the team might accomplish was to be almost totally of its own doing, a point executive director Wayne Gretzky was to make forcefully within the next few days.

First, the NHL executives had done next to nothing to help the players. They compressed the league schedule—which put a greater burden on elite players—and then opened a window so narrow that some players couldn't get to Salt Lake City in time for their one-and-only pre-Olympic practice unless they took charter flights.

Then, the COA, which was supposed to be the umbrella body representing *all* Canadian athletes, had made clear its resentment of its highest-profile team. And some of the more churlish members of the Canadian media had already started sniping, contending publicly that the team had cheated by staging a camp back in September.

But in typical fashion, the people who should have been most affected by this, the players themselves, shrugged it off. They had signed on for this challenge five months earlier and they were there to make amends for the 1998 embarrassment in Nagano, not to battle bureaucrats, to prove a point to the NHL or to justify their pre-tournament program to a segment of the media.

After all, the September camp made perfect sense. Gretzky had decided that because of the tight ten-day Olympic window—with the first game scheduled for the day after the players arrived in Salt Lake City—the team needed a training camp of some sort.

There had been proposals that the NHL's annual All-Star break might be used. Rather than take part in a meaningless, non-contact twenty-goal travesty, the national teams of the major countries could stage exhibition games.

But NHL commissioner Gary Bettman refused to depart from the traditional format, and he further refused to widen the Olympic window to accommodate Gretzky's requests for practice time.

Therefore, Gretzky proposed an August camp. But some players didn't want to meet in August. The concept of the camp was fine, they said, but not the date. If it were held right before the NHL teams opened their own camps, there would be no problem.

As one of the players explained, "At that stage of the summer, we'd be going full speed if we were back home. We'd be skating with a group of guys and getting into the final stages of preparation for training camp. We're skating every day anyway, so why not do it with the best players in the world?"

So they gathered in Calgary for four days of hockey-related events, combined with the usual bonding activities like golfing and team dinners.

It was staged as late in the summer as possible. The day after it ended, the members of the Colorado Avalanche headed for Sweden, where they were to open the team's training camp that year.

Team Canada coach Pat Quinn stressed that it was primarily an orientation camp, not a training camp. There were scrimmages, but bodychecking wasn't allowed, paving the way for the usual fantastic Team Canada spectacle as these superb players flew unhindered up and down an international-sized rink using Olympic rules, which meant the red line was not a factor in offside calls.

Technically, the Olympic teams weren't supposed to be staging summer selection camps. The European teams got around the prohibition by staging "charity games" which just happened to feature players who were being considered for Olympic participation. The Canadians simply held a camp and agreed that it would not be a tryout camp—that no one would be excluded from the team on the basis of his performance.

It was just as well that they did; even though they weren't dropping anyone from consideration, they were free to expand their list of prospective players, and without that camp, it is almost certain that they would not have had the services of Jarome Iginla, who became one of the most important cogs in the Olympic victory.

Iginla hadn't been one of the forty players invited to the evaluation camp, and had he lived anywhere in eastern Canada, he might never have had anything to do with the Olympic team.

But luckily for him, and luckily for Canadian hockey fans, Simon Gagne of the Philadelphia Flyers reported to Calgary nursing a minor and previously unreported injury. It was enough to keep him off the ice, and in order to balance the squads, a replacement forward was needed. So on the evening of the first day of camp, Gretzky called Iginla, who lived nearby in Edmonton.

"I'd watched the first day of camp on TV," Iginla recalled in 2005, "and I'd seen the highlights on all the sports channels. I went out to dinner with my brothers and my dad. My wife—my fiancée at the time—called me and she said, 'Wayne Gretzky just called and he'd like you to come down to camp.'

"I said to her, 'Ha, ha. Are you sure it was Wayne Gretzky? I can just see some guys playing a prank on me.' I said, 'What are the chances?'

"I told her there were some guys who thought it would be a pretty good joke to have me go in there with my equipment bag and everything."

Iginla was laughing as he considered what would happen next. "They ask me what am I doing there? 'Oh, I want to try out, coach.'"

Iginla was even too leery to call the number Gretzky had left, thinking that it could also be a part of the set-up— that a number of his buddies would be waiting by a speaker phone for him to call it. But he had a number for Kevin Lowe, Team Canada's assistant executive director, and he called it. Sure enough, the Team Canada officials wanted him in camp if he could make it.

Iginla made it clear that he'd be only too delighted to get up at the crack of dawn the next morning and drive to Calgary.

Had he not done so, he almost certainly would have been left off the Olympic team. Every player eventually selected for Team Canada 2002 attended that Calgary camp, even though some of them were hurt at the time and could not scrimmage. If you wanted to be a part of the team, you had to participate in as many functions as you could, even if you couldn't play.

That "non-selection" camp was only an opening step towards building a team, but to Gretzky and his support staff, it was a giant step. There was not a single participant who would not have acquitted himself well wearing a Canadian sweater. Every one was a superb player.

Therefore, when the time came to select Team Canada 2002, the organizers had to base their decisions on the most minute differences between players. Was one player just a little bit more outgoing and friendly than another? Was one forward just the tiniest fraction of a second faster than another? Was one defenceman just an ounce more resolute than another?

To the average fan, the differences were imperceptible. But to Gretzky, Lowe, director of player personnel Steve Tambellini and the others who would make the final selection, those distinctions were at least identifiable, if not always clearly evident. The merits or drawbacks of each player, however minuscule, were duly noted and filed away in the minds of the selectors for future reference.

It is never easy to select a team to represent a country that is as full of experts as Canada, and the task was no easier this time, even though it was Gretzky who was in charge.

One Toronto radio analyst announced that, since Patrick Roy had refused to be the goaltender this time around, Canada could not possibly win. The rest of the selections didn't matter. There were those who said Eric Lindros should not be on the team, and others who insisted Canada couldn't win without him. Some "experts" argued that Mario Lemieux was the key to success. Others said that because of Lemieux's recurring injuries and his long absence from the game, he wouldn't be effective in the Olympics.

And so it went.

By the end of November, the brain trust had narrowed their list to thirty potential players. Eight had already been selected in March—even though the Games were nearly a year away—in accordance with a typically bizarre Olympic rule.

A few others were certain selections (Al MacInnis, for example, had been left off the March list only because his eyesight had been in jeopardy at the time). But seven men still on Gretzky's list of candidates needed to be excluded to meet the Olympic requirements of a twenty-three-man roster.

With only one week to go before the December 15 deadline, Gretzky and his staff were no closer than they had been at the end of November. If anything, they were farther away. Ryan Smyth was out of action with a broken ankle. He was due to resume skating, but would he be ready for the Olympic opener on February 15? And even if he were, would he be in game shape? It was almost certain that Lemieux would play only sporadically, if at all, before the Olympics. Could he be counted upon to be healthy in time? If not, how would his absence affect the selection of the other forwards? Derek Morris was a candidate for a spot on defence, but he injured his wrist early in December. Even though it was expected to be healed in time for Salt Lake City, wrist injuries, like concussions, are notorious for lingering longer than expected.

It was one thing to take a chance on Lemieux. He was such a sure pick that he had been named to the team in March. But Morris was borderline.

Popular sentiment dictated that of the team's seven defence spots, five would go to established veterans. Three of the five—Rob Blake, Scott Niedermayer and Chris Pronger—had been March selections. Two others, MacInnis and Adam Foote, were evident to almost everyone. It was possible that Scott Stevens could be a selection based on his outstanding career, but he was having a sub-par season.

If Stevens were not included, the two remaining spots would go to young players who figured to be on the national team for years to come. In that regard, the four most likely prospects were Wade Redden, Ed Jovanovski, Eric Brewer and Morris, but the uncertainty about Morris's wrist injury could make his inclusion too risky.

As a result of Roy's decision to spend the Olympic break with his family, the selection of the goaltending corps was the most difficult of all.

Roy had been vilified in many parts of Canada for opting out, but it was not a decision he made lightly. He discussed it with friends and his Colorado teammates before making it public, and the widely held opinion was that his departure would not harm the team. Canada had goalies who could perform just as well, everyone said. It would just be a matter of agreeing on who they were.

As incumbents from the 1998 Olympics, Curtis Joseph and Martin Brodeur were virtually assured of spots. In the weighted system that Gretzky has insisted upon in choosing his teams, those who have represented Canada in previous events are given greater consideration than those who haven't.

But who would be the third goalie? Here, Gretzky also leaned towards the concept of passing of the torch and bringing in an element of youth. If he acted on that inclination, Roberto Luongo or Jose Theodore would get the call. But the NHL team of which Gretzky was a part owner, the Phoenix Coyotes, appeared poised to make a playoff run, an achievement that was almost totally attributable to the play of Sean Burke. If Gretzky didn't push for Burke, his employees might see him as disloyal.

In Dallas, where Hitchcock was head coach, Ed Belfour had been outstanding, and there was no doubt that Hitchcock would promote his cause.

Finally, on December 15, two months before the Olympics were to open, Gretzky named his team.

"It kept coming back to the same thing," he explained. "Just take the best players."

That sounds simple enough. Just one question, though: how do you know who the best players are?

The committee, which had included Gretzky, Lowe, Tambellini, Quinn, Hitchcock, Fleming and the other assistant coach, Jacques Martin, hadn't always been able to answer that question. Sometimes, there was not unanimity. The third goalie, for instance, was selected by consensus. Even though Gretzky preferred Burke, and there was some sentiment for a youngster, the man who got the most votes was Belfour. According to Gretzky, "It got down to the fact that these are the three goalies the coaching staff was very, very confident with."

Stevens was not selected for the team. But neither was Morris. Jovanovski and Brewer got the remaining defensive spots. Brewer was having an outstanding season, and Jovanovski earned his selection by virtue of his ability to join the rush and make an impact once he got there.

As it happened, there were no serious disputes among the selectors. Any disagreements that did arise were minimal and within well-defined boundaries. Gretzky and his staff had worked so hard over the previous year to whittle down the options that when they met in a Toronto hotel room, they needed only ninety minutes to finalize the team.

The selection of the forwards followed the same process as the other positions.

Five had been pre-selected—Lemieux, Steve Yzerman, Joe Sakic, Paul Kariya and Owen Nolan. At that stage of the NHL season, six others were simply too far ahead of the pack to ignore. Included in that group was Iginla, who had built on the confidence he acquired from being invited to the September camp and was having a breakout year. The others were Lindros, Smyth, Theoren Fleury, Mike Peca and Brendan Shanahan.

Joe Nieuwendyk, who owned two Stanley Cup rings at the time and was a veteran of the 1998 Olympics, was producing some of the best hockey of his life. He had to be given a spot. That made the selectors' job fairly simple because there was only one opening remaining.

There were four serious candidates—Anson Carter, Joe Thornton, Keith Primeau and Gagne—but Gretzky and his associates had already decided that this was not to be a defensive-minded team. They felt that Canada had some of the most explosive players in the world, so in any close calls, the nod would go to an offensively oriented player.

Following that criterion, and ignoring the many passionate advocates of the bigger, more rugged Joe Thornton, they chose Gagne.

Gretzky explained the committee's approach to building a team with the best Canada had to offer. "We wanted speed," he said. "We wanted size. We wanted emotion. We really wanted emotion.

"Everyone loses. Everyone makes mistakes. But we wanted our mistakes to be made out of caring, out of wanting to do well. We wanted that to really be a part of our team."

He cited the example of Peca who, despite missing the previous season in a contract dispute with the Buffalo Sabres, went to Germany in the spring to play in the world championship, suffered a shattered orbital bone on the first shift, but continued to play and was named the game's most outstanding player.

"That kind of attitude, that kind of atmosphere, is what we really want," said Gretzky, "because it's a disease that spreads through the team and you want that."

Because the selections had been made so quickly on that Friday night, the organizers had time to turn their minds to other matters, so they applied themselves to the task of fitting together other parts of the puzzle. They discussed possible line combinations. They worried about the balance of right- and left-handed shooters. They debated the pairing of roommates. They considered the most recent (and probably not final) International Olympic Committee edict regarding practice times. They pondered possible matchups against other teams. They tossed out hypothetical defensive pairings. They talked about the merits and deficits of moving certain players to unaccustomed positions. And on and on it went.

"We really turned over every stone throughout this whole process," said Gretzky.

It made sense. At this level, that kind of minute attention to detail is what it takes to be successful. And even then there are no guarantees.

The next major problem facing the organizers was about as basic as it could be. How were they going to get the team to Salt Lake City?

The NHL had scheduled six games for Wednesday, February 13. Team Canada had been allocated ice time at 10:30 a.m. on February 14 for its only pre-tournament practice. Those players who were in action on Wednesday night would have to get to Salt Lake City—never an easy task—not only in time to get to the rink for a 10:30 practice, but also in time to pick up their Olympic accreditation. They were coming in from St. Paul, Denver, Dallas, Anaheim and Los Angeles.

As a result, Team Canada had to tentatively arrange a series of charter flights to get the players to the Denver staging point. One, from southern California, would bring Kariya and Iginla. Shanahan and Yzerman needed one from Minneapolis, and a third would pick up Lindros, Fleury and Nieuwendyk in Dallas.

With the Olympics coming only five months after the September 11, 2001, terrorist attacks on New York's World Trade Center, security was extremely tight. No flights would be allowed to land at Salt Lake City unless they had first undergone a rigorous inspection in Denver.

Whatever arrangements were made, one point was clear: those players would have no chance whatsoever of getting a full night's sleep before the one and only practice.

And the first game was the following day.

There did appear to be one positive aspect to this development: Canada's first game was against Sweden, a high-quality team whose coaches wanted to use the torpedo defence that was all the rage in the Swedish Elite League. It's essentially an aggressive forechecking scheme in which two forwards apply heavy pressure in what is basically a 2–2–1 formation rather than the standard 1–2–2 or 2–1–2.

It had its complexities in that it could be a one-defenceman system or a three-defenceman system, and as a result, it would probably give the Canadians a great deal of difficulty.

The concept had not spread to North America and they could hardly be expected to adapt to it in one day. But the time squeeze worked against the Swedes as well. Much as their coaches loved the torpedo system, they didn't have time to teach its variations. They just used a simplified version.

Considering what they did to the Canadians with the simplified form, that was just as well.

Not to put too fine a point on it, the game was a disaster.

Canada's stated intent of hanging onto the puck and using possession as a form of defence went out the window early. The idea of playing as a tight five-man unit and eliminating the gaps so there would be no seams for the Swedes to exploit was forgotten almost as quickly. The awareness of the long pass, which the defencemen promised would be their primary concern, was rarely in evidence.

"They kept throwing the long pass and we cannot allow them to do that," said Brewer afterwards. "They exploited us in terms of stretching us out with the long pass. They were able to make plays and we weren't."

"We just got too spread out," said MacInnis. "In the second period, we really broke down."

Canada emerged from the first period in a 1–1 tie, but gave up four goals in the second. "It was embarrassing to have a period like the second period," said Kariya.

The final score was 5–2, but the imbalance was much greater than the score would indicate as the Swedes made all of the Canadians' pre-tournament worries seem well founded. They used the big ice to their advantage, not only with the long pass but also with creativity near the net. They maintained possession of the puck and stretched out the Canadian defenders.

The defencemen, concerned about the home-run pass in a game which does not use the red line for offside passes, were bailing out of the Swedish zone in a hurry, thereby leaving the Swedes with lots of room to break out.

"I think the [absence of the] red line had a big effect on us," said Gretzky. "The Swedes handled it very well. We didn't know how to offensively handle it, and we had no idea how to defend it."

Quinn, whose postgame comments are always succinct after a loss, said, "They had the long pass. They had the short pass. We were Swiss cheese."

But to be fair, Quinn's performance was no better than that of his players. He offered no suggestions to his players other than to wander into the room after the second period and say, "Let's play Canadian hockey," before walking out.

The players looked at each other. "What did that mean?" they asked each other. "Does he want us to goon them?"

Fortunately, Hitchcock arrived on the scene and offered some advice on how to shut down the Swedish attack. The only third-period goal was scored by the Canadians.

Even though Peca was on the team because of his superb checking skills, Quinn hadn't bothered to match him against Mats Sundin, the mainstay of the Swedish team.

Sundin scored a pair of lovely goals, an achievement made all the more embarrassing by the fact that he played for Quinn's NHL team, the Toronto Maple Leafs.

Although Gretzky wouldn't dream of criticizing Quinn, he did make a telling statement. "If we play Sweden again," he said, "Mr. Sundin will see a lot more of Michael Peca."

A further problem became evident. The Swedes had better goaltending.

Curtis Joseph had been given the start, a decision that was not universally accepted by Canadian fans. But then again, there was no clear-cut choice. Had Brodeur played, he wouldn't have met with universal approval, either.

Joseph is one of the finest people in any sport anywhere. He devotes not only a large segment of his income, but also a substantial portion of his time to children's hospitals. He's a strong family man and invariably a pleasure to be around.

As a result, it was difficult for the Canadian media to put any pressure on him after the game. After all, he had been no worse than the rest of them. But he had been no better, either.

"It was a humbling experience," he conceded.

From coast to coast, Canadians who had expressed reservations about the Olympic team's goaltending feared the worst.

A greater cause for concern should have been the play of Joseph's teammates, who allowed the Swedes to roll in on him with abandon time and again. But fans don't always see the big picture.

"I don't think I let any bad ones in," said Joseph, "but you're a professional, and any time you let five go by you, you're not happy."

He had plenty of company. Gretzky wasn't happy. Quinn wasn't happy. The rest of the players weren't happy. And the Canadian fans were the unhappiest of all.

Even though the entire Canadian entourage had been pointing out for months that the first three games were totally irrelevant, the fans refused to be mollified. Radio call-in shows, letters to the editor and barroom talks all came to the same conclusion: Team Canada was in trouble.

But the Olympic format should have given the detractors a reason to reflect. Even if Canada lost all three opening games by 10–0 scores, they were still on an even footing with all the other teams in the quest for a gold medal. The round robin merely decided the seeding for the medal round.

Lemieux tried to offer some solace. "Remember that the Swedes play a totally different style than all the other teams," he said. "So maybe that's not a good indication of what we're up against.

"They have a really unique style and it's very difficult to defend if you're not ready for it. We knew exactly what they were going to do, but being able to defend against it is a different story. If we play them again, I'm sure we'll have to play a different style."

Lemieux himself was another cause for concern. The Team Canada captain didn't look good against the Swedes— so much so that on Swedish television, Curre Lundmark, the coach of Team Sweden in the 1994 Olympics, said, "Lemieux is skating like an old tractor."

The following night, Lemieux's hip was acting up so much that he tried to get an injection from one of the Team USA doctors, a man who had treated him in the past. He could have approached a Canadian doctor, but thought that for the sake of continuity of treatment, it made more sense to see the doctor who was familiar with his problem.

But according to IOC regulations, which would dwarf the *Encyclopaedia Britannica* in their scope, a team doctor from one country is prohibited from administering injections to an athlete from another country, even if both parties approve of the treatment.

Lemieux and Gretzky spent most of Saturday evening tracking down the American doctor, only to finally find him and learn of the regulation. By that time, the Team Canada doctors had gone to bed. As a result, Lemieux did not get the shot, and team management thought it best that he skip the Sunday-night game against Germany. Surely Canada, with all its stars, wouldn't need Lemieux to defeat Germany.

They didn't. But the game was no cakewalk, either.

The game wasn't played in the main arena. Instead, it was in Provo, where the ice was atrocious. The players frequently fell when it gave out underneath them, and pucks sometimes changed course when they hit a rut or a pile of ice chips.

Even so, the Canadians managed to open a 3–0 lead, only to see the German amateurs and part-timers make it 3–2 before time ran out.

Only two German players, Jochen Hecht and Marco Sturm, were NHLers. A third, goaltender Olaf Kolzig, was on the roster, but he was recuperating from arthroscopic knee surgery and decided not to press his luck.

The close loss thrilled the Germans. "You've got to be honest. It's a dream come true to play against a team like that," said forward Stefan Ustorf. "We are not just talking about NHL players—which are great, don't get me wrong—but these are all-star teams.

"You take a face-off against Steve Yzerman and Joe Sakic—that's awesome. It's a lot of fun. It's a dream for many of us."

It was more of a nightmare for the Canadians. Two of their goals were attributable to a foolish five-minute major assessed to Germany's Daniel Kunce, and the final German goal was a weak one. Hecht took a shot from the side that Brodeur deflected away with his blocker. But the puck hit the upper shaft of his stick and dropped into the net.

The fact that Brodeur was in goal came as something of a surprise. It also marked the beginning of the rift between Joseph and Quinn that would culminate in Joseph leaving the Maple Leafs and going to the Detroit Red Wings.

Joseph was not as upset about the selection of Brodeur as he was about the way Quinn handled it. Joseph found out he wasn't starting only when he saw the lineups Quinn had written on the board.

He felt, with considerable justification, that as Quinn's starting goalie in Toronto and a seasoned veteran, he deserved to be told about the demotion face to face.

The narrow victory over the ragtag Germans did nothing to increase the confidence of Canadian fans. E-mails started pouring in to those covering the event, most of which suggested that any journalist not heaping abuse on this team was either seriously deficient in hockey acumen or in the pocket of the organizers—or both.

But there was no time for the Canadians to work on solving their problems. They had another game the next night, this one against the Czech Republic.

Although it wasn't evident to the fans at the time, this was the game in which Canada's fortunes started to turn.

Nieuwendyk converted a beautiful pass from Fleury into a late goal to make it 3–3 and there was no further scoring. It wasn't a particularly great game for the Canadians, and they gave up too many good chances for the coaches' liking. But they were starting to look more like a unified group, and there were none of the glaring mistakes that had been so evident in the game against Sweden.

All of a sudden, the parts were starting to fall into place. Lemieux was back in the lineup and looking far better than he had against the Swedes. The defence pairs were synchronized with each other, and the forwards were feeling confident about their linemates.

And Brodeur had won the job as starting goaltender.

Coming into the tournament, Joseph had the inside track, but when he didn't make any great saves against Sweden, Brodeur got his chance. With so many minor-leaguers on their team, the Germans could hardly be considered a true test, so Brodeur played again against the Czechs. And he was outstanding. After that performance, it was clear that, barring disaster, he'd be the starting goalie the rest of the way.

It would mean playing five games in eight days, but that didn't bother Brodeur. "I play every day in New Jersey," he said, "so I've got it in my mind that I'm going to play every day here.

"My first goal was to play in the Olympics, and after that to carry the torch all the way to the end. This is an opportunity. Like any athlete, when we see something that's going to be exciting and we're going to remember all our lives, we don't want to miss the boat."

As for the rest of the team, Nieuwendyk summed up the mood when he said, "Our performance was much better than our game against Germany, and that was much better than our game against Sweden.

"I really felt that today, our team felt a lot more relaxed. We just kind of said, 'Enough is enough.' We just jumped over the boards and played as hard as we could.

"It certainly helped to have Mario back and playing as well as he did," he added. "Now we're going into the elimination round feeling pretty good about ourselves."

Then he paused and amended that. "We feel great about ourselves," he said.

To top it all off, Gretzky made them feel even greater. Public tirades had never been a part of his repertoire, but after the tie against the Czechs, he fumed for a while, then took to the podium and teed off.

An incident late in the game gave him his springboard. Fleury had absorbed a violent and unpenalized cross-check from Roman Hamrlik, and Gretzky was livid about it.

"I think the guy should be suspended for the rest of the tournament," he thundered. "If it was a Canadian player who did it, it would be a big story. A Czech player did it and it was okay."

Gretzky then expanded on his us-against-the-world theme, taking on the Europeans, the Americans, the media and pretty well everybody who wasn't on Team Canada.

"I'm very proud of all the players in our locker room and it makes me ill to hear some of the things that are being said about us," he said.

There was more: "Am I hot? Yeah, I'm hot, because I'm tired of people taking shots at Canadian hockey and when we do it, we're hooligans. When Europeans do it, it's okay because they're not tough or they're not dirty. That's a crock of crap."

There had been stories in the media—and they were accurate—that some Canadian players were not enamoured with Quinn's coaching. But Gretzky was having none of it.

"American propaganda," he said. "If you want to talk about hockey, you want to talk about Canadians. We're the biggest story here. They're loving us not doing well. They loved the start we had. It's a big story for them.

"I don't think we dislike those countries as much as they hate us. And that's a fact. They don't like us. They want to see us fail. They love beating us. They may tell you guys something different, but believe me, when you're on the ice that's what they say. They don't like us."

The speech was so out of character for Gretzky that it was the immediate talk of the Olympics.

There were those in the media who suggested Gretzky had lost his cool, but anyone who took that tack didn't know Gretzky very well. As Lowe, his close friend and former teammate, pointed out, "Anybody who knows Wayne Gretzky knows that everything he has ever done has been contemplated and calculated."

Gretzky was simply following the course of action that his former coach Glen Sather used to take when times got tough for the Edmonton Oilers. He would create a diversion and take the heat upon himself, thereby easing the pressure upon the players.

"You have to react when there's a need to react," explained Lowe. "The most important thing is to keep the troops and the organization focused. That's what he was doing."

To those outside the team, it was not clear what was going on. The Canadians had mustered only a 1–1–1 record in the opening round and had been outscored 10–8, even though the schedule had allowed them to avoid a couple of powerhouses, Russia and the United States. They had looked confused at times, and their vaunted offence had yet to kick into gear. And now their general manager was acting in a manner that was totally out of character.

But within the team, the attitude was excellent. There was a quiet confidence there, and it had been boosted by Gretzky's affirmation of his belief in their abilities. Those who knew the players and chatted with them every day couldn't help but be aware of that confidence.

Making others aware of it was a different matter altogether. Despite its arcane licensing laws, Salt Lake City during the Olympics was a sociable place, and the arena was right downtown. As a result, the media covering the games often would be found relaxing in a restaurant or a bar near the rink. On those occasions, it was not unusual to be accosted by a disappointed fan dressed in Team Canada regalia who wanted to know what was wrong with his team.

"There's nothing wrong. They'll be fine," was somehow not the answer those fans wanted to hear. They had convinced themselves that disaster loomed. Some wanted to press home their point of view, but most just delivered one of those looks that people reserve for the terminally clueless and closed the conversation.

But the players knew what was happening, and so did the coaching staff. Even though there was only one day between the round robin and the medal round, the Canadians were given that day off. The feeling was that these were world-class professionals. They knew what to do and they needed a break more than a practice.

The next day, they prepared for Finland by getting into a comfortable frame of mind and following the familiar schedule for a typical NHL day—a late-morning skate followed by an afternoon nap and the evening game.

While the Canadian fans were writing them off in the early going, the players had been concerned only with gearing up for the first sudden-death medal-round game. And now, it was upon them.

In that Canadian dressing room was a group of guys who had a history of doing far better than average in the must-win games. It was a team of character and poise. Of the twenty-three players, twelve had won Stanley Cup rings. Kariya and Lindros had Olympic medals. Sixteen had medals from the World Junior Championships. Except for the younger players, almost every one of them had experience as a captain or alternate captain.

They were determined to advance through the medal round, and over the years, that kind of Canadian determination has rarely proved to be fruitless.

A further incentive, if they needed it, was a stunning upset in the afternoon game.

The Swedes peppered Belarus goalie Andre Mezin with forty-seven shots while allowing only fifteen on Tommy Salo at the other end. But Belarus, a team with only one NHL player, Ruslan Salei, won 4–3 when Salo allowed a late shot from just inside the red line to bounce off his head and drop into the net.

"If I'd said I was trying to score," said Vladimir Kopat, "no one would have believed me. I just shot from the red line and that's what happened."

As for Mezin, to say that he was a journeyman minor-leaguer would be something of an understatement. He had bounced around Europe, and most recently had managed to catch on with a team in Berlin. He had a ratty two-year-old catching glove, but he was happy with it. He'd had to make its predecessor last six years.

The rest of his equipment was even more decrepit. "My chest protector is nine years old," he said. "Every shot, I'm scared."

Before their game against the Finns, the Canadians reminded each other of the afternoon result and made the point that a sudden-death game can never be taken for granted. They also made the point that if they got past the Finns, they had to beat only Belarus to be in the gold-medal game.

Of course, the Finns were as aware of the potential subsequent matchup as Canada, and the previous time these two teams met in the Olympics—in the bronze-medal game in Nagano—Finland had won. If the Finns were able to beat Canada again, they were all but assured of at least a silver medal.

The confident Canadians started cautiously, pressing an occasional early attack when the opportunity arose, but never doing so recklessly. They had hoped that they might be able to take advantage of Finnish goaltender Jani Hurme, who had a reputation for giving up easy, early goals. And sure enough, Hurme lived up to that reputation to the fullest. Somehow, he allowed Sakic's routine backhander to float between his legs with only three minutes gone.

The assistant coaches, Martin and Hitchcock, recognized the importance of that opening goal and made frequent line changes to keep fresh troops on the ice. Then the troops fulfilled their part of the bargain, working relentlessly to win the battles along the boards.

As the evening progressed, the concern for Canadian fans was that it might be one of those games where one team spends most of the night in the other team's end, but eventually, against the play, the other team comes back and does enough scoring to win the game.

There was no doubt which team was by far the better in such aspects as shots, puck possession and territorial domination, but even so, late in the game, that domination had still not made its impact on the scoreboard.

After Hurme's early weakness, he settled down and played well. Team Canada built a 15–5 edge in shots in the first period and pushed it to 29–13 after two, but Hurme kept them at bay.

When the Canadians finally did ease the pressure by opening a two-goal lead, they were able to hang on to it for only twenty seconds. The many Canadian fans in the building were still letting off tension, whooping and shouting their praise for Yzerman, who had converted a perfect pass from Lemieux, when Niklas Hagman shoved the puck past Brodeur to build the tension again.

In many ways, it was like a typical late-round NHL playoff game, and as is often the case under those circumstances, the team that won most of the little battles won the big one.

In the final minutes, the Finns launched a furious attack, but the Canadian defenders were just as resolute. "We had half a dozen chances there, but no luck with those chances," said Finnish coach Hannu Aravirta.

That was because at that point, and at so many others

throughout the game, the Canadians were the better team.

Even though the margin of victory was only one goal, Canada had persevered against a team that had produced a tenacious effort. As Nieuwendyk said, "It was right up there with a late playoff game. It felt like a game six or game seven. Everyone is so up for the next shift, and you don't want to make a mistake.

"There's a sense of real urgency in the room now. We're sixty minutes away from a medal."

By this stage of the tournament, the Canadians had become comfortable with each other and were honing some of the finer points of their game.

The penalty killing had been superb, thanks largely to the tutorial that Hitchcock had delivered. He had pointed out that the defencemen are the quarterbacks of the power play and as such, are limited in their manoeuvrability. Forwards routinely slide pucks back to the point without looking, and the defencemen are expected to be there. Therefore, they had to maintain their station near the boards.

But on the wide surface, that put them about fifteen feet further from the net than they would be on an NHL rink. With Olympic goalies being so good on long shots (with the occasional Swedish exception), the shot from the point isn't much of a threat.

Therefore, Hitchcock told the penalty-killing forwards to cheat a bit by leaving the defencemen alone and collapsing on the opposing forwards near the goal.

In the NHL, power-play forwards score on redirections of shots from the point, rebound conversions and bang-bang plays—all of which are often available because an opposing forward has had to rush out to the point and leave a man unchecked near the net. But in Olympic play, the point men could be virtually ignored, so if the attackers wanted to get someone open around the slot, the only way to do it was to bring in a weak-side defenceman from the point.

The Canadians were alert for this and had created their share of shorthanded two-on-one breaks when that poaching defenceman got trapped. Even when the Team Canada penalty killers didn't get the break, they were able to move the puck through the area the defenceman had vacated and thereby ease the pressure.

The Canadian staff also knew that despite all their team's offensive firepower, they still had to pay close attention to defence. As a result, Lindros had seen very limited action in the second half of the game against Finland. It wasn't that he was having a bad game, but the Finns relied heavily on Teemu Selanne and were double-shifting him. Every time he showed up on the ice, Peca joined him—the strategy that Gretzky had promised would be used against Sundin had there been a Canada-Sweden rematch.

With one Canadian centre doing the job of two, it meant that one wouldn't get his turn. Dropping Yzerman off Lemieux's line was out of the question, and Nieuwendyk was having such a strong two-way game that he, too, had to get a regular shift.

So, for the second half of the game, Lindros languished on the bench.

Naturally enough, he was discouraged, but he got some support from Fleury, his New York Rangers teammate who had made it back to the NHL after a rehabilitation stint to combat his alcoholism.

Fleury urged Lindros to take the tack he himself had taken—to be positive, to recognize that the past is prologue, to be aware that merely being a part of this team was an indication of great talent and to be proud of that fact.

The victory over the Finns, which had required discipline, perseverance and tenacity, was a team victory, Fleury said, and Lindros had been a part of it. Now, the Canadians were in tremendous shape and apparently bound for the gold-medal game. Who knew what might happen there?

In the interim, however, there was the matter of beating Belarus, something that pretty well everyone in the hockey world expected Canada to do. When asked to comment on the upcoming game, most of the Canadians offered the usual platitudes, but Fleury, in typical fashion, had a different view.

"We're underdogs," he announced.

And how did he arrive at that conclusion? "We lost to Sweden and they beat Sweden," he said trying to hold back a smile. "They solved the torpedo and we didn't."

It was just another example of Fleury's self-motivation. "Everybody considered us underdogs after we played the first game," he said. "That's the way we like it, so we're going to go with it."

In fact, they were heavy overdogs. In the two games prior to that stunning upset of Sweden, Belarus had been outscored 16–2. They weren't likely to give the Canadians much cause for concern.

And they didn't.

Team Canada cruised to an easy 7–1 victory, the only Belarus goal coming when Brodeur set visions of Salo dancing through everyone's head and misplayed a long shot by Salei.

Yzerman summed it up best. "In this game, we did what we had to do," he said.

So they were off to the final, a chance to win the nation's first Olympic gold medal since the Edmonton Mercurys had done it fifty years earlier. A picture of that team had been hung in Canada's dressing room, and as the oldest player, MacInnis was the target of his teammates' humour.

"The boys were asking what the team was like in '52," he laughed. "I've been taking a little bit of a ribbing. They wanted to know which one was me in the team picture."

To win the gold medal this time around, Canada would have to defeat the Americans, who had eliminated the Russians to create a dream gold-medal match up for the NHL. It was such a dream, suggested Russian coach Viacheslav Fetisov, that it had been a virtual fix.

International Ice Hockey Federation president Rene Fasel issued a rebuttal, saying, "When a coach of a team tries to undermine and question the integrity of the Olympic ice hockey tournament, it makes me very angry and disappointed.

"Everyone who has seen the games must agree that the officiating in this tournament has been of the highest possible level. The referees' decisions were not the reason Russia lost."

Asked to comment on Fasel's statement, Fetisov said, "What's the point? I said this before. I watched the game. The NHL referees are professional people. They live here. They make their money here.

"For referees, for teams who participate, it's too much pressure. They missed some calls on the US team. We review evidence of this stuff. Competitions like this are supposed to be neutral.

"Listen, you've got problems. You have two referees. These guys do not know international rules."

The Canadians had no interest in the Russians' complaints. Their only concern was to get ready for the Americans, a team staffed by players they knew too well.

In the 1996 World Cup, Canada and the United States had advanced to the final, and even though the Canadians outplayed the Americans throughout, Mike Richter outplayed Curtis Joseph in goal.

It wasn't that Joseph was bad. Far from it; he was outstanding. But Richter was absolutely phenomenal, turning in by far the best short-term performance of his life. The Canadians rolled in on him time and again and peppered him with point-blank shots. But in the end, they lost because Richter kept his team in it long enough to allow Brett Hull to score a tainted winner that the Canadians felt was scored with a stick that was above his shoulder.

Now, in 2002, it was to be one game for the gold medal and with two teams as evenly matched as this, neither one could be considered a pronounced underdog.

As far as Team USA's offence was concerned, Hull was still Canada's primary worry. In NHL history, only Gretzky had scored more goals in a season than Hull.

"The thing about Brett is he knows where to find space," said MacInnis, who had spent years playing with and against Hull. "He's probably one of the smartest players in the game in knowing where to position himself to make a defenceman make a tough choice—whether to leave the front of the net or not."

Hull, MacInnis said, finds that never-never land where there is no certainty.

"There are a lot of guys who come in front of the net and bang away," MacInnis said, "but he's the guy who knows just where to go to find that space that makes you think, 'Should I go? Shouldn't I go? Could I get a stick on him?'

"And you know that he needs no time at all to get a shot away. That's where he makes it tough for a defenceman.

"Brett is great at finding space and he doesn't need a lot of chances. He can get one chance a game and it's a goal."

But the Canadians had the kind of team defence that could handle people like Hull, Jeremy Roenick and the other American snipers as long as the forwards came back and paid attention to their responsibilities in their own end. Richter was back in the American goal, and that was a concern. But on the other hand, their defence corps was the Americans' greatest weakness. The American defence was primarily oriented towards offence, featuring players like Tom Poti, Gary Suter, Brian Leetch and Phil Housley. As a result, it could be exploited by strong forechecking, and that's exactly what Canada intended to do.

The Americans knew that the Canadians would be inspired. "We're both proud nations," said Roenick. "We're both proud of our accomplishments so far in this tournament.

This is a religion in Canada, is hockey. Anything less than a gold would be hard to swallow."

Sometimes, when covering an event of this nature, you can underestimate its importance to the people back home. This is especially true of something like the Olympics where, because of security, you're in a virtual cocoon, surrounded by people for whom participation in major sporting events is a standard occurrence.

Two hours before the game, Bruce Garrioch of the *Ottawa Sun* and I had already staked out our seats in the second row, and Garrioch, a telephone junkie, started to pass the time in his usual fashion. He called Ottawa. He called Toronto. He called the Maritimes. It wasn't yet noon in British Columbia, which meant that none of Bruce's friends there would be up yet. Even so, the trend had been established.

"You wouldn't believe it," he said. "All the bars in Canada are already full. Everybody I call is either standing in line outside a bar trying to get in or inside a place that's packed."

We were aware that Canadians would be paying close attention, but we had seen it as something like game seven of a Stanley Cup final. This went far beyond that. This was a national event, a Canada-wide recognition of the country's passion for hockey, the kind of demonstration that seems to happen every fifteen years. In 1972, there was the Summit Series. In 1987, it was the Canada Cup. Now, in 2002, it was the Olympics.

Apparently, it was a worldwide Canadian phenomenon. For weeks afterwards, stories came in about Canadians who found a way to see the game in some far-flung corner of the world: on a beach in Australia, in a small village in Chile, in a hotel in South Africa. There were all kinds of anecdotes like the one about the Canadian working in a pub in North London who was asked by one of the regular patrons to turn off the TV so he could play the jukebox. "Not a chance," said the Canadian, putting the game ahead of his vocation. "We're watching the Canadian hockey game."

Even Gretzky, who had been through so many high-level games in his career, got caught up in the anticipation. "This is the first time since I retired," he said, "where I wish that I could be out there getting ready for a game like this and just focusing on playing."

It didn't start particularly well for Canada—at least as far as the scoring was concerned. At 8:49, Tony Amonte put the Americans in front.

It was Doug Weight who made the initial play, diving for a loose puck in his own end and knocking it ahead to Amonte to create a two-on-one break with Mike York. Even though he didn't need to do so under international rules, Amonte paused ever so briefly to allow the puck to precede him across the red line, then moved down the right side and took the shot himself, beating Brodeur through the five-hole.

In NHL rinks, the media are usually dispatched to the nether regions, so far from the playing surface that you couldn't reach it with a Scud missile. But at the Olympics, the press seats are near the ice. At that range, you get much more of an intuitive sense of the situation. You can see the looks in the players' eyes. You can sense their attitude. You can hear them shouting to each other.

And in this case, there seemed to be not the slightest reason for Canadians fans to be concerned. Even though their heroes were down by a goal, they appeared to be in control. The score did not represent the balance of the play, and the turnaround appeared to be just a matter of time. I expressed this opinion to my other neighbour at rinkside, Mike Brophy of *The Hockey News*. He agreed wholeheartedly.

Sure enough, about six minutes later, Lemieux made a dazzling play to set up the tying goal. From the right point, Pronger sent the puck across the deep slot and it seemed certain to everyone that Lemieux, who had stationed himself perfectly, would corral the pass and take a shot. The American defencemen—Aaron Miller and Brian Leetch—were just as certain and started to move towards him. But Lemieux just let the puck go between his legs—right to the edge of the left face-off circle, where the unattended Paul Kariya fired it past Richter to tie the game.

Mike Richter played farther out of his net than most of today's goalies, so when Lemieux let the pass go through him, Richter had to cover a lot of ground to block Kariya's angle. Lemieux's play had made sure that Richter would be out of position.

"He's sneaky," conceded Richter afterwards. "It was a beautiful play."

Then, with eighty-seven seconds left in the period, Iginla showed the kind of attributes that had earned him his selection to the team. As Sakic came down the left side with Gagne in the middle, Iginla drove into his favourite territory on the edge of the crease. Sakic, the crafty veteran, held the puck along the boards, looked at Gagne and poised his body as if he were going to put the puck into the middle. Then he snapped a pass right across the top of the crease.

American defenceman Gary Suter was backing in and was so concerned about the advancing Iginla that he couldn't see what Sakic was doing. The puck landed on Iginla's stick and he knocked it past Suter and Richter and into the net.

"That pass was exactly right on my tape," recalled Iginla. "I think Suter was on me, and I was trying to drive by him and trying to go to the net. I could see the puck coming, but I lost it at the last second. I was just trying to hold my stick firm and keep it on the ice. Joe hit it right in the middle.

"I was really excited. There are so many times as a winger when you drive to the net and you try to score and you hear the crowd go, 'Oooooh,' because it just missed the net or you just lost it. To lose it just for a split second is very common because of all the melees in the crease. But it was such a good pass that it didn't matter whether I saw it or not. Joe had seen me."

One period was gone and the Canadians were in front. But late in the second period, Team USA got one of those lucky breaks that make sudden-elimination games such a precarious proposition.

With the Americans on a power play, defenceman Brian Rafalski took a wrist shot from the circle—not a high-percentage play under the circumstances. But the puck hit the heel of Pronger's stick and deflected between the legs of a helpless Brodeur.

There may have been serious concern, perhaps even borderline panic, for those in Canada watching the game on television. But once again, from the rinkside vantage point, matters appeared to be under control. There wasn't the slightest hint of panic on the part of the Canadian players. The look in their eyes was not one of fear. It was pure composure tinged with determination.

When Roenick was sent off for tripping Kariya at the 17:30 mark, the Canadians went to work. Finally, with eleven seconds left in the penalty, Sakic snapped one of his trademark blazing wrist shots past Richter.

Again, Iginla was doing yeoman's work in front of the net as Sakic moved in to the top of the circle to take his shot, and in the heavy traffic, it appeared that he had deflected the puck.

Not so, he said afterwards. "It hit the defenceman [Leetch]. Joe got a lot of wood on it and if that had hit me, I would have felt it."

Now two periods had gone, and the Canadians were still in front.

The next goal would be of monumental importance. If the Americans got it, they would have erased a Canadian lead for the second time. No matter how much confidence the Canadians had shown to this point, doubts would subsequently begin to creep into their minds.

But if Canada scored next, it would represent a two-goal lead in the third period and with a quality team like this, that would be an insurmountable margin.

The first half of the period rolled past with the Americans trying to press. They did have a territorial advantage, but the Canadian defenders quickly collapsed on them, and as a result, Brodeur wasn't forced to make any great saves. In this way, Canada remained in control, but they weren't able to get that crucial insurance goal. They were in defensive mode again, with Lindros getting less ice time and Peca double-shifting to keep the American snipers under wraps.

Then the clock hit the eleven-minute mark. Twelve minutes. Thirteen minutes. Canadian fans were in the mental countdown phase.

But at 13:43, there was an ominous development. Yzerman was sent off for tripping Suter. While the Canadian penalty killers were proficient, this was still a occasion of crippling anxiety for their fans. The Americans had no shortage of forwards who could score, and they had been moving the puck crisply in the Canadian zone. It was clear to everyone that under these circumstances, they would pull out all the stops to tie the game.

And if they were to succeed, then what? Overtime? Another shootout? Canadians watching around the world found it hard to come up with many optimistic answers to those questions.

The two minutes dragged on interminably for the exuberant Canadian fans who made up most of the sold-out crowd of 8,599. But Hitchcock's penalty-killing tutorial had not fallen on deaf ears, and Brodeur had to make only one great save—on a quick shot by Hull. With Canadians everywhere emitting a sigh of relief, the penalty-box door opened and Yzerman returned to the ice.

Still, a one-goal lead was unduly precarious. The Canadian players remembered a similar situation in the 1996 World Cup, when Hull redirected a puck into the net with a stick that Canadians still maintain was above his shoulder.

The poised Canadian team had no intention of dropping back into a defensive shell that invited just such an occurrence. Right from the beginning, when he was explaining the selection process, Gretzky had said that he wanted an offensive team that could play defence rather than the reverse.

The line of Iginla, Sakic and Gagne had been superb throughout the tournament, but at this stage, with Yzerman coming back onto the ice from the penalty box, he was out instead of Gagne.

Rob Blake corralled the puck in his own end and sent Sakic away. Sakic roared up the middle of the ice, crossed the blue line and fed to Yzerman on the far right. Yzerman wasted no time sending the puck over to Iginla, who was cruising in near the top of the left circle. Iginla one-timed the pass, and although Richter got a glove on his shot, he couldn't hold it. The puck hit his glove, looped up in the air, fell into the crease, bounced off the post and trickled over the goal line.

"It was a good pass and I kind of didn't get all of it, but I still got enough of it," recalled Iginla. "It started fluttering after I hit it. I think maybe Richter was expecting it to be harder. It came across and I put everything into it, but it didn't come out as a really hard shot for whatever reason. I don't know if I missed it a little bit, or if it was wobbling at impact."

Either way, Richter was caught off guard, just like a batter in baseball who thinks he's getting a fastball when the pitcher has thrown a change-up.

For a brief moment, Iginla thought he might have missed an excellent chance.

"I could see the pass coming," he recalled, "and I was thinking, 'Oh, my gosh, what a good opportunity.' Then as soon as I hit it, I thought, 'Aw, I didn't get all of it.'

"But I knew it still had a chance when I saw it go off the glove and up in the air. I couldn't tell if it was going to go in or not. There are so many that hit the post and so many close calls that I couldn't say for sure. But it was nice to see it go across, and Joe was right there to make sure that it did."

US defenceman Tom Poti made a desperate stab at the puck with his stick but couldn't keep it out. The clock showed less than four minutes left to play.

It was time for Canada to start celebrating.

Later, it was reliably reported that all over the country, impromptu renditions of "O Canada" broke out in bar after bar. It had taken hundreds of flawless plays for Canada to get this far. It had taken twenty-one goals. But this was the one that made the difference. This was the one that gave Canada a lead that would surely not be relinquished. This was the one that gave Canada its first gold medal in fifty years.

As it turned out, there was another goal to come. With the Americans pressing, Sakic got a break, darted in alone and popped his second of the game. Iginla assisted for his third point of the afternoon.

But it was that fourth Canadian goal, the one by Iginla, that made the difference. That was the one that put the game away.

Seeing the fifth goal go in with only eighty seconds left, Owen Nolan celebrated with his teammates, took the briefest of shifts, then headed to the dressing room to get his video camera. As the game wound down, he was back on the bench with his camera rolling, and when the celebration began, he was not only a part of it, he was video-taping it for posterity.

What would have happened if Quinn had been looking for him to take a shift?

"He'd have had to do without me," laughed Nolan in the jubilant postgame media scrum.

What if Quinn had sent him back on the ice after he'd retrieved the camera?

"I would have said, 'I can't. I'm busy.'"

Iginla was the undisputed star of the game. He led the team in shots with six, put Canada in front in the first period, scored the insurance goal that clinched the gold medal and added an assist on the one that erased all doubt.

Additionally, even though he didn't get an assist on the play, he created the traffic that allowed Sakic to score the game winner.

"This is definitely the biggest day of my career," he beamed afterwards. Perhaps that's a bit redundant. Iginla is always beaming.

"I've been fortunate to play for Canada before [in junior hockey and at the world championship], but this is the best feeling. I'll be telling my kids or someone about the whole game—the atmosphere in the building. I loved having the crowd right on top of us and hearing both sets of fans going at it. I'll definitely be telling some stories.

"It's the biggest game I've ever played in and probably the most fun. Each period it was so intense. Winning and hearing the buzzer go off it's an unbelievable feeling."

All the Canadian players expressed their pride, not only in their own achievements, but also in their country. Because MacInnis knew it was to be his last Olympics, he was able to savour the moment.

"It's huge for Canada," he said. "People ask me what can compare to this in the US. I've lived in the US for eight years and I can't find anything to compare with what this means to Canada, because sports down there are shared—football, baseball, basketball.

"I don't think there's one sport that brings the country together the way hockey does in Canada. After Nagano, I was depressed for two weeks," he said. "I didn't know if I'd get another shot."

He paused for a moment, then looked around. "Oh, God," he said with heartfelt emotion. "To hear the national anthem out there at age thirty-eight, I'll tell you. It feels good.

"You look at young guys like Gagne and Iginla. I told them to cherish this day because you never know. With these moments, you never know."

"This is awesome," said Lemieux, who as captain had been one of the players who stood up before the game and told his teammates that they knew what needed to be done and to make sure they did it.

"Three and a half years ago, I was sitting on a beach in Florida, so to come back and have a chance to play with these great players is very special," he said. "All we've talked about since August is winning the gold. I brought my three daughters, my son and my whole family down for this because it was the chance of a lifetime. When you're born there, you're always going to be Canadian and will do whatever you can for your country. That's what I did this week.

"My goal was to come here, win a gold medal and play with these great players. You don't have that opportunity too often in life. I certainly took a lot of grief in the last couple of weeks, but this was worth it."

"We feel that Canada is where hockey was born," said Foote. "To be able to bring this back to fans is awesome. To be a Canadian today is unbelievable."

Yzerman, whose knee was so bad that he was always limping whenever he was spotted away from the rink, played a superb series, always dangerous offensively and a major force defensively.

"When I made the decision to come, I was committed," he said with his typical no-nonsense resolve. "There was no turning back. I just wanted to come here, play my best and forget about the injury.

"Everybody in the dressing room believed. It didn't shock us when we got off to the tough start. People thought we were going to walk in here and win. We knew that wasn't the case. We knew we had to work for it. We knew it wasn't going to be easy."

Roenick, who had said the day before that he was sure his team would knock off the Canadians, was gracious in defeat.

"It was a dream matchup," he said, "one that all of us were so excited to be a part of. I know I was so very proud to be a part of it. Unfortunately, we didn't come out victorious, but I think if we're going to lose to anybody, to lose to Canada, probably the best team in the world, helps ease it a little bit.

"It was a real honour to be out there playing against them. You can tell that they needed it. You could tell they were eager to win after fifty years.

"It seemed like fifty years of emotion were pent up in the way they played out there today.

"You could just tell by looking at them that they meant business. They did the things top players and top teams do. They came through when they needed to. It's unfortunate that we lost, but we didn't lose to a bunch of scrubs. We lost to the best players in the world, bar none."

"We had a good team," said Gretzky, "and our guys really came together. From the first game against Sweden when we got beat, they handed us our lunch and we admitted to it, and each day, our guys worked harder and harder. Those guys and the coaching staff, they deserve all the credit."

The experience made Iginla a better player and taught him important lessons that he hopes to some day pass on to other young Team Canada players.

"The whole tournament was amazing," he said. "I was a pretty young guy and I was pretty excited about it—all the emotions for the whole tournament, but especially that final game. The excitement. The nervousness. The energy.

"It was great to watch the leaders on the club. Even early, when we had such a bad game against Sweden, they were always so calm, and it was so interesting to watch them because here are some of the best players in the world and we're in one of the biggest games of our lives—my biggest game of my life.

"It was nice to see that they were confident and they were focused but they were still enjoying themselves.

They definitely led the way and it rubbed off on the group. It rubbed off on me.

"I would go on the ice in that whole final game and I couldn't imagine what it would have been like if those guys had been wound up. I was already so wound up; it was nice to see them be so calm and composed. It definitely made me a little but more relaxed."

Iginla remembered that between-period speeches were made in that final game, but he couldn't remember what was said. "It was just the way they carried themselves," he said. "They made you confident."

For some of the Canadian players, this was the high point of their careers. Some went on to further glory. But in one case, it was all downhill after the Olympics.

Fleury had beaten alcoholism and had defied his critics by playing a disciplined, productive series.

"I've been through personal hell and back with what I've been through in the last twelve months," he said afterwards, still carrying the Canadian flag that he waved so proudly after collecting his gold medal.

During the ceremony, no one seemed to be enjoying the occasion more. "It's just being aware," he said, "being present and savouring every last moment you can on the ice. Those are the things I have always taken for granted before.

"This is the proudest moment of my career, and I'm so happy that I've been able to be a part of this experience and play with twenty-two great athletes who are great people."

It had been almost a year since Fleury entered a rehabilitation clinic in New Mexico. "When I left the game, I never thought I'd be standing here," he said, "but I do think I deserve this, I really do.

"I've worked really hard away from the rink and got rid of a lot of personal demons that I had been carrying around for a long time."

"You can have as much skill as you want," he said. "I've played with a hundred guys who had more talent and skill than I have who are working in restaurants. They're not playing in the NHL.

"What sets it apart is how we play, and that's with grit, determination and heart. I'd take twenty Canadian guys on any team in the NHL and nine times out of ten, we'd win the Stanley Cup.

"Nothing comes easy in life. I could have folded up my tent a long time ago and just said 'screw it.' But I knew there was something better in life.

"There's no better feeling than winning, especially at this level and this magnitude. We all believed when nobody else did."

But shortly afterwards, the demons came back to revisit Theoren Fleury and this time, he couldn't fend them off.

He got in trouble with the Rangers, then was released outright, and during the summer, had a relapse. Before the next season began, he signed with the Chicago Blackhawks, but the troubles continued there, and finally, less than nine months after his Olympic triumph, Fleury went back into rehab, never to return to the NHL.

Of all the players on the Canadian team, the person who enjoyed the Olympic experience the least was Joseph.

Like any true professional, he's proud of his achievements, but he doesn't want to accept plaudits that are not deserved.

When he returned to Toronto, Maple Leafs president Ken Dryden, who had been all but shunted out of the management picture by that time and had little to do except arrange the game-night production, insisted that Joseph be honoured as part of a pregame ceremony.

Joseph, not particularly proud of his one-game, five-goal Olympic performance, wanted no part of it. Dryden stood firm. He had arranged for the involvement of Catriona Le May Doan, a multiple gold-medal winner at the Olympics, and she too was to be honoured, along with Quinn.

As part of the ceremony, Quinn tried to shake Joseph's hand, but he appeared to refuse. The rift that had been quiet burst into the open, and from that time on, until Joseph's contract negotiations with the Leafs broke off in the summer, the Toronto newspapers were full of stories of the feud.

Finally, Joseph signed with the Detroit Red Wings, and I caught up to him in San Jose, where he was preparing for the Wings' season opener. He set the record straight on what had happened.

"I just wanted to get back and play a game," he said, "get a win for the Toronto Maple Leafs and be between the pipes. The PR staff was saying that they were bringing in people and going to have a big Olympic thing.

"So I phoned Ken on the way to the rink and I asked him what it was all about. 'What's it going to be? I don't really have an Olympic highlight film and I don't want to be embarrassed.'

"I told him, 'I don't want to be honoured. Quinn did his job and Catriona did her job. Which highlights are they are going to show of me?' I told him I was really uncomfortable with it."

But Dryden considered his game-night productions to be sacrosanct and refused to put the feelings of his goaltender ahead of his pet project.

"Of course, I'm put on the spot," said Joseph, "and Pat comes over. I can't take my blocker off. I've got my stick, and everybody makes a big deal of that. It was just putting me on the spot and I didn't like it. I just wanted to get in there and do my job."

So he didn't intentionally spurn Quinn?

"No, I didn't. I do that all the time. I would have to throw my glove off. I just felt very uncomfortable in that situation. If they would have asked me or said something about it, it wouldn't have been so bad. I had to ask [director of media relations] Pat Park to find out about it. No communication."

In the summer, Quinn, who was also the Leafs general manager, appeared on TSN and said that he hadn't signed

Joseph because he had asked for an $11.5 million US salary.

"That's insane," said Joseph. "That's utterly insane." But he felt the statement was typical. "I don't think they negotiated in good faith—ever. Not at all."

But unlike Joseph, most of the Olympic players had an experience that was not only pleasant, it was memorable.

For Iginla, it represented the first serious recognition of his star quality. Riding his Olympic success, he went on that year to win the Art Ross Trophy as the overall scoring leader and the Maurice Richard Trophy as the top goal scorer. In 2004, he led his Calgary Flames to the Stanley Cup final, where they lost in seven games.

Quinn's Olympic experience with Nolan led him to make a trade to acquire his services in time for the 2003 playoffs.

Lemieux was unable to immediately overcome the hip problems that had plagued him, but after surgery, he came back to captain Team Canada again and lead them to another victory, this time in the 2004 World Cup.

Once again in that tournament, Gretzky was the general manager, and this time things ran so smoothly that there was no need for any impassioned speeches. The Canadians breezed through undefeated.

But after the Olympics, Gretzky did admit that his mid-tournament rant was not just some half-baked spur-of-the-moment tantrum.

"I learned that from Glen Sather," he admitted. "There are times when you have to stand up and take responsibility. At that time, I didn't think our team was very comfortable or relaxed. The hope was to take some heat off the guys and it did."

"Gretzky was the big force," said Hitchcock. "He took the heat off us. He took all the crap. He put himself in the position to blame him. These guys wanted to play for him. They didn't want to let him down."

A short time after the game, it was revealed that the ice maker in Salt Lake City was a Canadian and that a

Canadian dollar coin, a loonie, had been buried at centre ice for luck. The coin ended up in the Hockey Hall of Fame, and there were those who gave it credit for Canada's success.

It's a nice story, but luck had nothing to do with it.

Canada won its first gold medal in fifty years because it had a team that refused to be beaten, a team that had its own program and so many leaders on the roster that it didn't need much serious direction from elsewhere.

Before the gold-medal game, some of the veterans took the dressing-room floor and spoke to their teammates. These were the guys who had been through games like this before and had the Stanley Cup rings to prove it: Steve Yzerman, Al MacInnis, Joe Sakic, Mario Lemieux.

There were no jokes, but there was no falsely enthusiastic rah-rah boosterism either. There was some Lord Horatio Nelson in it: Canada expects that every man will do his duty.

The speeches were mostly statements of fact. We're Canadians. We know what we have to do. We don't back down. We don't lose confidence. We don't take the easy road.

Years later, Lemieux confirmed the overriding message that was delivered by those speeches in that room.

"Gentlemen, losing is not an option."

AFTERWORD

THE ENTRY DRAFT IS TODAY ONE OF THE NATIONAL HOCKEY League's annual extravaganzas, awarded to a different city each year—often as a means of increasing the credibility of the local franchise. When I started covering hockey in 1973, the draft was conducted by conference call and was generally ignored by the media.

In Montreal, where hockey was part of the city's life-blood, the draft was normally accorded more news cover-age than in other cities, so the Canadiens rented a suite in the Queen Elizabeth Hotel and allowed the four or five interested reporters to monitor its progress.

In that era, training camps were what the name im-plied: a pre-season conditioning session that allowed play-ers to work off the weight they had gained over the summer and get back into shape. Modern players never get out of shape, and in the week or two immediately prior to training camp, they ramp up their conditioning pro-grams to make sure they're ready to start the season imme-diately—even though meaningful games are still four weeks away.

In the seventies, the initial phase of training camp would be succeeded by a series of preseason exhibition games that were played in small cities that otherwise would never see an NHL team in action. Now, virtually all preseason games are played in NHL rinks—at NHL prices.

The rink of 1973 had no advertising on its boards. All the players wore tube skates. Every stick was made of wood. Most players didn't wear helmets. The crease was rectangular. Goalie pads were heavy and made of leather. By the end of the night, they were heavier still because they were waterlogged. On most teams, the coaching staff was one person. With only one or two exceptions—such as Stan Mikita of the Chicago Blackhawks, who emigrated from Czechoslovakia as a child—all the players were born in Canada.

Charter flights were rare and for the most part weren't coveted. When they did occur, the plane was usually a noisy, propeller-driven relic that struck fear into the hearts of even the bravest players. The Canadiens tended to use a rickety crate of dubious origin, painted a hideous shade of yellowish-orange. Defenceman Pierre Bouchard dubbed it "The Flying School Bus."

Most of today's teams either have their own jet aircraft or have a contract with a firm that caters to their needs with specially designed planes. The typical one would seat 300 passengers if it were in commercial use, but it has been reconfigured for the comfort of the modern athlete. It usually has about eighty first-class seats spread over two sections with ample leg room. There are open areas that can be used for socializing, but there's also enough room for the team's physiotherapist to set up his massage table. In the third section are another thirty seats for support staff, families, media or anyone else who might be travelling with the team.

These are just a few examples of the way the National Hockey League has evolved over the last quarter-century or so. And while the equipment and the customs were changing, so was the way in which the game was played.

In 1979, as a result of the infamous Challenge Cup, there was no escaping the fact that at the very highest level, Canadian hockey was inferior to its Soviet counterpart. It was probably true—as Canadians repeatedly insisted in the hope of providing each other with some solace—that if the top five Canadian teams played the top five teams from the Soviet Union, the Canadians would triumph on four occasions. But the fact remained that even if Canada could indeed lay claim to more high-quality hockey players than the Soviet Union, the very best of the best were to be found in Europe, not North America.

On this side of the ocean, there was confusion and uncertainty about the essence of the game itself. Somehow, the purpose of the competition had become less clear. While Canadian hockey had never been a sport for the faint of heart, the ultimate aim of the game always had been to outscore the opponent. But the focus had been diverted, and the rugged nature of the game had taken precedence over its more ethereal side. Even though it would be an exaggeration to say that fighting had become more important than scoring, it would not be the least bit inaccurate to say that if a team were to have any hope of success, it had to be among the league's toughest. It had to have not one fighter, but a stable of fighters.

In international hockey, where pugilistic intimidation was not a part of the game, the Canadians found themselves in trouble. It would have been easier for them to play without the forward pass than to play without fighting.

The Challenge Cup made that point forcefully. The Canadians, even with a trio of Swedes thrown in, couldn't match the skill and conditioning of the Soviets. Being unable to call upon their standard tactic of physical intimidation, the NHLers were embarrassed.

So ingrained was the malaise that it couldn't be eliminated overnight. But by 1984, the best NHL players had not only caught up to the Soviets, they had surpassed them. They could beat them using the pure hockey skills without resorting to violence. They still played the game hard, and their rugged body checks were certainly a factor in their triumph. But the physical play was within the rules of the game.

Over the years, the "goon" (a word that is used by fans but not by hockey players themselves) was phased out of the league. There were still the so-called enforcers or policeman, but in today's hockey, the guys who can fight can also play the game. A team like the Detroit Red Wings can operate at the highest level of the game year after year without a single enforcer. It does have players like Brendan Shanahan and Darren McCarty, who will get involved if need be, but neither of those players needs to fight to keep his job.

Today's players have remarkable skills, and their level of conditioning is nothing short of superb. Many of them have personal trainers to make sure that they stay fit, and the coaching style demands that they play short shifts at full speed. Long gone are the days of three-minute shifts with players gliding up and down the wing to conserve energy.

The debacle of the Challenge Cup precipitated a Golden Age of Canadian hockey. But unlike great civilizations, which have one golden age and disappear forever, a sport can regenerate. The victories in three successive Canada Cup tournaments left little doubt about the stature of Canada in the hockey world.

There was a hiatus after the 1991 Canada Cup victory when the Americans won the 1996 World Cup and the Czech Republic won the 1998 Olympic gold medal. But in this century, Canada has come back to the fore and is now universally recognized as the top hockey nation in the world.

Unfortunately, however, the fans of the NHL don't always get to see the skills that make these players so great. In the 1990s, the coaches hijacked the game, and people like Jacques Lemaire and Roger Neilson stressed the skill-killing defence-first game that had as its principal weapon the neutral-zone trap.

When Lemaire's New Jersey Devils won the Stanley Cup in 1995, it was a dark day for hockey. As is the case with every sport, success breeds imitation, and as of this writing, the lawyers who run the league from their New York office and the governors who regard the teams as nothing more than investments had been unable to find a way to allow the players to take back the game from the coaches.

It was the intention of those who chart the course of the NHL to return from the devastating 2004 owners' lockout with a new product that would win back the fans. With new rules in place and a new focus on offence, it was hoped that the game might return to its glory years.

But unfortunately, those glory years, when they existed, were all provided by the players. The game has never had any glory years off the ice. It has been perennially mismanaged and misgoverned, with Band-Aid solutions always being favoured over properly researched long-range plans. It has been run for the most part by people who don't know the game and who therefore have not the slightest idea how to improve it.

For sixteen years, the NHL was governed by John Ziegler, whose favourite saying was, "If it ain't broke, don't fix it." The problems with that attitude were twofold. First, Ziegler and his colleagues were not qualified to determine whether it was "broke" or not. Secondly, that approach, by definition, indicates a total disdain for preventive maintenance.

In 1993, Ziegler was succeeded—after the forgettable, unlamented interregnum of Gil Stein—by Gary Bettman, another lawyer whose knowledge of hockey could have been written on the head of a pin with a chisel. Bettman came from the National Basketball Association, and to this day there are conspiracy theorists—who may well have spent too much time reading John Le Carre—who insist that Bettman was a mole sent over by the NBA to destroy hockey from within.

That's something of a stretch, but the fact remains that under Bettman's stewardship, the NHL's slide has been precipitous. Bettman is the first commissioner of a major professional sport to lose an entire season because of a labour dispute.

At the nucleus of that dispute was the size of player salaries, which had indeed skyrocketed during Bettman's regime. But they did so under a collective bargaining agreement that Bettman forged—and which he and his staff bragged about for its first two years, insisting they had crafted a one-sided agreement that would work in their favour. Then Bettman extended that agreement—not once, but *twice*—before deciding in 2001 that it was fatally flawed.

Eventually, the dispute boiled down not to money but to the system. At no time has the players' association demanded higher salaries—or even the status quo. In fact, they offered a 24 per cent rollback, along with other concessions. But they wanted, they said, a free-market system where the owners could subsequently decide players' worth based upon the traditional principles of supply and demand.

The owners, however, insisted upon a hard salary cap that would mandate the upper limits of all the teams' payrolls.

It made no difference that the two sides were in agreement on the numbers (the 24 per cent rollback created an average annual salary that was identical to the level Bettman had demanded for his salary cap). The league was to be shut down for a year.

In the United States, no one seemed to care. In Canada, fans tended to side with the owners, having been deluded into believing that if salaries were reduced, ticket prices would also be cut and the quality of the spectacle would somehow be enhanced.

Not even Bettman would say that his salary cap would reduce ticket prices. But he definitely said, on a number of occasions, that his system would result in a more entertaining product for the fans to enjoy.

In December 2004, I asked him why, since there are only 700 or so elite-level players in the world, he thought that the NHL game would be enhanced if salaries were reduced. After all, the same players are used in either scenario. Why would the game be better with the same players playing for less money?

He said he was surprised I would disparage the players—whatever that meant—and moved on to the next question.

The fact that public opinion was solidly on the side of the owners probably had a lot to do with Bettman's decision to stay the course. But fans have a right to believe whatever they want, and at least, for once, the NHL was taking their opinion into consideration.

The lockout and the inevitable resultant drop in the NHL's popularity forced the league to respond to the fans in other areas as well. The game was to get a new streamlined look with shootouts, smaller goalie pads and other adjustments to help it return to what it once was—a high-speed, high-intensity game with the ability to excite and amaze, to arouse our passions and inspire our awe.

Today's players are bigger, faster and stronger than their predecessors. They're also more articulate, accessible and insightful than players in any other sport. They are often accused of being greedy by the same fans who readily admit that the greatest effort is always expended in the playoffs when only two things are at stake—a relatively small bonus cheque and the bragging rights that come with winning the Stanley Cup.

If the players were truly greedy, they'd be winding down during the playoffs, not gearing up.

If the game is given back to the players, it will thrive. If they are allowed to show their skills and play the game the way they played it as kids—and still want to play it—the spectacle will be magnificent.

Think about it. Think about the way you played as a kid. Did you fantasize about scoring the winning goal in the seventh game of the Stanley Cup final, or did you dream about dropping out of the attack to make sure the opponents didn't counter with an odd-man rush?

The players still picture themselves scoring those memorable goals. Unlike the rest of us, they have the opportunity to realize their dreams.

If the coaches and the governors ever allow them to do so.

ACKNOWLEDGMENTS

FEW LIFESTYLES ARE MORE LIKELY TO CREATE AN UNREPENTANT cynic than lengthy exposure to the newspaper business. People lie to you as a matter of course to further their aims. Your heroes let you down when you're counting on them. You're constantly exposed to the worst side of humanity.

But the creation of this book went a long way to suspending that cynicism. The outpouring of kindness and cooperation that came my way was something I'll never forget.

Everyone quoted in this book deserves, and receives, my heartfelt thanks, especially the four people who subjected themselves to lengthy in-person interviews and so willingly gave of their own time. They would be Don Cherry, Wayne Gretzky, Mike Keenan and Glen Sather.

But there were many others who helped in so many ways. Marian Strachan edited every word with her usual perspicacity and saved me, I hope, from grammatical errors worthy of a public flogging. She did so with good humour and remarkable insight.

My son Andrew also read most of the manuscript—he would have read it all had I got around to sending it to him—and pointed out a number of shortcomings. He not only caught the specific errors, such as my assertion that Ernie Hicke averaged 16 goals a game, he also offered some valuable insights as to the overall tone of each chapter.

Even my younger son Ian, who is not a hockey fan, did what he could to further the cause.

When the task ahead seemed to be looming a bit too large, Lucie Leduc was always there to provide encouragement and to help me get to the next stage.

At every step along the way, help was offered and received from people like Scott Bowman, Kathy Broderick, Dave Carter, Tony Gallagher, Bob Goodenow, Pierre LeBrun, Jim MacDonald, Roy McGregor, Don Meehan, Scott Morrison and John Shannon, They too receive my thanks, as does anyone else whose support I may, in typical fashion, have overlooked.

Thanks also to Chris Cuthbert and Scott Russell who pointed me in the right direction back when the book was nothing more than a muddy concept.

Nick Massey-Garrison of Doubleday played a major role and was, to my mind, the perfect editor in that he left me alone to let me write it my way. Therefore, while I fervently thank all those who gave their help, I must accept total blame for any errors that might appear.

NAMES INDEX